CURIOUS SURVIVALS

CURIOUS SURVIVALS

HABITS AND CUSTOMS OF THE PAST THAT STILL LIVE IN THE PRESENT

BY

DR. GEORGE C. WILLIAMSON

PARKGATE
BOOKS

First published by Wyman & Sons, Ltd, 1924
This edition published in 1997 by

Parkgate Books Ltd
London House
Great Eastern Wharf
Parkgate Road
London SW11 4NQ
Great Britain

9 8 7 6 5 4 3 2 1

ISBN 1 85585 395 7

Cover design by Book Creation Services, London

Printed and bound in Finland by WSOY

PREFACE

AN American writer some time ago stated that, in his opinion, England was like a house where nothing was ever thrown away, where not only the family pictures but "the old meat-tins, nutshells, cracker-cases, empty bottles, old gowns, discarded collars and worn-out boots" were carefully kept, and although this is perhaps rather a crude statement, yet it has a certain element of truth about it, and is an acute observation. We in England have a strange capacity for preserving things. It extends not merely to objects, but actually to forms, and we retain the forms of things in this country long after their meaning has been forgotten.

It was my good fortune once to see an amazing collection of treasures that had been retained in a house belonging to a member of the Touchet family, where the costumes and ornaments of the members of the family had been treasured from a remote period. There were velvets, silks and brocades that went back to the time of Elizabeth, and with them were the gloves, sashes, stockings, and even corsets, that had formed part of elaborate costumes. There was a long series of the magnificent attire of the men of the family in the time of Charles II, beautiful silk and velvet costumes complete and hats magnificent with fine ostrich feathers.

There were all the garments worn by ancestors in Queen Anne's time, and the series went right down to the early days of Victoria, and included elaborately flounced costumes worn over crinolines at the time of the Queen's wedding. Shoes, gloves and sunshades were preserved, and there was also a quantity of old jewellery, tortoiseshell combs, wigs, snuffboxes, old spectacles, rings, chatelaines, and all the paraphernalia that went to make up the attire of the members of this ancient family. The collection was one of survivals, illustrative of manners and habits of the past.

I have striven, in these pages, to bring together a somewhat similar collection of forms, habits, ceremonies and customs equally reminiscent of days that are past. The idea of the volume originated in some remarks made by an American correspondent, to whom I had occasion to write concerning a fee charged to him by a man of my acquaintance, and set out in terms of guineas. He was puzzled by the word. He had never been in England, and he did not know that a coin called a guinea, now obsolete, was still used in reckoning out certain values.

He could not understand why professional fees were still reckoned in a term which is nothing more than a survival from times past. I explained the circumstances to him, and the resulting correspondence showed me that there are many habits in England which puzzle even those who are of English parentage, and who speak the same language as we do. It was at the desire of this correspondent, and of others in America, that I have brought together these chapters.

I make no claim to originality. The information they contain can be had from many sources, some of it less well known than other. Part of it is constantly cropping up in the newspapers and periodicals of the day, and for much I am indebted to the ordinary works of reference, notably to Dr. Brewer's *Dictionary of Phrase and Fable*, a marvellous mine of unexplored and very useful material; to Professor Skeat's *Etymological Dictionary* (from which, as far back as 1889, when some first thoughts on this subject came to me, he gave me, in Cambridge, full permission to quote); to the *Encyclopædia Britannica* : to Scriven's *Law of Copyholds* : Carter's *History of Legal Institutions* : Hood's *Conveyancing Acts*, and Halsbury's *Laws of England*, Vol. 8; to an exceedingly useful book by Ackermann, called *Popular Fallacies* : to the pages of *The Antiquary* and the *Antiquarian Magazine*, *Notes and Queries* and similar sources; to a volume called *Curiosities of the Church* ; a delightful book by Mr. Walter W. Skeat, called *The Past at our Doors* ; and to the various volumes concerning the different Companies of the City of London, with Mr. Carew Hazlitt's wonderful work on the Livery Companies· which summarises the results of considerable investigation.

For information on Parliament I am deeply indebted to that famous book, *The Pageant of Parliament*, by Mr. Michael McDonagh, and to the new edition of *The Complete Peerage*, now in course of issue.

All these works have been laid under contribution, and I am indebted also to many anonymous writers in the Press, who, from time to time, record with much delight the existence of some of these ancient customs. I have also had occasion often to refer to those important books by Mr. and Mrs. Quennell, *Everyday Life in England*; *In Feudal Times*, by Dr. Tappan; Traill's *Social England*; *London's Story*, by Mullins; Wright's *Homes of other Days*; Turner's *Domestic Architecture in England*; Ollard and Crosse's famous *Dictionary of English Church History* (1912); Litchfield's *Antiques*; Bell's *Unknown London*, and the same author's *More About Unknown London*; to various publications of the Royal Numismatic Society, the American Numismatic Society, and other kindred learned bodies, to the *Westminster Cathedral Chronicle* and to various religious pamphlets.

Many of the customs I have personally investigated, but for others, I have had to rely on those who have already written about them, and the references that occur in the journals. Where it has been possible, I have acknowledged the sources of my information, but in many cases, especially with reference to the books I have just mentioned, it would have overloaded my pages with foot-notes to have referred in every case to the source of the material.

I have endeavoured not to be unfair with regard to quotations, and would beg leave to offer my hearty thanks to the authors and publishers of the various works which I have ventured to lay under contribution for the material that has been used in this book. My object has simply been to bring together, for the sake of interest and convenience, such of these strange survivals as seemed important to mention, in order that in one volume there should be a series of references to old customs still remaining in England, and tending to recall the interesting days of the past.

If I should have misquoted, or drawn too freely on the writings of any of those who have preceded me, may I beg leave, in advance, to offer my apologies. Every writer on a subject of that kind has to furnish himself with material from those who have been in the field before, but I hope that, in gleaning from the ripe cornfields of other authors, I have not infringed too much on the privileges that are customary in the harvest.

I have to thank Mr. G. Rooke Collingridge for the loan of a rare book concerning the ceremonials of the City, and for several valuable hints which he gave me in connection with it. I am, moreover, particularly grateful to my friends, Dr. Laing and Mr. C. J. J. Bolton-Clark, and to my son, Mr. C A. Williamson, for their kindness in reading my proofs, and making many important suggestions and corrections. My publisher and friend, Mr. Jenkins, also made many happy suggestions and supplied important information.

I have to express my very hearty thanks to Mr. R. P. Stone and to the members of his family for the graceful permission they have so generously afforded me, and which has enabled me to copy certain of the excellent photographs taken by Sir Benjamin Stone, and deposited at the British Museum and at the Corporation Gallery of Birmingham for the advantages of students ; this permission having allowed me to produce scenes of which there are no other photographs. I have also to thank the officials of the Print Room, notably my friend Mr. Hogg, for the courtesy extended to me, and to my photographer, Mr. Oswell, who prepared the negatives, and I have to thank the officials of the Birmingham Art Gallery, the London Press Agency, and Mr. Norman Grut, of Guernsey, for similar permissions, most obligingly rendered to me for the purposes of this book.

I am also warmly grateful to the Mayor of Ripon, the Rectors of Helston, Painswick, Knutsford and Corby, the Archdeacon of Man and Mr. Camburn of Hungerford for loans, gifts and information relative to their respective localities, and to many correspondents all over the world, from Shanghai and Singapore and Kuala Lumpa to Patagonia, South Africa, British Columbia, Lapland, Siberia, New Zealand and the Solomon Isles, for suggestions, corrections and additions. To all of them I am very much obliged, and many of their suggestions are incorporated in this new edition.

GEORGE C. WILLIAMSON.

MOUNT MANOR HOUSE,
    MOUNT STREET,
        GUILDFORD.
Christmas, 1924.

CONTENTS

ILLUSTRATIONS

The illustrations Nos. II. and III., representing the scenes before the King's Remembrancer, are reproduced by kindly permission of the Managing Director of the London News Agency Photos, Ltd., 46, Fleet Street, London.

CURIOUS SURVIVALS

CHAPTER I

IN THE CITY OF LONDON

CONCERNING THE LORD MAYOR AND ALDERMEN

THERE is no place in England in which old customs have been more carefully preserved than the square mile known as the City of London, and within its boundaries there are probably enshrined more of these ancient habits and survivals than in any other place in the world.

The City of London is, by very instinct, conservative. In antiquity, it has been stated to precede every other corporation in the Kingdom, although I believe there is still a certain amount of dispute between London and Winchester in relation to precedence, but in importance and dignity it leaves the Hampshire cathedral city far behind, and in its ancient and unrivalled Corporation, London possesses a body which has stood for English freedom and English liberty from the days when William the Conqueror granted its earliest charter. This the City still preserves as its greatest treasure, though the charter itself is preceded in antiquity by the famous crystal sceptre still used by the Lord Mayor, the mounting of which is believed to belong to Anglo-Saxon times.

It should be remembered that, although the privileges of the City are carried on under the charter granted by William the Conqueror, yet that charter contained words saying that the citizens were to be " as they were in the days of King Edward," and therefore these privileges were only re-granted by the Conqueror, when he said " I grant you to be all law-worthy," and then, further on, " I will not suffer any person to do you wrong, God keep you."

So that, although Norman regulations were introduced for the rest of the kingdom, London was to possess the ancient privileges it had held from Anglo-Saxon times, and it is under these that it is still governed.

The City of London and its officials are exceedingly tenacious of all the customs which link them with remote antiquity, and year by year the question is put by the Livery, who are the electing body, to the various candidates for the office of Lord Mayor, as to whether they are prepared to protect the liberties and the customs of the City, and much depends upon the manner in which the answer to that question is given.

Perhaps the oldest ceremony that has been handed down from ancient times to the present day is that by which the Corporation of the City pays its rent to the King for two pieces of land, by the presentation of horse-shoes and horse-shoe nails, and by the cutting of faggots with a bill-hook and a hatchet. The first reference to this remarkable quit-rent ceremony occurs in 1118, when the piece of land in question is described as being situate at the north-west corner of what is now called Chancery Lane In 1162, the Knights Templars were in possession of very much land bordering on the River Thames, to-day represented by the estates known as " The Temple," and still belonging to the Benchers of the Inner and Middle Temple.

Adjacent to this was a field called The Thickets, upon which the Knights Templars held tournaments, and it is stated that in 1235 a certain Walter le Brun, who was engaged in a tournament, required the assistance of a smith for shoeing the forefeet of his horse, and called in the aid of a man who, at that moment, was in possession of a forge erected in the field for carrying out repairs to armour. In consideration of the assistance given by this smith, he appears to have been granted the privilege of building a forge on this corner of land, and placing his services at the disposal of the knights who fought in the tournaments, and who might require repairs to their armour, at a rental of so many horse-shoes and nails, but how exactly it fell about that the Corporation of London came into possession of the site of this forge, no one can in the least explain.

It has been stated that, when Wat Tyler got into the

City, and burned in Holborn a large quantity of papers belonging to the Temple, the documents relating to the descent of this property were destroyed, but the one thing certain is that for over seven hundred years the Corporation, claiming to possess this piece of freehold land, now covered by the Law Courts, has paid its feudal quit-rent to the Crown, year by year, by presenting to the King's Remembrancer, who represents the Sovereign, certain gigantic horse-shoes, suitable for the fore-feet of a great Flemish mare, and sixty-one nails, to be used in fastening them on. The shoes are six in number ; they are solemnly handed to the King's Remembrancer by the City Solicitor, and the nails are counted out. The warrants from the Sheriff and the Remembrancer respecting this ancient quit-rent are duly read out by the Secondary, and ordered to be filed and recorded, and then this strange ceremony of the presentation of horse-shoes is followed by another of almost equal antiquity.

A piece of land, known as " The Moors," near Bridgnorth, Shropshire, was granted to the Corporation in 1211, the rent to be paid to the Crown, consisting of two knives, one blunt and the other good. In process of time, this rent appears to have been changed to a billhook and a hatchet, although no one is able to explain why the change took place, or at what date the alteration was made, but the City Solicitor produces a small bundle of faggots and proceeds to chop them in pieces with a billhook and with a hatchet, and then he solemnly presents to the King's Remembrancer this billhook and hatchet ; and so the rent is satisfactorily paid to the Crown by the City for a piece of land which cannot now be identified, which the City does not appear ever to have occupied, or to have received rent for, but for which the Crown makes its annual demand of this quit-rent, and this demand is duly paid by the Corporation year after year, and has been so paid for 700 years.

Probably there is no other ceremony performed in England, other than the Coronation, older than this strange payment of quit-rent. It has gone on century after century in exactly the same fashion. It is conducted with the gravest of judicial importance, the King's Remembrancer attending at a special court, in complete judicial attire with full-bottomed wig, and taking away with him, on behalf of the King, the billhook and hatchet which the City Solicitor hands over.   It would appear that the horse-shoes and the nails are not actually taken away, although by a fiction of the law they are supposed to have been transferred to the King, but they appear year after year in the ceremony, and are on each occasion duly counted and handed over. A new hatchet and a new billhook, however, are provided annually by the Corporation and presented to the Crown.

I have referred in a previous sentence to the Livery. The word perhaps needs some explanation. The election of Lord Mayor does not rest in the hands of the general citizens of the City of London. It is still the peculiar prerogative of the members of the ancient City Companies to elect the chief magistrate. They are termed the Livery. They originally wore the gowns pertaining to the Company, which at one time were coloured in accordance with the field and principal charge of the armorial shield appertaining to the Company.

Livery is just simply that which is delivered, and we now apply it almost exclusively to the clothes of a man-servant, delivered to him by his master as an emblem of his service ;   while it is also used for the stables to which a horse is delivered for keep ; but it originally referred to the costumes worn by persons attached to great establish-ments, such as the members of a Royal household or the retainers of a Baron or high official. The only persons who now are called " The Livery " are the members of the ancient Trade Guilds which have their home in the City.

When a man becomes a Liveryman of the City he is clothed with a fur gown, and the shape, colour and char-acteristics of these gowns differ in the various Companies. As a rule, it is only the Master and Wardens of the Court of a Company who continue to wear the gowns, and they do so when presiding in the Halls of the various Companies, or attending on official occasions either at church or at the Guildhall. Each Liveryman, however, in his turn, has to be clothed with the Livery of his Company, and is entitled to wear, if he chooses to purchase it, the fur gown appertaining to the Company in question.

The members of the Livery are summoned to attend at

Guildhall on the 24th of June for the election of Sheriff, and on the 29th of September for the election of Lord Mayor. Prior to these dates, a barrier is stretched across King Street, shutting out all unauthorised persons from the entrance to Guildhall. This barrier is composed of a series of small doors, and over each door appear the names of certain companies. It would be impossible to have nearly a hundred doors, and in consequence the companies divide the doors between them, and three or four names are on each. Behind these doors stand the Beadles of the various Companies in their rich and varied costumes, carrying their maces and wearing their three-cornered hats, ready to identify the Liverymen as they pass in, for no one who does not belong to one or other of the City Companies is supposed to enter Guildhall on these occasions.

Each man presents himself at the door over which appears the name of his Company, is identified by the Beadle in charge, and then passed in, to hear, before the commencement of what is known as Common Hall, a solemn proclamation, stating that all unauthorised persons, who do not belong to the Livery, are to leave the Hall, under pain of being committed to the Tower by the Lord Mayor.

The election of Lord Mayor is from a certain group of the Court of Aldermen, those who have not yet passed the Chair but have served the office of Sheriff, no one being eligible as Lord Mayor unless he has been Sheriff. As a rule, the election is a matter of precedence, the next senior Alderman receiving the suffrages of the assembled Liverymen. The names of the Aldermen who are next in succession to the Chair have already been painted upon large boards, and these are exhibited to the assembled Liverymen, who vote by acclamation for the favourite candidate.

Prior to this election taking place, the Lord Mayor and the Aldermen who have passed the Chair retire into the Court Room belonging to the Aldermen, in order that the election should be free and unfettered. The names are announced, the voting is taken, and the two Aldermen who are next on the rota are sent in to the Court of Aldermen as the selected candidates. The final selection rests with the Court of Aldermen, and the signal pointing out the person selected is given to the assembled Livery when the procession returns, and it is noticed which of the two candidates is walking by the side of the Lord Mayor.

Well can I remember how in 1883 a change from the ordinary procedure took place and the Alderman whose name was second on the list was found, when the procession returned, to be walking by the side of the Lord Mayor, instead of the man who had been accepted by acclamation, and whose election was most confidently anticipated. The Court of Aldermen was in possession of some information respecting the rejected candidate which was not generally known, and very wisely they passed over the popular choice, selecting the man next in succession.

There was at first great disturbance in Common Hall and considerable anger was expressed at the action of the Court, but a few weeks later it was proved how wise had been the decision of the Court of Aldermen, and, as Mr. Welch writes, " subsequent events fully justified the course taken."*

The procedure when the candidates reach the Alderman's Court is remarkable. The City sword is laid in a bed of roses, recalling the old classical legend, when Cupid gave to Harpocrates, the God of Silence, a rose, to bribe him not to betray the amours of Venus. The flower has therefore been taken as the emblem of silence. The phrase " sub rosa " or " under the rose " still means that a statement is made in strict confidence, and roses have frequently been sculptured on the ceilings of banquet-rooms, to remind the guests, as has been well said, that what was spoken " sub vino " was not to be uttered " sub divo."

The banqueting-room ceiling at Haddon Hall is one of those which survive with its original decoration of roses. The rose, in 1526, was also placed over the doors of confessionals, with similar intent. When the sword has been deposited on its bed of roses, a high official of the Corporation addresses each Alderman in turn, and receives a whispered reply. These replies are duly noted down, and the choice is made by the majority of the Aldermen. Then the Lord Mayor calls to him the selected candidate and conveys the congratulations of his brother Aldermen, and the procession returns to Guildhall in the manner just mentioned.

There follows an interesting ceremony connected with

* Welch's *Modern History of the City of London*, p. 362.

the congratulations offered to the Lord Mayor Elect and his speech in reply. These are followed by speeches referring to the year of office that has just expired, and to the excellent manner in which the Lord Mayor has carried out his duties. Almost without exception, expressions of warm gratitude to the Lord Mayor are presented by certain spokesmen acting on behalf of the Aldermen, and he is congratulated upon whatever honours may have accrued to him during his year of office.

Then the insignia pertaining to this high dignity are duly presented to the Lord Mayor Elect by the various officials who hold the keys, the purse, and the City sceptre, who, making solemn obeisance to the new Chief Magistrate, proffer to him these insignia of his office. He signs certain documents, acknowledging to have received into his custody the City plate, and to have taken upon himself the position of Lord Mayor ; and shortly after that the proceedings terminate.

Prior to the assembling of Common Hall, the Lord Mayor and Aldermen attend a religious service in state, in the church of St. Lawrence Jewry, immediately adjacent to Guildhall. The newly chosen Chief Magistrate is then known as the Lord Mayor Elect, but his appointment awaits the confirmation of the Crown, because, although the Livery, in the exercise of their " free and undoubted privilege," select the Lord Mayor ; yet he does not possess full jurisdiction over the City until his appointment has been ratified by the Crown. This ceremony takes place at the House of Lords, and the consent of the King is given to the election of the Lord Mayor by the Lord Chancellor, still called in England " the Keeper of the King's Conscience." This title points back to the days when the Chancellor was an ecclesiastic, and the King's Confessor. Evidence of this old ecclesiastical position is seen in the fact that he is still the chief custodian of parochial appointments in the kingdom, having at his disposal a far larger number of livings than appertains to any other person, and to these he appoints in the name of the Crown.

The Corporation of the City attends at the House of Lords to receive the Royal approval, when the Recorder introduces the Lord Mayor Elect, testifying to his character and repute, and dealing at some length with his career.

The Lord Chancellor at once announces that the King ratifies the choice of the Livery, and drinks to the health of the Lord Mayor and the Corporation in a loving-cup, which is then passed round to the assembled officials.

There was at one time a peculiarly interesting ceremony which took place on these occasions, but, for some reason or other, I am given to understand, it has been allowed to lapse. The City sword, covered with an elaborate velvet scabbard, used to be borne in the presence of the Lord Chancellor as the representative of the King. This scabbard was removed by the Lord Chancellor and retained as the Royal perquisite, evidence of the fact that the crown alone possessed the right to sheathe the sword, and that it was to be borne naked in the presence of the Sovereign, to protect the Crown from any source of danger, the Lord Mayor having no power to sheathe it because the scabbard was retained by the King.

The Beadles who attend upon the Aldermen occupy an office at least six hundred years old. The very earliest records of the City of London refer to the fact that each " Bedel " should make arrangements in his own ward for setting two men to watch at the gates of the ward. His own duties consisted in warning the inhabitants who were liable to serve as watchmen, supporting the Aldermen in their efforts to keep the peace, and he had also to do with the arrest of evil-doers and the searching for and reporting upon, any nuisances that occurred in the ward. The duties are now much simpler than they were, but the Beadles are in evidence at any Ward-Mote, and whenever the Aldermen are carrying out their special official duties, and it is they who prepare the lists of the various licensed victuallers within the ward, and who wait on the Aldermen with them. The Beadles have in their custody the maces belonging to the wards, and many of these maces are of extreme importance, and of considerable beauty. They date back to the sixteenth and seventeenth centuries, and they vary in appearance according to the nature of the ward, usually having upon them some representation of an important building or buildings in the ward, as, for example, the mace of the Tower Ward is in the shape of a representation of the White Tower. These maces, which have been the subject of a special book, are carried by the Beadles upon all important occasions, and are placed on the table before the Aldermen, when the Ward-Motes are held, and without their presence, as in the House of Commons, the Ward-Mote is not legally constituted.

I have referred to the ceremony of the loving-cup. Drinking from a loving-cup is one of the notable features of the feasts that take place at the halls of the various City Companies. The cup, as a rule, is a very large one, of silver or silver gilt, filled with a special spiced wine, which from time immemorial has been known as sack. The word is simply a corruption of the French word " sec " or " dry," but it used to be applied to various kinds of wine, as one spoke of Canary sack, or Madeira sack, or sherry sack.*

To return to the ceremony of the loving-cup. It takes place immediately after dinner and grace, when the Master and Wardens drink to their guests a hearty welcome, and the cup is passed round the table. Then comes the interesting ceremony whereby three persons stand up at the same time. The person who pledges with the loving-cup bows to his neighbour, who, also standing, removes the cover of the cup with his right hand,† and holds it while the other one drinks, a custom said to have originated in the precaution to keep the right, or dagger hand, employed, that

---

* It has no connection, as such, with the word that is generally applied to a bag, and which, of itself, has a strange origin, and is connected with a curious story. We probably got that word " sack " from a Coptic or Egyptian word " sok," applied to a kind of canvas or cloth from which a bag was made, and we still have the word in use, when we speak of sack-cloth. It has been said, however, that this word " sok " was the very last word uttered before the tongues were confounded at Babel, and that in consequence it appears in every language, almost in identical form. Curiously enough, this is very much the case. The Irish " sac " is the same as the French word, the Latin " saccus " is closely attached to the Italian " sacco " and the Spanish " saco." In Greek it is " σάκκος," in Hebrew " sak " or " saq," in Egyptian or in Coptic " sok," in Dutch " zak " and Swedish " sack," and the same result is seen in many other languages, the word having only slight changes. As is well known, we now apply it in quite another fashion, when we talk of a person getting the sack, or having the sack given to them, as a felicitous way of describing his being discharged, and this use we probably derive from the Eastern habit of putting a person into a sack and throwing him into the Bosphorus, in order to get him out of the way.

† Or left, I suppose, if he is left-handed.

the person who drinks may be assured of no treachery, like that practised in mediæval times, when people were often slain while drinking.

As an even greater precaution, the person who has next to drink from the cup stands up also behind the cover-bearer, so that three are standing at the same time, and it is to keep up this old custom that the loving-cup possesses a cover. The drinker solemnly bows to the person who is opposite to him, drinks, applies his napkin to the mouth of the cup, bows again to his neighbour, who replaces the cover, and then turns round to the person who is behind him. We retain the same old idea in our habit of removing the glove before we shake hands with an approaching friend, in order to show quite clearly that no weapon is concealed in the right hand.

It must be remembered in this connection that the gloves formerly worn were large and loose about the hand, more like our gauntlet or gardening gloves, not close-fitting like the modern kid glove. It would have been easy in these old gloves to conceal a knife or other short weapon.

Guildhall, to which reference has so frequently been made, is the scene of the most ancient Court which still sits in England, that which is known as the Court of Hustings, otherwise " Housethings," or personal matters connected with the House, that is with the City itself. The Courts at which the Lord Mayor, Sheriffs, Bridgemasters, Ale conners and members for the City are elected, are still known as Courts of Hustings. They have enrolled wills and deeds in the City since 1252, but their origin is far more remote. They date back to Anglo-Saxon or Scandinavian times.

Their proceedings are still opened by the following quaint proclamation : " Oyez, Oyez, Oyez. All manner of persons who have been five times by virtue of any exigent directed to the Sheriffs of London, and have not surrendered their bodies to the said Sheriffs, this Court doth adjudge the men to be outlawed and the women to be waived."

The proceedings are closed by a somewhat similar declaration : " Oyez, Oyez, Oyez. All manner of persons who have any more to do at these hustings, of pleas of land, may depart hence at this time, and keep their day here again at the next hustings of pleas of land."

The bridgemaster elected on such an occasion is still regarded as an important official of the Corporation, and is associated with the Bridge House Trust, when leases of the property are to be executed. The ale conner has not, however, any duties now connected with the tasting of liquors sold in the various City taverns.

The dais on the occasion of the sitting of this Court is still sprinkled with aromatic herbs. These recall the dangers that used to arise from the presence of gaol fever amongst those persons who were brought up for judgment, and the idea was that the perfume of these aromatic herbs would help to ward off the risk of infection from the judges who were sitting on the dais. This custom is a relic of the same thought which causes the Masters and Wardens of the various Companies to carry sweet-smelling bouquets with them, as they pass through the streets, on the occasion of their visits to the various churches of the City, either prior to their elections, or in order to hear certain sermons, which have been endowed by citizens in past days to commemorate particular events. Cardinal Wolsey, when he used to pass along the streets, was, it is stated, in the habit of holding an orange to his nose, and in it certain spices had been inserted, in order to keep back the evil smell that filled the streets. He is so represented in various contemporary portraits. The Masters and Wardens of the City Companies use their nosegays for the same purpose, although the streets in the present day are very different indeed from those of mediæval times, and, happily, the necessity for the precaution has passed away.

There is another curious evidence of the filthy condition of the City streets in mediæval times. The Vintner's Company, in connection with their annual procession to church, still keep up the ancient custom of having the roads swept in front of the Master and Wardens as their procession advances. The porters of the Company, wearing clean aprons, wield new brooms, and precede the procession from the Hall to the Church, and vice versa, sweeping a path clean where the procession should move. This custom goes back, of course, to the days when the streets of London were full of mud and mire, and it was necessary that a clean path should be swept for the fur-robed officials of the Company as they made their progress. The necessity for doing so no longer arises, but the ancient habit is still kept up in all its detail.

One of the most ancient privileges belonging to the Lord Mayor concerns the possession of venison. There is in the British Museum a warrant from the Crown, granting to the Lord Mayor of London six bucks from the Royal forests. It is in Norman-French, dated 1428, and bears the seals of the Archbishop of Canterbury, the Bishop of London, and various other Privy Councillors, who in Henry V's time were administering public affairs. It refers to the granting of these bucks as though it was, even then, a generally accepted privilege, perfectly well known, and therefore, in all probability, the right of having deer from the Royal forests had belonged to the Mayors of London from a period long anterior to that date.

The same privilege still exists, and once a year the venison warrants are issued by the Crown, when the Lord Mayor receives four bucks, the Sheriffs three, the Recorder, Chamberlain, Town Clerk, Common Sergeant and Remembrancer one each, while in December similar warrants are sent in exactly the same proportions for does. The privilege is one that is very highly valued, especially by all officials of the Lord Mayor's establishment, and there are few rights in the kingdom that extend back to such a remote period and are even still in force.

Another privilege which belongs to the City of London, and about which it is very tenacious, is that its maces and its swords may be carried upright. This privilege was granted to the City in 1354, and where other Corporations slope their maces and their swords, the City maces may be carried upright, and the City swords generally are so borne, in the same way as the State sword is borne before the King, as an emblem of Sovereignty. The privilege was contested at one time by the City of York, which claimed to have an equal sovereign right, and to be able to carry its maces and swords in the same fashion as the City of London, but in 1873 the question was fully considered, and the Corporation of York relinquished its claim.

The connection between the City and its great cathedral has always been an intimate one. The Lord Mayor has always been, and still is, a trustee of St. Paul's Cathedral, and it falls to his right to audit the accounts of the cathedral, a privilege which has always belonged to the Mayoralty, and is still exercised. He is sovereign within the City, and as long as Temple Bar stood, when the King or Queen desired to enter the City, the heralds knocked at the gates of Temple Bar, and requested permission. The Corporation of the City, representing its citizens, claimed their ancient privilege that they could, if necessary, bar out the Sovereign from their boundaries, and refuse him permission to pass along their streets.

Even now, since Temple Bar has passed away from its old place, the same arrangement is kept up. A cord or chain is stretched across the City boundaries, and when the Sovereign is to pass through the City the Royal herald still halts at the boundary and asks permission to do so. The permission, of course, is instantly granted, the Lord Mayor and Court of Aldermen are all ready and waiting on horseback on the other side of the chain, and the Lord Mayor, dismounting, kneels and hands the crystal sceptre of the City to the King, who touches it, and returns it into the custody of the Chief Magistrate. The Lord Mayor then precedes the Sovereign through the streets of the City, and generally has the opportunity of offering refreshment at the Mansion House.

The Lord Mayor's state robe of office is that of an Earl, and while wearing it, he has the special precedence of an Earl. Moreover, the old London records state that, should he die in the presence of the Sovereign, he is entitled to such funeral ceremonies as will be rendered to an Earl, and his wife becomes a Countess, and their children take precedence and enjoy proper rank accordingly. The event has never taken place, and therefore there has been no opportunity for this old regulation to be carried out. The robe, by ancient custom, is always provided and paid for by the Court of Aldermen, and presented to the Lord Mayor, and it becomes his property. At the demise of the Crown, the Lord Mayor is the first person who is informed by the Secretary of State, and he is requested to give instructions for the tolling of the bell of St. Paul's. The right to give these instructions, which in any other cathedral would be given by the Dean, belongs, in the case of St. Paul's, to the Lord Mayor absolutely.

Furthermore, the Lord Mayor is the first person who is

summoned, as a member of the Privy Council, to the meeting of that Council, when the new Sovereign is proclaimed, and he signs the proclamation at the head of the other Privy Councillors. It is generally stated that his is the only Privy Councillorship which actually remains at the demise of the Crown, all others *ipso facto* lapsing out of existence, and having to be renewed by the succeeding Sovereign, but the position held by the Lord Mayor renders his Privy Councillorship unique.

At the Coronation, the Lord Mayor is placed in a prominent position, near to the Sovereign, and the City has always claimed that it should be consulted in the election of a King, however formal that election may be. Hence it is that the Lord Mayor is summoned, as I have just mentioned, to the Privy Council.

He is the only person who is provided with the password to the Tower, and this privilege has belonged to the City ever since the erection of that stately fortress. It has been said that on one occasion the pass-word was sent, signed only by the Secretary of State, inasmuch as Queen Victoria was at the moment at Balmoral, and the official in charge thought it was needless to trouble the Queen, and so forwarded the document without the Royal signature. I am told that the paper was at once returned by the then Lord Mayor to Balmoral Castle, with a humble petition that the right of the City should be maintained. It is said that the Queen was most indignant that the paper had not been submitted to her, for her signature, and the official responsible for the error received a somewhat severe reprimand. The forms are sent in to the Mansion House quarterly, and they give the pass-words for every day in the month.*

I have heard that the same kind of mistake occurred once in connection with the ceremony of the Maundy money, to which some reference will be made later on in this volume. The Maundy money has always been handed over in small leather purses, white and red, and to these are attached the

---

* In a book written by the late Sir William Treloar called *A Lord Mayor's Diary*, 1906–1907, there appears opposite p. 208 a representation of the form sent to the then Lord Mayor, giving the pass-words for every day in the month of October, signed by King Edward.

long leather thongs, which were, in mediæval times, used to fasten the purse to its owner's girdle, and which now are merely long, narrow strips of leather, passed through holes in the mouth of the purse, enabling it to be drawn up, as is a schoolboy's marble bag.

It is stated that there was once an officer who thought that these leather thongs were unsightly, and replaced them by silk cord and tassels, and that his mistake proved somewhat costly, as when the news of this innovation reached the Sovereign, he was ordered to pay for the silk cord and tassels out of his own pocket, and at the same time to replace the leather straps or thongs which had always been in use, and were so to continue.

It is an interesting ceremony which goes on night after night at the Tower, and concerns its safe custody. Every evening, just before midnight, the chief Warder proceeds to the guard-room, in his hands carrying a bunch of keys. At the guard-room he requests an escort. The officer of the guard details an escort of one N.C.O. and four men, and it is marched off with fixed bayonets, carrying a lantern, closely guarding the chief Warder and the Keys. In ordinary times the chief Warder would salute an officer, but when he carries the King's Keys, an officer salutes him, or rather the King's Keys, and a civilian would take off his hat. The Spur Guard turns out and presents arms to the Keys as they pass out. The chief Warder and his escort march to the Outer Barrier, where they are joined by a second warder, who assists in shutting the gates, and while this process is going on, the escort turns inwards and is ordered to present arms. The procession then re-forms and marches back to the Middle Tower, where the Spur Guard again presents arms. The escort comes to the " Present " while the gate is locked. Then the Keys and the escort march back over the moat to the Byward Tower, and there the same ceremony is repeated. There the assistant warder leaves the procession, and remains on guard all night at the gate. The procession then turns in opposite the Traitor's Gate, and as soon as it is observed, the sentry on the main guard lowers his bayonet to the charge, and challenges, " Who goes there ? " The chief Warder replies, " The Keys." The sentry then calls, " Whose Keys ? " " King George's Keys," replies the chief Warder. " Pass, King George's Keys ; all's well," and the sentry lifts his bayonet point, the chief Warder with the Keys advances, and when opposite the guard halts, whereupon both guard and escort present arms. The chief Warder then, stepping to the front, takes off his hat, and pronounces the words, " God preserve King George," to which the officer and men of the escort and the guard answer, " Amen."*

The Keys are then carried by the same guardian to the King's House, or, as it is frequently called, the Governor's House, and placed for the night in the custody of the Constable of the Tower. From that moment, it is impossible for anyone to proceed in or out of the Tower, unless he possess the special pass-word, which is changed every night, and which, as just mentioned, is sent to the Lord Mayor of London under the sign manual of the Sovereign.

This ceremony of locking the gates, saluting the Keys and providing the pass-word, are the survivals of a custom which has now been in existence, it is said, for over six hundred years.

There was a well-known instance in which a high official of the Tower was himself locked out of his own residence, having arrived from a dinner-party a few moments after the gates had been closed. As he was not in possession of the pass-word, it was quite impossible for him to enter the fortress, and he had to spend the night at a neighbouring hotel.

There is an exceedingly ancient privilege attached to the office of the Keeper of the Jewel House of the Tower. It has been in force from remote antiquity, and is still held to, with great tenacity. It is that the Keeper of the Jewel House " hath no superior officer in Court or Kingdom." He accepts no instructions whatever, except from the King himself or conveyed from the King through the Lord Chamberlain, and they then have to bear the King's signature or sign manual. No judges, no military authorities of any kind, and not even the Houses of Parliament, have any power whatever to give instructions to the Keeper of the Jewel House, and the origin, no doubt, of the privilege was that in turbulent days it would have been easy for

* I am indebted to Sir George Younghusband, K.C.M.G., for details concerning this interesting ceremonial.

some traitor to order the Keeper to hand over the King's jewels to him. Hence the existence of this privilege, which is declared to date further back than the time of the Conquest, and even now on the occasion of the Coronation, or the opening of Parliament, no jewels can be removed from the Tower, or even transferred to any other place, except under the distinct instructions of the King himself.

It is also of interest to remember that the Executioner's Axe is still carried in the Tower by the Yeoman Gaoler, and also sometimes in Royal processions, even though it is not now the actual axe, but a smaller axe, an emblem of the ancient weapon.

The Lord Mayor has the sole power to determine what troops shall pass through the City. One regiment, the Third, or the Buffs, the modern representative of the Train-Bands raised in the City in ancient days, claims that it has a prescriptive right to pass through with fixed bayonets and colours flying.

The power of the City of London to forbid the beat of drums, the display of colours or the fixing of bayonets on the part of the armed forces of the Crown when moving through its precincts, is referred to as existing in the time of Charles II. The regiments that had the privilege were the Grenadier Guards, the Buffs, the Royal Marines and the 7th Royal Fusiliers. The privilege for the Grenadier Guards for generations belonged to the Third Battalion, but was afterwards extended to all the battalions. No regiment, however, has any " right " to march through the City, but the privilege is established by ancient usage. When Charles II became King in 1660, having disbanded nearly the whole of the army, with the exception of the King's regiment of Foot Guards (now the Grenadier Guards), the Holland Regiment (now the Buffs), and the Duke of York's regiment (now the Royal Marines), he authorised officers of these regiments to raise recruits by beat of drum in the City, and the Lord Mayor's permission was given for the purpose. The recruiting was done by the regiment marching through the City in full panoply in order to draw attention.

The third battalion of the Grenadier Guards was the only complete battalion formed from the original regiment, when, in 1686, the regiment was divided, and this was raised by leave of the Lord Mayor, in part from recruits within the City boundaries.

The privilege is claimed, moreover, by the Honourable Artillery Company, and by the 5th Northumberland Fusiliers, the first by reason of its descent from the City Trained Bands, the second because it was quartered in the City during the Gordon Riots in 1780. There appears to be some evidence in favour of the Honourable Artillery Company, but nothing of any importance in favour of the Northumberland Fusiliers.

During service on Sunday, at the Chapel of St. Peter ad Vincula in the Tower of London, the great entrance gate at the Byward Tower is closed, and a Yeoman Warder stands on guard over it. In days of old, this gate was thus closed and guarded, and the portcullis was dropped while the garrison were engaged in their devotions, so that there should be no chance of their being taken unawares. Although no such danger now exists, the ancient custom still holds good.

Further interesting evidence of the historic continuity of the City consists of the fact that the seal still in daily use in the Mayoralty and City of London Court is the very one first used by William Walworth, then Lord Mayor of London, on April 17, 1381, and the Common Seal of the City, also still in use at the present day, is even of an earlier date. It was made in 1225, and has been continuously used ever since. No other Corporation can boast of such important relics still in use at the present day.

The traces of the ancient ecclesiastical or Guild life of the City are still apparent in the hoods to the gowns worn by the Aldermen. They represent those worn by the Capuchins, who derived their nickname from the capuce, or pointed hood, which they wore.

It should be remembered that persons who obtain the freedom of London have still to be warranted for, however exalted may be their position, by six individuals who are termed their compurgators. They testify that the person in question does not desire the freedom of the City whereby to deprive the King or the City of their rights, customs and advantages, but that they will pay their scot and bear their lot.

It should be remembered also that the annual procession

which takes place in London in connection with the installation of a new Lord Mayor on Lord Mayor's Day, in which he is attended, not only by his own great officers, but by the representatives of all the various trading Guilds with which he and his Sheriffs have been associated, is the last remaining example of the trade pageants which used to take place so frequently in connection with Guild life, especially upon days on which the Saints were commemorated to whom the particular Guilds were dedicated. This procession, and a somewhat similar one which takes place every twenty years at Preston, are the last remaining evidence to the public eye of the existence of these Craft Guilds, whose origin goes back in English history almost to time immemorial.

CHAPTER II

IN THE CITY OF LONDON

CONCERNING THE CITY COMPANIES

THE election of the Master and Wardens of a City Company is still attended with a certain amount of ceremony, and in one instance affords a remarkable example of the survival of ancient habit. In one of the Companies, the Chaplain has to attend at least one hour before the Master and Wardens go to church, and he has to spend that hour in a quiet room now known as the coffee-room. Here, for the most part, he sits alone, until he has the signal from the Beadle that it is time for him to go to church to receive the Master and the Wardens. Unless, however, he passes this length of time in his room, he is not entitled to be considered the Chaplain to the Company, and to receive the emolument which is his due.

I can quite well remember the horror of a comparatively venerable Low Church clergyman, when it fell to my lot to explain what he had not hitherto known, the reason for his presence in that room. It was, of course, that he might receive the confessions of the members of the Company, before they attended at Mass and took Communion. Even now the service, which, by reason of alteration of time, takes place in the afternoon, is not Evensong, but is the ante-Communion service, pointing out the connection it had in old times with the service of the Mass. The duty has still been kept up that the Chaplain should be there in attendance, although, as a matter of fact, in the Company to which I refer, there are hardly any Catholics at the present moment, and even if there were, they would not go to an Anglican clergyman for confessions, or make them in the afternoon, prior to going to church. Still, there is the interesting survival, connecting the City Company with the religious guild out of which it sprang, and retaining under changed circumstances its habit of attending at Mass, and giving the opportunity to its various members of visiting the priest, to receive absolution before the religious service took place.

Some of the Companies retain other ceremonies. In more than one, the fiction is carried out of trying a crown or wreath on to the heads of various persons, and of announcing that it only fits the head of the one who has just been selected for the dignity, and who will therefore be authorised to wear it.

The ceremony of the coronation of the Master and Wardens of the Girdlers' Company is unique amongst the City Companies, and it is one of particular charm and interest. After the loyal toasts have been duly honoured, the toast-master gives notice that the coronation of the Master and Wardens is about to take place, and thereafter the sounds of distant, slow music are heard outside the hall. Through the windows of the hall a charming little procession can be seen winding its way across the paved garden attached to the building, a garden that has a delightful old-world charm, and is ornamented in its centre with an exceedingly fine lead cistern, which has belonged to the Company for generations.

The procession is headed by the Beadle, bearing his beautiful silver-mounted staff, and he is followed by various musicians, playing the March from Scipio on an ancient hautboy and some flutes. These musicians wear heavy cloaks, adorned with the representation in silver of the arms of the Company, and the March they play has been used ever since it was composed by Handel in 1726. Following them, comes an official of the Company bearing a blue velvet cushion, on which are set out the four embroidered crowns to be used in the ceremony, beautiful pieces of old English embroidery, in gold and silver thread, each ornamented with the shield of arms of the Company. The last persons in the procession are the Clerk of the Company, in his black velvet gown, and the Butler with the Loving-cup.

The little procession, having traversed the garden, enters the hall, marching slowly to the sounds of solemn music, and proceeding up to the dais. The musicians surround the Master, the Clerk takes the principal crown from the cushion, and in a clear voice, announcing the name of the Master, crowns him as Master of the Girdlers' Company for the year ensuing. Another official of the Company, who takes part in the procession bearing in his hands a large silver loving-cup, then presents it to the newly crowned Master, who drinks to the health of the Livery and gives thanks for the honour that has been done him. The procession then moves towards the Upper Warden, who is also seated on the dais, and he likewise is crowned as Upper Warden of the Girdlers' Company for the year ensuing. Then the procession leaves the dais, and comes to the head of the right table, at which sits the Middle Warden, and he, and then his companion, the Renter Warden, who is at the head of the left table, are in due course crowned in similar fashion. The full names of each of the Wardens are clearly announced by the Clerk, when in the act of placing the crown upon the head of each of the persons referred to. Then each of the Wardens is presented with the loving-cup, drinks from it, and expresses his thanks to the Livery for the honour done to him, and announces his intention of doing his best to justify the confidence shown in him.

While the officials are still wearing the beautiful and symbolic crowns, the little procession, to the strains of the same strange, old-world music, passes solemnly down the centre of the hall, encircles the garden, and returns to the offices of the Company. A few minutes later, the crowns are quietly removed, and taken back again, that they may be used in the following year, and then the toast of " The Worshipful Company of Girdlers, root and branch, and may it flourish for ever," is given by one of the guests, and is honoured as an upstanding and most important one. The coronation has been conducted in this way for at least four hundred years, the ritual being slightly curtailed during recent times of stress, but now revived in all its full charm, alike of colour, melody and manner.*

Another Company which carries out the Capping ceremony, as it is called, is the Fishmongers, but their ancient

* I am indebted to the Clerk of the Company for having been given an opportunity upon a recent occasion of witnessing the whole ceremony in all its details.

custom was suspended for a great many years, and has only recently been revived. From 1922 it has been carried out with all its customary significance. The Clerk, wearing his gown, went behind each of the outgoing Wardens, and placed a crimson cap, decorated with silver medallions, on his head. The retiring one then drank to the health of the new Prime Warden, and wished him prosperity during his year of office. His cap was then removed, and placed upon the head of the second in seniority, who had previously removed his third warden's cap. Then the existing second warden drank to the new second warden, and he was followed by the existing third warden, who drank to the new third warden, and so through the fourth, the fifth and the sixth, and the appropriate caps were at the same time placed upon the heads of the new office-bearers.

The Wardens then withdrew to make their declarations, and the senior member of the court assumed the chair, and proposed the health of the new Prime Warden. When that had been honoured with all enthusiasm, the Wardens returned, and the new Prime Warden took the chair, wearing his cap of office, and he was followed by his five companions, garbed in similar fashion. The new Prime Warden then gave the health of the outgoing Prime Warden, and the ceremony was at an end.

Perhaps the most interesting of all the survivals in connection with the City Companies is that strange one which persists in relation to the precedence of two Companies who follow one another in the City lists, the Merchant Taylors and the Skinners. The order in which the City Companies placed themselves had relation to the dates of their charters. It was uncertain and irregular for a long time, because there were disputes as to the dates of these charters and the origin of some of the Companies. In the early years of Henry VIII's reign, the Court of Aldermen formulated a list, intended as a definitive rule for observance. In that list the Mercers were put at the head, although at the coronation of Henry VIII the Merchant Taylors had claimed to stand before them.

In the Aldermen's list the Merchant Taylors are put down as sixth, and the Skinners appear as seventh. The Clothworkers are described as Shermen or Shearmen, and the list includes only forty-eight Companies, the one at

the end being the Fruiterers. For some reason or other,
the Skinners had always been touchy regarding their precedence. There had been a dispute in 1339 between them
and the Fishmongers, that had assumed the proportions
of a riot, and then, in 1483, there came a big altercation
between them and the Merchant Taylors, which was decided
by Lord Mayor Robert Billesdon, who said that alternately
the Skinners and Merchant Taylors should take precedence
of one another, and this interesting arrangement has been
carried out ever since that remote period.

It is said that the actual words of the Lord Mayor were :
" If you Skinners go before the Merchant Taylors this
year, then the Merchant Taylors will go before you next
year ! " and on St. John the Baptist's Day the Merchant
Taylors still give a dinner to the Skinners, and the Skinners
later on return the compliment. The Skinners took precedence on the first occasion, it is not known why ; the
Merchant Taylors declared it was because they were the
weaker party, but the only rivalry that now exists between
these two Companies is in hospitality and in support of
charity.

The toast which the Master of the Merchant Taylors'
Company gives at the banquet reads thus : " The Master
and Wardens of the Worshipful Company of Merchant
Taylors drink health and prosperity to the Worshipful
Company of Skinners ; Skinners and Merchant Taylors,
Merchant Taylors and Skinners, root and branch, and may
they flourish for ever." In return, the Master of the
Skinners' Company gives the toast of the Merchant Taylors'
Company, in the following words : " The Master and
Wardens of the Skinners' Company drink health and pros-
perity to the Worshipful Company of Merchant Taylors.
Merchant Taylors and Skinners, Skinners and Merchant
Taylors, root and branch, and may they flourish for ever."
In this way the old habit is sustained, and year by year,
on the printed list, ever since the eventful year 1483, it
will be found that alternately one of these Companies
takes precedence of the other.

The Vintners' Company is the only one, so far as I know,
which still retains a certain definite commercial privilege
belonging to its members. A free Vintner is still entitled
to sell wine, irrespective of the Customs regulations. The

charter to this effect was granted by Edward VI, although it only confirmed a previous charter of Henry VII, but the important right was renewed by Elizabeth twice, by James I twice, and in 1685 by James II. Elizabeth's charter also lays down most clearly that the widow of a Vintner, if she remarried within the freedom of London—or the wife—or the apprentice—or the chief servant of a Vintner—or of his widow was entitled to keep a tavern for the sale of wine.

In 1829, however, at the earnest request of the Excise Department, the Court dealt with this matter, and removed this regulation, or varied it, so that now the privilege is only exercised by the actual members of the Guild. It is still a question whether the widow of a Liveryman of the Vintners' Company could not claim to exercise the right that had been given to her husband, and probably could enforce that right in a court of law. It is important, however, to notice that the Elizabethan charters clearly lay down amongst the provisions under which the free Vintner is to hold his house, that he should not " sanction or connive at any bawdry on the premises," and that he should " enforce good and honest conversation by frequenters thereof."

The Vintners used to enjoy the exclusive right of " loading and landing, rolling, pitching and turning," of wines and spirits imported into or exported from the City of London, and all places within three miles of the same, and it used to employ its own tackle porters, and hold itself answerable for their faults. These privileges still hold good ; but there is hardly any opportunity for their being carried out, and, to a great extent, they are only nominal rights.

About one other power the Vintners' Company is very tenacious. It has, in conjunction with the Dyers' Company, the right to keep a certain proportion of the swans on the Thames, and the three Swan Wardens, representing these two Companies and the Crown, make an annual expedition, in order to inspect the swans on the river, and to make the marks upon their bills, known as the nicks, by which the swans are attached and marked as the property of the respective owners. It is from this custom that the old inn sign which generally appears as the " Swan with Two Necks " is derived. It should really be " The Swan with Two Nicks."

With regard to these swans, the privilege possessed by the Vintners' Company goes back for many hundreds of years. The earliest record relative to it is in an ancient book dealing with the accounts of the Vintners' Company for 1509, now preserved in the British Museum. From the entry in this book it is quite clear that the privilege of keeping swans was ancient even at that time, and it is impossible to say when the right was first created. In 1609, a hundred years later, in the first Court book of the Company that has been preserved, appears the record of the appointment of Swan Uppers, and that is so worded as to show that these officers were simply appointed in succession to others, who had held the office before, and that there had been a long succession of officers preceding them.

The younger of the three Wardens of the Company is always known as the " Swan Warden." It is his special province to see to the safety of the birds, and to direct his swan markers, when necessary, to inspect them. The inspection takes place on the last Monday in July, when the cygnets are about two months old. It is called the " Swan Voyage," and the swan markers belonging to the Crown, and to the two Companies of the Vintners and the Dyers, meet at Southwark Bridge, and proceed together on the journey. The excursion is made under the direction of the Swan Warden, but is at the instance of the Crown, and in order to induce the fishermen on the river to preserve the birds, a very liberal remuneration is made to those who succour them.

The practice of marking the birds appears to have arisen first of all in Buckinghamshire, and to have been judicially established in the second year of the reign of Richard III, wherein, after an action taken by Lord Strange and Sir John Charlton, a decision was arrived at concerning the owners of swans. The plan was then adopted of giving a pecuniary reward to those who nested or protected them. It must be borne in mind that the swan is still regarded as a royal bird by law, and by a statute of Edward IV no persons otherwise than those connected with the Crown are able to keep swans on the Thames, while in Queen Elizabeth's time, in the thirty-fourth year of her reign, the question of marking swans was especially set forth, and swans that were not marked were declared to belong to the King by his prerogative.

The Vintners' Company is sometimes in possession of as many as five hundred swans.

The Fishmongers' Company still retains its rights in respect of the fish that enters London, and does magnificent service, through its fish inspectors, in protecting the inhabitants of London from bad fish. This power of inspection and condemnation it has always possessed, and still exercises it to a very complete extent.

The Goldsmiths retain in their hands the right of the inspection of gold coin on the occasion of what is known as the Trial of the Pyx, but, moreover, they have the right of inspecting all gold and silver plate, which has to be marked at Goldsmiths' Hall with certain marks which guarantee the year in which it was made and the quality of the metal. They also, in certain circumstances, denote the name of the maker.

The Gunmakers still retain the privilege and the right of inspecting barrels for rifles, and the Plumbers undertake a series of examinations by which the ability to carry out certain work on the part of plumbers is carefully tested, so that those who are able to pass the examinations are entitled to term themselves registered plumbers, and to belong, if they so desire, to the Company, taking up their Freedom by what is called Redemption.

The Apothecaries, for many generations, have carried on a wholesale and retail business in drugs, retaining certain ancient recipes in their hands, which have considerable value even at the present day, and anyone desiring drugs that were absolutely pure, could, until the year 1922, purchase them at Apothecaries' Hall, with a degree of greater assurance than when the same drugs were bought from an ordinary chemist. The Company in 1922, however, decided not to enter into further competition with the ordinary trade, and closed its retail establishment, disposing at the same time of its wholesale business to a well-known firm. It still, however, retained in its own hands a privilege of far higher value, namely, that of certifying concerning the skill of medical men and admitting them after an elaborate and rigid examination to be Fellows of the Apothecaries' Company.

Beyond these, I do not know of any City Company that retains any of its greater rights concerning the inspection of things belonging to its particular trade. The Painters still have the privilege of examining paintings that are exhibited within the City of London, and condemning them, if they are thought to be contrary to the morals of the King's lieges, or if the manner in which they are painted is regarded by the Court of the Company as unsatisfactory, but, so far as I know, it never exercises these rights. The Pewterers still retain the touchplates containing the marks upon pewter, and I am inclined to think as there are several members of the trade belonging to the Company, that their pewter *is* still marked in accordance with the ancient habit, and at the old Hall.*

The Stationers, for many generations, had the " sole and exclusive " power of registering all books that were issued, and "Entered at Stationers' Hall" was the customary imprint to be found upon the volumes. This privilege does not now survive in its original form—it has been taken away by Act of Parliament—but a record is still kept on the same lines concerning the publication of all books, and the ancient records of the Company are of the highest possible value to bibliographers, with regard to the history of all the volumes entered at the Hall in days past.

The Spectaclemakers undertake examinations with regard to optical matters, and have interested themselves very largely in the investigation of the optical qualities of certain glasses used for spectacles. Many of the Companies are keenly interested in the crafts with which they were originally concerned, and spend considerable sums in the advancement and improvement of these crafts, but I believe one Company *only* continues to confine its membership actually to members of its craft, and that is the Scriveners, the people who in the early days were the writers of deeds, who had to do with conveyances, and who were also intimately concerned in the

---

* The Pewterers' five touchplates are reproduced in Mr. Welch's *History of the Pewterers' Company*, but are also described in very clear language by Mr. Massé in his work on *Pewter Plate* (Bell, 1904), in a lengthy appendix, and the touches are separately indexed also in that book.

In the *Pewter Collector*, by the same author (Jenkins, 1921), the touchplates are again reproduced, and fresh information concerning them is given.

duties of banking and agencies. So far as I have been able to understand, *all* their members are still connected with the profession. The Law Stationers have undertaken the work of the writing, but the Scriveners are still the notaries in connection with the City of London. The Company is therefore a true survival of ancient form.

The Weavers claim to be the oldest of all the Companies ; they were recognised as having a corporate existence in the time of Henry I, and Henry II granted them a charter in 1184. Edward III gave many charters to Livery Companies, for example to the Goldsmiths, Vintners, Fishmongers and Skinners, and he himself became a member of the Merchant Taylors' Company.

There are many ancient survivals in connection with Sermons, the Courts of different Companies attending at different City churches on various occasions in accordance with regulations laid down by the wills of past benefactors, listening to particular sermons, and distributing alms after the service. One of the most interesting is in connection with the Stationers' Company, when, in accordance with the bequest of Richard Johnson, who died in 1795, the Court attends at Hendon Parish Church to hear a sermon by the Rector on the text " Vita humana bulla est "— " Human life is a bubble." The Rector receives a certain fee for preaching this sermon, and immediately after Divine service the Court inspects the tomb of this benefactor, in Hendon churchyard, to see that it is in good order. On the tombstone is inscribed the text which has to be used annually as the subject of the sermon.

For a long time there were sermons preached in the City of London at what was known as the Spital Cross. The custom is said to have originated in the time of Edward IV, and to have been continued down to the Reformation. The sermons that are still preached annually in connection with what are known as the Royal Hospitals—Bridewell, Christ's Hospital and Saint Bartholomew's—are even now called the Spital Sermons, and an allusion is usually made by the preacher to the fact that these sermons have continued in London annually since that very remote time.

Of all the City Companies, however, the one which retains the largest number of mediæval ceremonies is the only one which, to use an accepted Irishism, is not a City Company in the ordinary sense. It is the Worshipful Company of Parish Clerks, which, although a City Company in one sense, is, more strictly than the others, a survival of a religious guild, and is not counted as one of the Livery Companies. To this Company, no one can belong who is not an actual parish clerk; and there are only certain parishes whose clerks may join the Company. It is the parish clerks of the City churches within a certain fixed limit, forming the boundaries of the ancient City, and of one or two adjacent small villages attached to the City at that time, as for example, Hackney and Islington, who alone are eligible. In consequence, every member of this Company must be an actual practising parish clerk, with, of course, the curious result that, although the direct descendant of an ancient Catholic guild, and in closer connection with that guild than is the case with any other Company, it is impossible for a Catholic to belong to it, as no Catholic could be an acting parish clerk in an Anglican church.

Moreover, this is the only Company which possesses its own organ and organist, and which still makes use of the " office hymn," and it is the only Company at whose banquets is read out the list of its early benefactors, going back to a period of very remote antiquity, certainly at least to 1233, when the Guild of Saint Nicholas of the Parish Clerks of London is first mentioned in the Company's books at the Guildhall, and after the roll of its early benefactors has been read, the Company still uses the ancient invocation that their souls may have rest.

The Company was originally founded for those who were in the minor orders of the Church, the grades known as the door-keeper, the reader, the exorcist and the acolyte, and the clerks were of course originally tonsured. After the Reformation, the minor orders were practically left out, being only regarded as subject to higher Orders, but the rights of the Clerk still continued, although he ceased gradually to be in Orders at all. In the first Prayer-book of Edward VI, and in the present-day Prayer-book, the existence of a parish clerk is still recognised, and he is, it may be presumed, deemed to represent the exorcist, the acolyte, reader and sub-deacon, all in one.

The Parish Clerks' Company still keeps up its definite

connection with ecclesiastical arrangements, having its feasts on the great ecclesiastical days (notably on Ascension Day), when its members attend church in procession, and each of them, in his own church, takes the position for which his office gives him authority.

The fact that they were a religious fraternity, and have continued to exist on those lines, is borne out by other of their present-day customs. They are members of the only Company whose meal is prepared in its own hall, and by its own servants, and whose servants actually serve at the meal. Moreover, they constitute the only Company who themselves take part in serving one another, and in serving their guests, who are, by the way, limited to two persons. The offices connected with serving wine, and other similar duties, are always taken by their own members in rotation, keeping up the definite assumption that they are all brothers, equal to one another in importance, even though, for a time, one holds the office of Master, and two those of Wardens, but these latter offices never prevent their holders as Wardens from waiting upon the other brethren in the ordinary routine.

Again, it is of peculiar interest to find that the Parish Clerks keep up the existence of what is known as the Bederoll, and perhaps a word or two here with reference to that may be of some interest, because the word, of itself, is a remarkable survival. It is an Anglo-Saxon word, meaning a prayer, and little balls with a hole through them, placed on a string, were used from quite early days for keeping account of the number of prayers repeated, and thus the word became transferred to those globular objects themselves, and hence the use of our word " bead."

There is exactly the same origin to the words " bidding prayer," which is the prayer for the souls of the benefactors said before the sermon, and such a prayer, although not actually in the Reformed Communion a prayer for the souls, as it was in Catholic times, is still used in cathedrals and University churches. The Saxon word " biddan " should be translated " to pray for the souls of benefactors."

The Parish Clerks have always taken notice of those who were benefactors to their religious fraternity, and in the Bederoll which is said after dinner, they refer to their founder, King Henry III ; to Edward VI, and to the three brothers who were uncles to Henry VI ; to Edward IV, and to the members of his family; to Margaret, Countess of Richmond; to various sovereigns who have from time to time been connected with the Company, and to a long list of religious; abbots, priests and others, who were closely associated with it. They do not pray for Henry VIII !

It should, however, be further mentioned in connection with this interesting Company that, in respect to its relation to the Corporation of London, one of its duties was to make returns of the deaths and christenings in the respective parishes with which the clerks were connected, and to print weekly what were known as Bills of Mortality. These bills were printed on a hand press, which actually stood in the Hall where the Parish Clerks still meet, and the duty of printing these Bills of Mortality extended from the time of Henry VIII down into the nineteenth century— indeed practically until October, 1858, when the arrange- ment, which had been the subject of considerable negotiation during the previous hundred years, definitely ceased, and the copies of the bills in the possession of the Company from 1664 to 1699, and from 1701 to 1829, were handed over to the library of the Corporation of the City.

It was my good fortune to have the privilege of giving over to the Parish Clerks an interesting collection of these Bills of Mortality issued during the time of the Plague, which had been preserved in their original condition amongst some family muniments ; so that they might possess in their Hall some of the original bills that were printed in the building where they still meet.

The Parish Clerks are also one of the few Companies (numbering less than half a dozen) in the City of London, who possess their original funeral palls. Theirs is an exceedingly beautiful one, of great importance as an example of fine needlework. They also possess a garland of crimson velvet embroidered, dated 1601, which is placed on the head of the Master when the result of the new election is formally announced to the assembled brotherhood. It is somewhat like a mitre without the crown, and after being placed on the Master's head is folded up and worn on his arm somewhat in the manner in which a priest carries a maniple. The hearse cloth was repaired in 1686, and it and the garland were lent recently to the South Kensington

Museum, where, as fine examples of old English needlework, they attracted considerable attention. Members of the Livery of the City, when they die, still have the privilege of having their coffins covered with the ancient palls or hearse cloths which belong to their own Company. The finest of these palls are those belonging to the Fishmongers, the Merchant Taylors and the Saddlers. They are composed of needlework of such superb quality that for some time past the privilege of their being used at a Liveryman's funeral has been suspended for fear of any damage occurring to them at a funeral. As a matter of fact, however, it is stated that the relatives of a deceased Liveryman belonging to either of these Companies could *demand* the use of the pall, and that belonging to the Parish Clerks is still in use and has been used many times since 1860, when after many years of disuse its original importance was revived.

The Fishmongers' pall is a sumptuous piece of work without parallel in this country, with superb colouring, the wings of the angels represented upon it being composed of peacocks' feathers. It has a splendid fringe. The Merchant Taylors have two palls : one is magnificent and both are exceedingly precious.

A presentation takes place every year of fine English fruit, given to the Lord Mayor by the Worshipful Company of Fruiterers. This Company had been accustomed to pay dues to the Lord Mayor for the rights exercised in the markets, but for the last two hundred years these dues have been commuted into a gift of fruit, and this arrangement is still retained.

In 1632, the Lord Mayor conferred a special favour upon the Gardeners' Company by issuing his warrant for the apprehension of any persons using the trade of gardening in contempt of the Company's charters, and ever since then, on the 29th of June, the date of the Lord Mayor's warrant, English flowers, vegetables, herbs and fruit have been presented by the Company to the Lord Mayor.

The Clothworkers' Company offers on certain occasions, to those who happen to be present at its feast, boxes of a large spiced sponge-cake. These are really Corpus Christi cakes, and are the survivals of the old cakes given away by the Company when it was a religious guild, and when its greatest and most eventful day was the feast of Corpus

Christi. The cakes are of unusual size, and of somewhat unusual flavour, and are said to be made from a recipe for their manufacture which has been in use since the time of the early Edwards and so still continues.

In Clothworkers' Hall, as Mr. Bell points out in his book about *Unknown London*, there is still retained an odd custom whereby guests are asked when the liqueurs are brought round whether they dine with Alderman or Lady Cooper, and according to the reply a glass of liqueur is handed to them. Two hundred years ago, a certain Alderman Cooper left to the Clothworkers' Company a sum of money to provide fine cognac to be handed round when the members of the Company dined. His wife left a similar amount for the provision of another liqueur, and in consequence, the memories of these two persons are preserved in this interesting ceremonial.

CHAPTER III

IN THE CITY OF LONDON

CITY PRIVILEGES AND CUSTOMS

A CURIOUS survival in London consists in the fact that certain lengths of cloth are still presented by the Corporation annually, and are known as the lengths of Livery cloth. This gift of cloth was really made by the City Corporation in order to give the servants of the Ministers an official livery when they visited the City. In the early days of London's history, the retainers of great lords, wearing their livery, were so numerous as to become dangerous to the King and his laws, so the wearing of liveries was prohibited, except by members of the Guilds and Fraternities. The old custom gives these high officials sufficient cloth with which to garb their attendants when they come into the City. Although there is no need now for this gift of cloth, it is still kept up with extreme punctiliousness, and lengths of green and black cloth are duly sent in by the authorities to the state officials and to those of the City.

The list of people who receive the black cloth, $4\frac{1}{2}$ yards each, is as follows :—

Lord Chancellor, Lord Chief Justice of England, Master of the Rolls, Lord Chamberlain of His Majesty's Household, Vice-Chamberlain, Lord Steward, Treasurer, Controller, Secretary of State, Home Department, Secretary of State, Foreign Department, Mr. Attorney-General, Mr. Solicitor-General, Mr. Recorder, Mr. Chamberlain, and Mr. Common Serjeant. The Town Clerk has six yards of black and six of green, his principal clerk four of each, and there are also five cloth-notes issued, four yards at sixteen shillings a yard to the Attorney in Exchequer, the Attorney in Chancery, and the Cashier in the Chamberlain's office, and four yards at twelve shillings a yard to Mr. Recorder's clerk and the

Usher to the Court of Aldermen. The cloth is inspected and selected by the Court of Aldermen on the 4th of December.

To show how tenacious is the City of certain survivals, it may be mentioned that the pillars of Guildhall still, up to a certain point, are dirty, while, above that point, they are clean, and it may be pointed out that the grubby appearance of the pillars was actually caused by the smoke from the Great Fire of London, the result of which has never been cleared away, from that date to the present day, and the smoky appearance of these columns recalls that terrible event, when a large section of London perished. It was in Guildhall that twenty-two of the judges met to settle the boundary disputes after the Great Fire, and the table at which they sat is still preserved in the building, an interesting relic of those days.

What we now call " spring-cleaning " is said to go back to the days of the Passover, for from that time there has been a custom whereby everything in a house should be cleaned in the early part of the year, so as to make it all fresh and tidy for the on-coming seasons. The custom was kept in full use by the Jews, and especially by those of them who settled in Holland, and gradually the whole of the Dutch nation became impregnated with this idea of cleanliness and tidiness, and hence arose, it is said, the love of cleaning which betokens the Dutch housewife. In the time of Sir Thomas More and Erasmus the idea of spring cleaning made great way in England, coming to us from the Netherlands. Thus, a custom which is understood and recognised by everyone at the present time, and which appears to have been carried out all over England, with the exception of Guildhall, came into full force.

A curious privilege, which used to belong to the Sheriffs of London, was that, in memory of the Great Fire, and to remind them of the services which the Sheriffs personally rendered, in their efforts to extinguish that fire, the Corporation of the City had a habit of presenting to each Sheriff twelve leather fire buckets emblazoned with the City coat of arms, and this custom was carried out from the time of the Great Fire, certainly down to 1883, and there is some evidence that it was continued even later than that date.

For a long time, certain ancient payments used to be made to the Sheriffs. These, in 1883, were commuted for a fixed annual sum of about £815, but, previous to that time, their origin was interesting for the side-light it threw on the habits of the times. The sum of £5 6s. 8d. was paid for a toll originally paid by German merchants in London for wax candles, for herrings and for sturgeons. Fifty pounds was paid for the benefit of poor prisoners in the City, to be given to them on the eves of Christmas and of Easter. Eighteen pounds was paid for a toll on London Bridge, and a rent that belonged to Bromley College. Fifty pounds was paid for an allowance in respect of London Bridge, two hundred and sixty pounds for the toll of Smithfield Market, sixty pounds for the toll of Bishopsgate and Aldgate, a hundred and fifty pounds for scavage, or scavengering fees, and nine pounds for the fire buckets just alluded to, so that in those days, from these various ancient payments made to the Sheriffs, each received £407 7s. 10d., and now the two of them receive a lump sum of £814 15s. 8d., and the details of the ancient payments have passed into obscurity.

The City still has possession of what is known as the Hospital of Bridewell, and since 1552, part of this hospital has had cells to which refractory apprentices could be committed. The power granted to the Corporation by Edward VI was to examine " all persons who wandered idly in the City, and to compel them to occupy themselves in honest labour," and it also gave permission for " searching out idle, ruffianly vagabonds," and for committing them into the cells, and for incarcerating apprentices who " did not do their work properly, or who spoiled their tools or quarrelled with their fellow-employees."

These rights were exercised more or less completely down to 1923, when it was pointed out that there had been but one case of an apprentice committed to a cell in 1916, and none since, and that, although the cells were still there, and there was either a beadle or warder for the " accommodation of refractory " apprentices, yet the use of this house of occupation, as it was called, had passed away, and in consequence it was desired to use that portion of the income which was applied to the warden and to the cells, for more needful purposes. Sanction was accordingly granted by Mr. Justice Russell, under which the scheme was modified, and a portion of the funds applied to maintaining a school for girls, which it was desirable should be placed in the country. The Judge pointed out, however, that so definite were the instructions in the Charters with regard to cells and apprentices, that he had no power to order them to be done away with, and that if the Corporation felt it was desirable to make that change, an Act of Parliament would have to be applied for, to carry it out.

Christ's Hospital has disappeared from the City now for some years, having been re-founded in Horsham, but, as long as it continued in its old place, one saw the boys about in the City streets wearing that extraordinary and delightful costume, which belonged to the time of Edward VI, and has been in use in that school ever since his days. It consists of a long blue coat, which falls nearly to the ankles, kept in position round the waist by a red leather strap.* With it are worn knee breeches, yellow stockings and low shoes. The costume has always been made specially for the school, and by tailors who are in direct succession from those who originally made it, and so carefully has its use been safeguarded, that it is practically impossible to obtain a suit as worn by a pupil of this school, for the purpose of a fancy dance or anything of that kind, the privilege of supplying it being definitely retained by the Hospital. For a long time Christ's Hospital had the right of minting its own money, certain tokens of differing value passing as current coin within the precincts, only, of the hospital, and there are examples of these rare tokens carefully preserved in the school museum, although the actual use for them has now ceased. During the time that the school continued in London, the ancient custom of Lent suppers took place, as it had always done from the time of its foundation, and on more than one occasion I have been present at these festivities, and seen the quaint observances, by which the boys set and cleared away the contents of the tables, and made their obeisance to the guest of the evening, who was, as a rule, the President of the school.

I am not likely to forget the Duke of Cambridge—who was an extremely popular President of Christ's Hospital, and whom the boys were always glad to welcome—making use of a characteristic habit in his speech. Talking to the boys in friendly fashion after supper, he warned them

* The strap worn by the Blue-coat Boy is still called by its old name as his " girdle."

against certain bad habits, more especially that of swearing, and then, in very simple fashion, added the words, which in a moment brought down the house, " Damn it all, boys, never swear ! "

There is a curious old custom in connection with Christ's Hospital which has been in existence since 1773, and which still continues. It relates to a certain Hampstead lady, Mary Gibson, who left five thousand pounds in three per cent. consolidated bank stock, directing the interest to be applied to " the preservation, beautification, and keeping in good and substantial repair " of her monument and family vault in Sutton in the county of Surrey. At the same time, she left five hundred pounds in the same stock, the interest of which was to be applied in the following fashion. Five pounds was to go to the Rector of the church for the service and sermon on every August 12th, five pounds for the poor of Hampstead, four pounds for the churchwarden of the church where the sermon was preached, and a pound for the clerk, but the money was only left on the condition that the Governors of Christ's Hospital opened the vault in Sutton every year, and saw that it was in good order, and if they failed in this trust, the money passed away to the Foundling Hospital. The vault has been opened annually year by year, on the 12th of August, and it is believed in the Gibson family that when the last member of the family has been buried in that vault, it is finally to be locked up, the key taken to Palestine, and thrown into the river Jordan, but Christ's Hospital have no information respecting this extraordinary statement, and are quite satisfied with the duty that does fall upon them of examining the tomb every year.

The tomb resembles a large room, around which are shelves bearing the various coffins, and is a very weird place to enter.

One of the sermons that is preached annually in the City is known as the Lion Sermon. It was founded in accordance with the will of Sir John Gayer, who was Sheriff of London in 1635, and Lord Mayor in 1646 and 1647, and was to commemorate the escape of Sir John Gayer from death by a lion, and also to commemorate his further escape from imprisonment in the Tower by the Commonwealth Parliament, for his ardent attachment to the cause of King Charles I.

Sir John had been a member of the old Turkey and Levant Company, which traded under a charter in the Sultan's wide domains on the shores of the Mediterranean, and he often went to the East, going inland with long caravans for the purchase of Oriental goods, carpets and spices, brought back to London by his ships, and by the sale of these he established his fortune. It was on one of these dangerous trading expeditions, when crossing the Arabian desert, that he had the encounter with the lion which he commemorated by this sermon. It has been preached year by year at St. Katherine Cree, and quite recently the preacher was the Rev. E. R. Gayer, a direct descendant of Hugh Gayer, one of the original founder's brothers, and he was accompanied to the church by a dozen other persons, who were all connected with the family. The lessons read on the occasion have always been those describing the deliverance of St. Peter from prison and of Daniel from the lion's den. It was Sir John Gayer and his brothers who built the present church of St. Katherine Cree, on the site and ruins of an older and smaller church, and the famous Merchant Adventurer and Lord Mayor was himself buried in the vaults underneath. There has been no single year since his decease in which this sermon has not been preached.

There is still preached at Huntingdon, I believe, every year, a sermon against witchcraft. The preacher is selected by Queen's College, preaches his sermon in the Huntingdon Parish Church, and receives two pounds for doing so. Whether or not he has still to entertain the Mayor and Corporation at lunch out of these two pounds I do not know ; but such was the original arrangement made some two hundred years ago by the person who left a sum of money to the College, and declared that this sermon must be preached annually, and that the preacher should never fail to point out the extreme wickedness of witches.

The ringing of certain bells has also been retained very carefully in the City, and in different churches the Angelus bell has been rung, although for a long time its purport had been lost sight of. It was originally, of course, intended to remind all who were round about to pay daily honour to the Incarnation, Passion and Resurrection of Our Lord. One of the churches where it used always to be rung was that of St. Magnus the Martyr. After a while, the ringing fell into disuse, but it has recently been renewed.

By the way, as an example of the manner in which hours have changed in the City, it should be mentioned that the bell of the Coal Exchange is still rung at two o'clock for the close of the coal market, although in the present day the coal market does not actually *open* till half-past two, and that which was closed in early days at two o'clock by ancient regulations, does not now even open its precincts until half an hour after that time.

Another curious custom relating to the City is that of the detachment of the guard that comes down to the Bank of England every night. During the Gordon Riots, some-one tried to break into the Bank, and the King's Guard was instructed to send a small detachment of its men to watch over the Bank at night. The Bank has been moved more than once, and is now housed in a building of extreme strength, which was built by Sir John Soane without any exterior windows, in order that it should be peculiarly strong against any such attack. It would almost stand a siege, but the guard, once appointed, has always gone down night after night into the City, and the privilege is highly valued, because the lieutenant in charge has a dinner provided for him, with a bottle of good claret and another of old port. To this he is at liberty to ask a guest, and he and his men remain on point duty all night, in order to protect the building against the possibility of an attack. The soldiers are, I understand, still armed with ball cartridge, so that an attempted entry is attended with considerable risk.

It might be well, before passing on to another subject, to note that there were originally many City Companies which have disappeared, and to refer to the interesting circumstance that the oldest and greatest of all London's Trading Companies, that of the Merchants of the Staple, still survives. It was a Company incorporated by Edward III, and actually still exists, although it carries out no duties connected with the trade of wool from which it originally took its name, and is nothing more now than a small community of persons, who hold in common a small sum of money which has always belonged to the Guild, certain seals, and above all, a series of minute-books.

These books, which have never been properly examined, contain details of the history of this ancient Corporation from very early times, down to a comparatively recent period, when the old hall, still known as Staple Inn, passed out of its possession. It is probable that, in the books of this Company, which are now preserved at its Bankers, could be found a history of the early trade of England, having far greater importance than any that could be produced from another series of documents. There was, at one time, in the City of London, a Company of Fullers. It has now disappeared in London, but I believe similar Companies still exist in some of the Northern towns, notably in Newcastle-on-Tyne. In the city of London it was absorbed by the Clothworkers.

One of the London churches, however, is still known as St. Mary Matfellon, the Matfellon being the fuller's teazle, largely used by the trade in its operations. It was culti-vated on a piece of land near to this church, and on another piece, which until quite recent times was known as " Teazel Close." The church is in Whitechapel.

There is still a building known as Pinner's Hall in the City, but the Pinners themselves have disappeared long ago. There was a Company known at one time as the Shearmen, and that name still remains in connection with a lane in the City, and with an alley; it has also become a family name, but there is no longer a Company of Shearmen— they are the Clothworkers now. The Spicers were another trading Company which became united with the Grocers, first of all being bound up with the far more important and wealthy Guild of the Pepperers, and their name survives as that of an important surname. The Woodmongers have disappeared as an actual Livery Company for a long time, but as an example of how a name and a characteristic survives, it is curious to note that coal merchants are still officially known at Guildhall as Woodmongers, and are considered as having a connection with the extinct Company of Woodmongers. This was because in the early days it was only the Woodmongers and Lightermen who handled the trade of coal, and they were the only persons regarded as owners of coal craft, and claiming to have any connection with the loading and unloading of the new material known as seacoal, which was to take the place of wood.

There are several relics of the Company of Woodmongers still in existence, and some interesting things which belonged to the earliest established society of owners of coal craft. These are preserved at the Coal Exchange, but for a long time the early minute books of that Company have been missing, and an effort has been made quite recently to discover what has become of these volumes, which date back to 1731. The Society of Coal-merchants is very anxious to acquire them. Curiously enough, although the Society retains its rooms in the Coal Exchange, it is unable to hold a meeting there, if any large number of persons are expected, as the Rotunda, which is the only suitable place for such a meeting, is a public exchange, and cannot therefore be used by one particular body.

It may be worth while to point out, in connection with this Rotunda, that it has a rather curious floor of inlaid work, and that it is stated in books about London that the black oak in this floor was part of a tree more or less fossilised, many hundreds of years old, which was found in the river, and that in the shield of the City arms which adorns the floor, the blade of the dagger is made of wood taken from a mulberry tree which Peter the Great had planted, when he worked as a shipwright at Deptford.

A visitor in one of the City churches a little while ago was puzzled to see in St. James's, Garlickhithe, at the back of the pulpit, on a level roughly with the preacher's head, a wooden peg which appeared to belong to the pulpit wood-work, and yet oddly out of place in its position. The explanation of the existence of this peg is a remarkable one ; and similar pegs are to be found in other parts of this same church and in other City churches. Wigs were in fashion in the old days, and even when other people had given up the use of the wig the parson retained it, but on an exceptionally warm Sunday he could remove his wig, hang it on a peg behind him and then resume it on con- clusion of the sermon. Other people could follow his example, and hence the pegs in other parts of the building.

CHAPTER IV

THE HOUSE OF LORDS

THE HOUSE AND THE KING

THE House of Lords has two distinct positions. It is a great legislative assembly, and it is the supreme Law Court of the realm. It constitutes the final Court of Appeal, and yet, at the same time, these functions are strangely united, because the decisions given by the House of Lords as a Court of Appeal are not given by judges delivering judgment. They are given by Members of the House as a legislative assembly sitting to debate the reasons why the *House* should take a particular course in relation to the questions before it, prefacing all the decisions by the words " My Lords," and not making or altering any law, but simply interpreting and fixing the interpretation.

The decisions are given " Content " or " Non-content," and every Peer has the right to assist in this Court of Appeal, whether he knows anything of law or not, and whether he has any interest or none, in the case under consideration. This Supreme Court is very differently constituted from any other Court ; it is extraordinarily simple, there is just a table covered with scarlet cloth, near to the bar, and the Lord Chancellor, who usually presides, alone wears wig and gown. None of the Law Lords follow his example, and all the others, whether Law Lords or ordinary Peers, wear ordinary morning dress. The decision why the House takes a certain course cannot be overruled by any person or by any body.

The Members of the Upper House attend in response to a writ, which is sent to each Peer, and is presented by him to the Clerk of the House when he takes his seat. The writ that is issued to all the Peers demands that they should be " personally present with Us, and with the said Prelates, Great Men and Peers, at the meeting of the House," and with regard to the temporal Peers, they are summoned upon " the faith and allegiance with which you are bound to Us," but, with regard to the spiritual Peers, " by the faith and love by which you are bound to Us," and this wording has been in use for over six hundred years.

The Roll of the Upper House, on which the names of the Peers appear in order of precedence, is an actual roll, and is wound round a roller ; it is a long strip of parchment some sixteen inches wide. The Royal Princes are named at the head of it, then follow the names of the Archbishop of Canterbury, the Lord High Chancellor (who was originally, as I have stated, an ecclesiastic, the King's confessor, and thence derives his title of " Keeper of the King's Conscience "), the Archbishop of York, the Lord President of the Council, and the Lord Privy Seal. Then come the Peers in rightful precedence, the Dukes first, the Marquesses next ; the Earls, headed by the Master of the Horse ; the Viscounts, headed by the Lord Steward of the Household and the Lord Chamberlain of the Household ; the Bishops, and the Barons. Many of the Peers do not, of course, sit in the Upper House under the titles by which they are generally known ; the Duke of Hamilton, for example, sits as the Duke of Brandon, the Duke of Abercorn, not as a Duke at all, but as the Marquess of Abercorn, the Duke of Buccleuch as Earl, for he is Earl of Doncaster ; the Duke of Montrose, also as an Earl, for he is Earl Graham, the Duke of Atholl as Earl Strange ; and the Duke of Roxborough as Earl Innes. The Marquess of Londonderry does not sit amongst his brother peers, but is summoned as Earl Vane ; the Duke of Leinster is summoned as Viscount Leinster, and the Earls of Donoughmore and Clancarty sit amongst Viscounts as Viscount Hutchinson and Viscount Clancarty ; while, amongst the Barons, appears the Earl of Bessborough who sits as Lord Ponsonby ; the Marquess of Waterford, who sits as Lord Tyrone ; the Earl of Shannon, who sits as Lord Carlton ; the Earl of Gosford, who sits as Lord Worlingham ; the Marquess of Huntly, who sits as Lord Meldrum ; the Earl of Enniskillen, as Lord Grinstead ; the Earl of Limerick as Lord Foxford ; the Marquess of Lothian as Lord Ker ; the Marquess Conyngham as Lord Minster ; the Earl of Longford as Lord Silchester ; and many others, who sit by titles differing from those by which they are generally known, but which happen to be the peerages of the United Kingdom which give them their seat in the Upper House.

Of the Dukes, the premier one is the Duke of Norfolk; the premier Marquess is Lord Winchester ; the premier Earl, Lord Shrewsbury ; the premier Viscount, Lord Hereford, and the premier Barony is that of De Ros, and, following this, the next Barony in priority is that of Mowbray.

The Scottish Peers, of course, do not all sit in the Upper House, but only sixteen of them, who have been elected as representative Peers. The same thing applies to the Irish Peers, amongst whom there are twenty-eight who sit in the House for life. The ordinary accepted statement, therefore, that every Peer is a Member of the House of Lords, is erroneous, for a considerable number of both Scottish and Irish Peers have never sat in the Upper House, and are never likely to do so.

The Roll of the House is compiled for each fresh Parliament, and is solemnly delivered to the Clerk by Garter King-at-Arms, who comes into the House wearing his tabard ; at the same time, the certificate respecting the Scottish Peers is also presented to the House. There is no Roll in the House of Commons, the list, to which the Members sign their names, being contained in a book.

The introduction of a new Peer is an exceedingly curious sight. The Peer comes in, with two Lords of his own rank, preceded by the Earl Marshal, Garter King-at-Arms, in his gorgeous heraldic tabard, and Black Rod ; the Roll and then the patent of creation, are handed to the Lord Chancellor on bended knee. The documents are read out by the Reading Clerk, the writ of summons is then produced, the oath is taken, and the Roll is signed. Garter then conducts the new Peer to the position in the House belonging to Peers of his own particular rank, and he takes his seat with his supporters on either side, all three of them wearing their State robes, the degree of the Peerage to which they belong being denoted by the number of bars of ermine on the velvet of the robe.

Having taken his seat, the Peer and his supporters rise three separate times, removing their cocked hats, and bowing low to the Lord Chancellor, who, having put on his

three-cornered hat, uncovers at every salute. The Peer
has then legally taken his seat, and in company with his
supporters he leaves the House, stopping at the Woolsack
as a rule, in going out, to shake hands with the Lord Chancellor. He then removes his robes of office, and returns,
if it pleases him, to the House, in ordinary morning costume.

The ceremony has an added interest when the Lord
Chancellor himself takes his seat as a Peer. He is the
representative of the Sovereign, but he cannot preside over
his own elevation, and therefore the empty Throne sym-
bolises the presence of the Sovereign. The covering is
removed from it, showing the richly embroidered representation of the Royal coat of arms, and the gilt rails usually
in front of the Throne are also removed, as if the King
himself was present to take his seat.

The usual complicated ceremony takes place, but the
new Peer, instead of bowing to the Woolsack, which is
unoccupied, bows before the empty Throne, makes his
obeisances to it, and at the end of the ceremony, when he
would usually have handed his patent to the occupant of
the Woolsack, and shaken hands with him, he walks up
to the empty Throne, and places his patent upon it. It
remains there during the rest of the time the House sits,
and is eventually removed by the Clerk of the House, when
the House has risen. It is *always* the custom, in the event
of the Lord Chancellor not being present, to allow the
empty Throne to be regarded as the presence of the Sovereign, and it is to this empty Throne that the Peers make
their bow, as though the Sovereign were himself present.

The Woolsack, the big settee stuffed with wool, emblematic of the staple trade of England in mediaeval times, is
technically considered as outside the House. If the Lord
Chancellor desires to speak he moves several paces to the
left, and is then regarded as being within the boundaries
of the House, where he speaks just as an ordinary Peer,
and not in any respect as the mouth of the House. He
has no authority to rule a Peer out of order, he cannot
decide which Peer is to be heard before any other Peer,
and he cannot prefer one Peer before another. All the
Peers in the House, whatever may be their dignity, are
regarded as being equal, all have a right to speak when
they desire, and the House only can determine who is to

be heard first; there is no one to speak in its name, and its proceedings cannot be adjourned without the consent of the entire House, which consent has to be taken before the sitting is at an end.

What is called a full dress debate in the House of Lords, a somewhat rare occurrence, is very important, because, as a rule, the Lords who speak on particular subjects do so with authority, and as the result of long experience. They give to the House the results of that experience, they are not bound to consider any person or any constituency, they can speak for as long or as short a time as they please, and no one but the House itself can stop them. The duration of each speech therefore depends very much upon the laws of courtesy, and the House itself is a very patient listener when a Peer who thoroughly understands his subject is giving his opinion.

Nothing is more interesting in the House of Lords than the ceremony by which consent is given to the Bills which transforms them into Acts of Parliament. It is almost invariably given by Lords Commissioners, of whom the Lord Chancellor is generally one, for the Sovereign does not come down to the House to give his consent personally —it is done by his Commissioners. The House of Commons is summoned to hear the Bills passed into Acts of Parliament, the names of the Bills are read out by the Reading Clerk, and the consent of the Sovereign is given in the Norman-French phrase that has been used ever since the time of the Conquest, " Le Roy le veult," or, in the case of a private Bill, " Soit fait comme il est desiré."

Money Bills receive a different reply. " Le Roy remercie ses bons subjets, accepte leur benevolence, et ainsi le veult." Should the Sovereign refuse his consent to the Act, the phrase is " Le Roy (or ' La Reigne ') s'avisera " (will consider it), but this phrase has not been heard in the House of Lords since 1707, when Queen Anne withheld her approval of a Bill for the Militia of that part of England called Scotland. This Bill, Mr. McDonagh tells us, had passed through all its stages, but there was in Scotland a movement for the restoration of the Stuarts which in the opinion of the Government of the day rendered the establishment of a Militia in that country very inadvisable.

It is to be borne in mind, with respect to the King's

approval of money bills, that his phrase " ses bons subjets "
applies both to the Lords and the Commons, and that the
money bills which are passed through the House are so
passed with the consent of the Lords and Commons, although
the Upper House has no control whatever over a money
bill. The Exchequer and the Treasury obtain their money
from the Bank of England by warrant under the Royal
sign manual, so that in this way the fiction that the money
belongs to the King, and the King himself distributes it
to the various departments, is still most definitely retained.

Twice, on the part of iconoclastic people, there has been
an effort made to do away with this extremely interesting
link with William the Conqueror, by which the King's
consent is given in Norman-French. The Bill introduced
in 1707 to establish the giving of the Royal assent in the
English tongue was quickly dropped. The one which
followed in 1772 was laughed out of the House, and nothing
has been heard since of any desire for a change.

On the occasion of conveying the Royal assent, there is
a little divergence between the costume of the three Commissioners, the Lord Chancellor wearing a three-cornered
hat, his colleagues cocked hats.

Two copies of every Act of Parliament are printed on
vellum, and one, which is kept amongst the Rolls of Parliament, is endorsed with the Royal assent, the other goes
to the Record Office. It must be borne in mind, as has
been pointed out, that an Act of Parliament is only an
expression of the will of Parliament at that moment; it
may be recalled, or it may be contradicted the very next
day.

It is rather amusing in the House of Lords to watch the
performance that has to take place when Bills are being
considered in Committee, and then passed by the House.
The Chairman of Committees, who is practically the Speaker
of the House of Peers, is in his position as Chairman when
the House is in Committee. As soon as the Bill is agreed to
he moves aside, the Lord Chancellor comes to the Woolsack, and the Bill is passed. The Lord Chancellor then
moves away, and his place is taken by the Chairman of
Committees, and this may happen half a dozen times within
as many minutes, when certain Bills finally leave the
Committee and are passed by the House.

There are some things, however, in the world that cannot be changed, and one of them is a patent under the Great Seal. It can have no alteration made in it whatever. There is more than one example of this, and one may perhaps be given. The patent creating the Earldom of Annesley gave a Viscounty of Glenawly, but the clerk who wrote out the patent by mistake spelt the word " Glerawly," and in consequence that is the courtesy title of the son and heir of Earl Annesley, and has been so since 1766. The title cannot be altered without the issue of an entirely new patent.

There is more than one case in existence, in which the patent for a peerage has never existed, and there is certainly one in which the patent cannot be produced. The patent for the Earldom of Cumberland in the time of Henry VIII was never executed. The King had created Henry Clifford, Earl of Cumberland, and when the College of Arms proceeded to demand its usual fee for the preparation of the patent, the new Earl refused to pay it, and said he understood that the King, in granting him the dignity, was prepared to pay the necessary fees. The King, on his part, steadily refused to pay the very high fee demanded by the College of Arms. He had signed the Bill creating the Peerage, and this Bill the new Peer had in his possession, and he demanded of the House that it should be regarded as representing his creation as an Earl.

Owing to the existence of the dispute Lord Cumberland was allowed to take his seat, having presented only the Bill to the Clerk at the table, but the dispute appears never to have been settled, and the patent, although actually presented to the King by Garter, was never enrolled. There were five successive Earls of Cumberland, but none of them was able to produce a patent when he took his seat, and eventually, with the demise of the last Earl, the Earldom expired. As a rule the patent has to be carefully safeguarded, because, on the death of the holder of the Peerage, the son has to produce it in the House, as evidence of his right to the Peerage, and it has to be accompanied by the necessary documents, proving that he is the son of the last holder of the dignity.

The patent creating the old barony of Ruthven cannot ever be produced. It was burned in a fire centuries ago, and in consequence there was, until recently, when a new patent was issued, some doubt concerning the devolution of the peerage, and whether or not it had descended to females.

In the House of Lords the announcements for the day are still given in the Latin form of the phrase, and one sees such words as " dies sabbati " on the procedure for a Saturday's gathering, and similar phrases with regard to the other days of the week.

The customs relating to the bowing towards the Speaker's Chair in the House of Commons have their equivalent in the Upper House, but there the matter has no religious significance. The bow which the members make on passing the Woolsack is to the Throne, and that bow is made, as I have pointed out, whether the Throne is occupied or empty, and is an act of obeisance towards the Sovereign. Members of the Upper House never pass the empty Throne without the obeisance. In earlier times, the Queen Consort of the day made a formal obeisance to the King when she entered the House with him. I believe the last occasion when this was made was in 1721, Queen Charlotte making a deep obeisance to the King, when her dowry was granted to her ; but still, in the present day, as the Queen takes her seat near to the King, there is a recognition paid to his sovereignty on the part of his consort by a bow.

No Peer comes to the House of Lords with his gloves on when the King is present. He appears unarmed before the Sovereign, and in order that it may be made certain that he carries no hidden weapon, his hands are bare.

The Bishops, by a curious fiction, are not regarded as Peers in one special respect. They cannot claim to be tried by their " peers " as can all other noblemen ; they were supposed originally to be only subject to trial by a Legate sent from Rome, and to be subject to penalties that could only be imposed by ecclesiastical courts, and this anomaly has still been kept up. It may be well also to notice here that the law does not recognise the existence of a Bishop's wife. She is really not supposed .to exist. She cannot be made the recipient of any of her husband's dignities. If a Bishop were to be knighted, his wife cannot claim to be called " My Lady." That is actually the case at the present day, as the Archbishop of Canterbury holds

a dignity equivalent to knighthood, although no ecclesiastic really receives the accolade, but the Archbishop's
wife does not take any dignity from her husband's knighthood, and, in fact, is not supposed even to exist. She has
no precedence, and at table, when the Archbishop of Canterbury formally entertains the Sovereign, his wife occupies
a subordinate position. The Bishops were, of course,
unmarried in pre-Reformation days.

The reason that the Bishops are not tried before Peers
is to be found in the effort made by the clergy for many
generations to get rid of secular jurisdiction. They con-
tended that they were not amenable to the ordinary course
of law, and only bound to answer to their own ecclesiastical
tribunals. There were at least three cases where Bishops
were indicted by the King's Bench, but pleaded under
protest of ecclesiastical privileges, and did not plead as
Peers. The Bishops rejected the right, which, as holders
of a Barony, they might have had, of being tried by their
peers on an indictment, and so, when the Court of the
Lord High Steward was instituted, the claims of the spiritual
Peers to be Peers of the Realm were extinguished because,
as they would not consent to a judgment upon themselves,
they were useless as judges in cases of treason and felony.

A curious piece of evidence in this matter came out quite
recently, when a Lord High Steward was appointed to try
the Earl Russell case, and the Peers received a summons
to attend him. The Bishops were not summoned on this
occasion, because they could not pass sentence.

It must also be remembered that the essence of a peerage
is its hereditary quality, so that Bishops, although Lords
of Parliament, are not in that respect actually peers, just
as there are many peers, Scottish and Irish, who are not
Lords of Parliament, and it is suggested from the House of
Commons Library that the Lords of Appeal are only Lords
of Parliament, and not Peers.

The King is termed in legal documents, especially those
connected with ecclesiastical arrangements, and in the
Prayer Book, as " Our Most Religious and Gracious King,"
and this is not flattery, as Dr. Johnson seemed to think,
when he once wrote, " It has always been the formula to
flatter Kings and Queens, so much so, that even in our
Church services we have ' our most religious King ' used

indiscriminately, whoever is King." The use of the phrase,
moreover, goes much further back than Dr. Johnson would
seem to imply, and comes from the custom of the Vatican,
the senior school of diplomacy in Europe, which has always
had a regular series of terms by which it addressed the
Catholic Sovereigns of Europe, quite irrespective of whoever
might be occupying the throne.

The phrase "Most Christian King," always meant the
King of France, "Most Apostolic King" meant the King
or Emperor of Austria, the "Most Catholic King" was
the King of Spain, the "Most Faithful" the King of Portugal, the "Most Religious" the King of England, and
these were the invariable phrases adopted, and in many
instances, the actual name and title of the King was not
used at all. "Therefore," writes Sir Robert Edgcumbe,
who looked into this matter some years ago, "the compilers
of the English Book of Common Prayer could hardly do
less than attribute to the Sovereign as good a character
as that bestowed upon him by the Papal authorities in
Rome." Hence it is that the term "Most Religious King"
found its way into the Prayer for the High Court of Parliament which appears in the Book of Common Prayer.

At the time when there was a dispute concerning who
had the right to occupy the English throne, and there were
adherents both of the Stuart and Hanoverian claims, it
was felt by the Hanoverian Kings that a definite step
should be taken to mark the honours which they created
from those that were even then being created by James II
and his successors. The colour of the Garter ribbon accordingly underwent a change, and it will be noticed, when
old pictures of that period are examined, that the Garter
ribbon worn by the Knights up to the time of James II
is of a much deeper blue colour than that which has been
worn since.

There was another more important change, however,
which took place at a much later period, which had nothing
to do with the trouble concerning the Stuarts. The Garter
ribbon was worn for many generations in a "V" shape,
the "George" being pendent from the point of the "V"
in the middle of the breast, and in this particular fashion
it appears on the early pictures. The change, by which
the ribbon is worn across the breast, is said to have taken

place in the time of George III, when a Duke of Richmond had an accident when dressing, and his ribbon was set on fire by the candle on his dressing-table, and the larger part consumed. As it was impossible to get a fresh ribbon in time, he used the perfect piece and strapped it across his breast in transverse fashion. It is stated that he apologised to the King for appearing with his ribbon in this way, but the Sovereign preferred the new method adopted, and from that time to this the Garter ribbon has been worn in that way.

It is well known that, in entertaining Royalty, no finger-bowls appear on the dinner-table, the origin of this custom going back to the days just alluded to, when there were many persons who regarded the Stuarts as the rightful owners of the throne, and who, in drinking the Royal toast, held their glasses over the finger-bowl, and were thus drinking " to the King over the water." In order to prevent any possibility of this act of treason being repeated, the custom was introduced of not having finger-bowls when the King or Queen was present, and this has been retained.

In connection with the Coronation, the Royal Standard of England is still borne by the descendant of the King's champion. The champion does not now ride in armour into Westminster Hall, and challenge in single combat anyone who should impugn the King's right to the throne, as the Marmions and their successors, the Dymokes, have done since the time of William the Conqueror, because the banquet is not now held, but it is a Mr. Dymoke who represents the last Baron Marmion who is entitled to carry the standard, and carried it at the Coronation of George V.

It is, however, impossible in these pages to deal with all the survivals that remain in connection with the Coronation Service, in itself a veritable treasury of ancient customs.

The Coronation has already been the subject of special books dealing with it *ad hoc*, and to such volumes the student and reader must be referred.

CHAPTER V

THE HOUSE OF LORDS

PEERS AND THEIR PRIVILEGES

THERE are many eccentricities with regard to the Peerage which have been handed down from remote times. There are peerages which fall into abeyance, and in some instances this abeyance lasts for many hundreds of years, during which time the particular title in question disappears altogether from the Roll of the House. This happens when it is a Peerage which descends to issue, and when daughters are the only surviving issue. For example, in 1426, on the death of the second Lord Camoys, the Barony fell into abeyance, and it remained in abeyance for over four hundred years, up till 1839, when it was called out in favour of one of the descendants of Mary Biddulph, who had been one of the co-heiresses. As long as there are co-heiresses remaining to these ancient titles, each heiress holds an undivided part of the Barony, and it is only when these heiresses have been proved to have had no issue, and one alone stands to represent the Barony, that application can be made to the Sovereign to call it out of abeyance in her favour.

It has twice happened with regard to the Barony of Braye, the first, a very long abeyance, occurring on the death of the second Baron, who held high military commands under Henry VIII ; the second, between the daughters of the third Baroness : and that is why the present Lord Braye is only the fifth Baron, and his mother, Baroness Braye, was only the fourth in the line, although the original barony was created in 1529. It went into abeyance between 1557 and 1839, and again between 1862 and 1879. Another case is that of the Barony of Vaux of Harrowden. Sir Nicholas Vaux, a soldier and statesman much in favour with Henry VIII, was awarded the Barony. The abeyance commenced on the death of the fifth Peer, and lasted from 1662 to 1838, a period of a hundred and seventy-six years, when it was terminated in the favour of G. C. Mostyn, who became sixth Baron, and whose grandson is the present Lord Vaux of Harrowden.

The two Baronies of Fauconberg and D'Arcy, now held by two sisters, went into abeyance for several hundreds of years, and then were called out as the result of a long and complicated lawsuit, undertaken before the Committee of Privileges of the House of Peers, in order to prove that Lady Yarborough, who was already Baroness Conyers in her own right, was entitled, with her sister, to these two Baronies. The Barony of Audley is now in abeyance, the last, the twentieth Lord Audley, having left two daughters only, between whom the Barony rests. On the decease of either of these two ladies, the survivor will become Baroness Audley in her own right.

This arrangement of abeyances does not take place with regard to Scottish Peerages. A woman succeeds to her father's Scottish Peerage on his decease, the Duchess of Norfolk, for example, being Baroness Herries in her own right, having succeeded to that Barony on the decease of her father, who was the last holder of the title.

There used to be a very interesting anomaly with regard to the position of the Bishop of Norwich and his seat in the Upper House. I had a long correspondence many years ago with Bishop Pelham, who was the last Bishop summoned to the House under a special arrangement made in the time of Henry VIII. The King demanded the large revenues of the See of Norwich, and forced the Bishop of the time to exchange these revenues for the far smaller emoluments appertaining to the Abbey of St. Benet in Holme. He caused the Bishop of Norwich of that time to be summoned to the House as Abbot of St. Benet, telling him to assume the less important title, but declaring that the Bishopric had been vacated and the revenues sequestrated to the Crown.

From that time downwards, the writ of summons for the Bishop of Norwich regarded him as a mitred Abbot, the only person holding such a dignity in the House, but from the fact that very few Bishops ever look at their writ of summons, and, if they did so, do not trouble to wade through its long phraseology, the Bishop himself, with whom I corresponded, was unaware, until his attention was drawn to it, of the anomalous position which he held. He was extremely interested in looking up the details which were to be found in the various books dealing with Norwich ecclesiastical history, but I believe that, by reason of his attention having been drawn to it, certain inquiries were made in the Writ Office, and this curious arrangement finally disappeared, all later Bishops being summoned in the ordinary way.

A strange position in the Peerage, sometimes forgotten, is the fact that certain Peers have no second title, or, if they have one, it is of the same name as their first, but lower in dignity. In consequence, there is difficulty in giving a courtesy title to the eldest son. Three cases stand out prominently in this respect : the Earl of Guilford is the bearer of two titles, both of them of Guilford, an Earldom and a Barony, and in consequence his eldest son assumes the family name of North, and is called only by courtesy, Lord North. He has, however, no actual right whatever to that title, because there already exists a Barony of North, of which the present holder is the eleventh Baron, a Barony which extends from 1554.

Again, the Earl of Huntingdon only possesses his Earldom, of which he is the fourteenth holder, the various other titles, which at one time belonged to the Earldom, having all passed away from the family, and his subordinate title of Baron Hastings de Hastings has been, in recent times, merged in the Earldom of Loudoun. His eldest son is styled Viscount Hastings, a courtesy Viscounty being given to him in respect to his father's Earldom, but his signature is liable to be confused with that of an existing Lord Hastings, who is the twenty-first Baron, holding a Barony created in 1295.

The third instance that may be stated relates to the Earldom of Lindsey, not to be confused with another Earldom of very similar name, that of Lindsay. Lord Lindsey is the twelfth Earl, the Earldom having been created in 1626. He has no second title, and therefore, as a rule, his son is called Lord Bertie, although from as far back as 1779, the Earls of Lindsey, who were in earlier days Dukes of Ancaster, ceased to have any Barony vested in them, but the name of Lord Bertie, when it is in use, is liable to be confused with that of Viscount Bertie of Thame, a Viscounty of the United Kingdom created in 1915 as a Barony, and raised to a Viscounty in 1918.

Another instance is that of the Earl of Devon, the present holder of which is the fourteenth Earl, the Earldom having been created in 1553. The eldest son assumes the name of Lord Courtenay, taking the family name, and in his case he is fortunate in the fact that there is no other nobleman whose name can be confused with his, although for a while there was a Lord Courtney, and the pronunciations were so similar that there was at that time a possible chance of some confusion.

There are many similar cases in the Peerage of a possible confusion between names, and the usual books of reference give explanations of many of them, but there are actually identical names to be found in the Roll. For example, there are two Lords Cobham, a Viscount and a Baron, two Lords Arundel, the Earl of Arundel and Surrey, and Lord Arundell of Wardour, and many other instances with which the student of the Peerage is doubtless familiar.

There are three, or perhaps four, Earls who sit in the House of Lords who are known as the Catskin Earls, Lord Shrewsbury, Lord Derby, Lord Huntingdon, and by some writers it is said Lord Pembroke, these four being the only Earldoms now remaining prior to those of the seventeenth century, several such Earldoms, like Arundel, Rutland and others, being now merged in higher titles. The curious word " catskin " is a corruption of " quatreskin," derived from the fact that in ancient times the robes of an Earl, as will be seen in many ancient portraits, were decorated with four rows of ermine, as are the robes of a modern Duke, instead of the three rows to which they have been restricted in later days. As a matter of fact, I think I am right in stating that the ancient robes of the Earls of Shrewsbury, worn until quite recent times by the holder of the Earldom, and which may be seen again when the present Lord Shrewsbury attains his majority, still possess the four rows of ermine, and I believe that, until quite recent days, the robes of the Earl of Derby had the same peculiarity.

There are not many of the ancient robes of the Peers now to be seen in the House, but where they do exist they can be quite readily distinguished by the beautiful dull rose-colour that they have assumed by reason of age. Amongst such robes are, I believe, those of the Earls of Stamford, which came to the last owner of the title through the Countess of Stamford and Warrington, and which had been carefully preserved by her. The robes of the extinct Earldom of Nithsdale are still in existence, in the possession of the Duchess of Norfolk, and are remarkable for this beautiful colour.

The Earl of Carlisle, it is curious to note, is the only remaining Peer who sits in the House by virtue of a patent issued in the time of the Commonwealth, and it is interesting to notice, by the way, in connection with the baronetcy held by the Eden family that it is the only one deriving its title from the United States. The family are the Edens of Maryland, and, to make the survival even more curious, there is the fact that the first Baronet married a sister of the last Lord Baltimore, the holder of the only Peerage that took its name from the United States.*

There are two noblemen in the British Peerage who have the privilege of standing covered before the King, Lord Kingsale and Lord Forester. Lord Forester's ancestor, William Forester, a commoner of Watling Street, Shropshire, received the privilege from Henry VIII, but the right that belonged to Lord Kingsale is far earlier. Seven hundred years ago, Philip of France summoned King John to mortal combat. The King was not disposed to accept the challenge, and he offered De Courcy, Lord Kingsale, freedom from imprisonment, which at that moment he was undergoing, if he would undertake the commission on the King's behalf. De Courcy was an exceedingly tall man, a magnificent soldier, very brave, and well known for his prowess, and when the French champion saw him, he declined the encounter. De Courcy heard, it is said, from the lips of the King his reward in these words, " Thou art a pleasant companion, and Heaven keep thee in good health. Never unveil thy bonnet again before King or subject."

* While these pages were passing through the press the Viscounty of Exmouth fell in to a citizen of the U.S.A. Lord Fairfax was also at the time a citizen of the same country.

The descendants of this famous Lord Kingsale have jealously guarded the privilege, and have even, at times, contested the point with the Sovereign. It was raised as lately as during the reign of George III, and he yielded the point, but with this comment, " The gentleman has a right to keep covered before me, by ancient privelege, but even King John could give him no right to be covered before ladies." Whereupon Lord Kingsale, having obtained the recognition of his right, promptly uncovered before the Queen, who was present on that occasion.

It is said that the same privilege was granted on November 6, 1522, to a certain Robert Morgan of Worcestershire, but the Crown claimed that this was for his life only, and that his successors were not entitled to it.

It may be well here to draw attention to the fact that there are certain families in England who have possessed the same land for very many hundreds of years. There are many who claim that this is so, but about one great family, known as Saltmarshe of Saltmarshe, there is no question, because William the Conqueror confirmed Lionel Saltmarshe in the possession of his lordship and knighted him, and the family claim that their seat, Salt-marshe, some few miles from Goole, has belonged to them since the days of King Harold, and has never passed out of their possession. A similar statement is made concerning the Berkeley family.

Berkeley Castle is perhaps the only house in England that has always been inhabited by the same family, since it was built in early Norman times. For a while it was transferred to Henry VII and his heirs male, but during the time that the King and his successors held it, a member of the Berkeley family was resident within its walls, so that the Berkeleys have never ceased to dwell within it. The castle did not descend to Queen Elizabeth or to Queen Mary, but Elizabeth claimed it and resided in it on certain occasions, when the Berkeley family did not think it was either politic or wise to dispute her claim to the property, although it had been distinctly understood that it was only to be held by the heirs *male* of Henry VII.

Perhaps older than the Saltmarshes in one continuous line is the family of the Derings, who claim to have been settled at Surrendon Dering, a property which they still own, and where a member of the family still resides, since 880. This family is one of the very few of undoubted Saxon origin that still remain in England.

It would be impossible to refer to the numerous instances in which land has passed from one generation to another down to its present owner, but it may be worth while to mention that Sir William Hulton possesses an estate in Lancashire which has come down direct through father and son, with one exception, when it descended from uncle to nephew; from 1120, still remaining in the possession of the descendants of the original grantee. It is perhaps an exceptional case, but there are others almost similar to it. Sir William Hulton has also pointed out to me that at West Houghton in Lancashire there was a large importation of Flemish weavers, and in consequence the dialect spoken in the district contains several words which are of Flemish origin. During the war many Flemish refugees settled down in that village, and found, to their surprise, that they were able to understand many of the peculiar phrases that were in use, and quite quickly to speak the local dialect.

It is not often remembered that, for a few months, England had a Queen who does not appear in the list of Kings and Queens, but who certainly had a very good claim to the throne. This was the Empress Matilda, or Empress Maud, as she is more generally called, the daughter of Henry I. She was acknowledged on April 8, 1141, at Winchester, as Lady of England and Normandy, and she took the title of Queen of England when, in the following June, she entered London in triumph., By September, 1142, her reign was really at an end, although for some five years longer she was still in England, and claimed her position, and in her charters she expressly declared herself as " Lady of the English." I remember seeing several of her charters in the Carthusian house at Pisa, and noticing several allusions in some of them, dated 1141, to a position she claimed as Queen of England.

It is interesting to remember that she was responsible for six Earldoms, for she created the Earldoms of Cornwall, Devon, Hereford, Oxford, Salisbury and Somerset, and that, although none of these Earldoms actually exist at the present time, there are Peerages still held by persons who descend from the same families as those who held the Peerages which this remote sovereign created during her very brief tenure of the throne.

There were Peerages, of course, created by Charles II, while he was in exile, and of these many of the names are still familiar ones. He created the Earldom of Balcarres, which probably is the one still existing, Baronies of Colville and Duffus, which are dormant at the present moment, and an Earldom of Ormond, which is also dormant. The Viscounty of Oxfurd, derived from a Scottish estate of that name and *not* from the English City of Oxford, is also probably still in existence and only dormant, and the same remark would apply to the Viscounty of Tara, which was conferred on one Thomas Preston, but others are certainly extinct, although the families that held them are still represented in the English Peerage.

Then there were also the Peerages conferred by James II when in exile, and two or three of these, e.g. Lucan, Abbeville, Loughmore and Ballyhigue, are probably still in existence, although dormant. There were also others created by his son (titular James III and VIII), amongst which still remains the Spanish Dukedom of Berwick and Alba, probably also a Barony belonging to Lord Falkland, and perhaps one belonging to Lord Jersey, while the Baronies of McLeod and Cameron of Lochiel and others, perhaps, still exist. The question as to the Earldom of Melfort created by James II is even now under consideration ; it probably exists in the person of a lady who does not, however, make use of the title. The connection of the Spanish Dukedom of Berwick and Alba, created by James II in 1687, with England has always been remembered in the family, and is perpetuated by a standing tradition that all the children who may in process of time succeed to the Dukedom are to be taught to speak the English language.

There used to be a power of surrendering Peerages in England, by which certain Peerages were surrendered to the Crown, sometimes regranted with special remainders, or to the original holder and his wife together, and sometimes actually cancelled, but since 1640 this arrangement has not been possible, because on February 1, 1640–41, the House itself resolved, in most definite fashion, that there was no possibility by which any Peer could " alien or transfer his honour, drown or extinguish it," but that it must descend to his descendants, and there was no form either " of surrender, grant, fine or any other conveyance to the King," by which its descent can be stopped. There certainly was a case almost immediately afterwards in 1660, concerning the Earldom of Buckingham, but it was not carried out in complete fashion, and there was a grave doubt as to the legitimacy of one person who was concerned with it. The decision adopted by the House is still believed to hold good.

Finally, it may be interesting to mention that there are certain Peerages which the Royal Family have generally retained for their own use. There are titles in connection with such places as Gloucester, Dublin, Edinburgh, Kent, Rothesay, Ulster, York, Albany, Carrick, Clarence, Connaught, Eltham, Milford Haven, Renfrew and Tipperary, that are always supposed to be Royal preserves, and these titles belong only to members of the reigning House.

The peerage of Athlone, now regarded as a Royal one, has not been retained by the Royal Family for its exclusive use, as the Earldom was created in 1692, and remained in the possession of the grantee's descendants until 1844.

One old privilege which members of the House of Lords used to claim has never had any justification and does not exist at all. It has been said that every Peer had the right to attend the Coronation of the King, and the demand has often been made that " by right " an invitation should be sent to all, but on the occasion of the Coronation of King Edward, a very particular examination was made of this claim, and it was found clearly proved that no such right existed, and that although the King was certainly in the habit of requiring the attendance of the Peers at his Coronation, he could summon whom he liked and pass over any person whom he disregarded. There was no inherent right in a Peerage to entitle the holder to be summoned on the occasion of a Coronation.

CHAPTER VI

THE HOUSE OF COMMONS

BOTH Houses of Parliament enshrine many interesting customs that have come down from remote times, but there is probably no body in existence, not even the Corporation of the City, that is so tenacious of its ancient rights, customs and privileges as the House of Commons, or one so determined to keep them in force, even though part of their meaning has for generations ceased to exist.

We have to remember, in considering questions of the procedure of the House of Commons, how necessary it has been in the past that this body should be independent and unfettered, how it has stood for the privileges of the English people, and how much we are indebted to this stalwart resistance to a power that was often inclined to be tyrannical ; for the existence of many rights which at the moment we take for granted. This has to be borne in mind in considering these customs, because many of them have arisen from the contests that the House of Commons had with the Crown, and from the way in which it maintained its own rights, that is to say, the rights of the people of the country.

One of the most impressive scenes in the ritual of the House occurs at the opening of a new Parliament, when a Speaker has to be selected. There may have been some informal consideration in the House of Commons as to who shall be Speaker, but in the actual election the Government of the day never takes any definite part, because any member of the House has a right to attain to this position, if approved by the majority, and everyone has an unquestionable right to nominate any other.

When the House first meets, the Mace is invisible, and, because there is no Chairman who can speak in the name of the House, the senior clerk may not make his voice heard.

He simply rises and points silently to some member who proposes the election of a Speaker, and to someone whom he knows to be ready to second the proposal. The proposer and seconder, having announced the selected candidate, he has to be called to the Chair by the House itself, and, as a rule, the result of the informal discussion beforehand has been of such a character that the call is an unanimous one. The proposer and seconder then bring up the selected member, and conduct him to the Chair, when he deprecates his election but "submits himself" to "the will of the House." He is then conducted to the Chair, but before actually taking it he thanks the House for electing him. Finally he takes his seat, the Mace is placed in position, and the House is constituted.

There follows the Speaker's speech to the House, and it may be noted in this connection, that the title of Speaker is a somewhat incongruous one, for he is the man who makes fewer long speeches in the House of Commons than does anyone else. He represents, however, the voice of the House, and speaks on its behalf. After his selection the Speaker is known as Mr. Speaker Elect, very much in the same way as I have already said the Lord Mayor on his election is known as the Lord Mayor Elect, and his appointment has to be confirmed by the Crown.

The Lords Commissioners, who act on behalf of the King, have already come into the House of Lords wearing the robes of their office, and having their hats in such a position that it is not at all easy to determine who are the actual peers representing the Crown. This of itself is intentional, because it is of no moment who the Lords Commissioners may be, they are, for the time being, the representatives of the Crown itself. Their names are, however, declared in the patent of appointment and the Clerk, when he reads it out, bows to each person as he is named. When they first take their seats, Black Rod is sent to the House of Commons to announce to that House that he is their representative, and on this occasion, Black Rod knows perfectly well what he has to do, he leaves the House retreating backward before the Lords Commissioners, but neither he nor the representatives of the Sovereign say a word, the procedure taking place in dumb show. The

Commissioners sit solidly in their seats, they neither rise nor lift their hats, and away goes Black Rod.

When the Speaker has been elected, he comes into the Upper House, surrounded by various members of the Commons. He is not yet Speaker, and in consequence, the Mace is not carried by the Serjeant-at-Arms over his shoulder, but rests in the hollow of his arm, and the Speaker does not wear his silk gown, nor his full-bottomed wig, but has just an ordinary small wig, such as a barrister wears. On his arrival in the Upper House, the Commissioners bow three times to him. He informs them that the choice of the House has fallen upon him, and he submits himself " in all humility " to the King as the person selected by the Commons to represent them.

The Commissioners convey the Royal approval of the selection, and then comes a notable scene, for the Speaker claims from the Commissioners all the " rights and privileges which are the undoubted possession of the House " of Commons, including those of " free speech " and of " free access to the Sovereign " and of " freedom from arrest." Then the Speaker goes still further, and prays that, should the faithful Commons fall into any error with regard to their actions or their position towards the Sovereign the blame should not be imputed to them but it should be laid on his shoulders, he only being held responsible for the action of the House of Commons. It was for this same reason that the memorable scene took place in Stuart times, when the Speaker announced to the King, who had forced his way into the House of Commons, that he was unable to see the persons whom the King pointed out, as his eyes were entirely under the control of the House, and he could only see as its representative.

The position which the Speaker occupies in the House of Commons is entirely different from that of the Lord Chancellor in the House of Lords. The Lord Chancellor has no power to keep order in the Upper House, he is not its President, he actually sits outside of its precincts. He represents the Sovereign, and does not sit as Speaker, or Chairman, of the Upper House. The Chairman of Committees occupies the position (if there is such a one) coming nearest to that held by the Speaker in the Lower House.

The Lords Commissioners having assured the Speaker

that all the privileges demanded by the House of Commons
are freely granted, and that he alone will be blamed for any
wrong action that may take place in the House, they bow
again to him, and then the Mace is lifted to the shoulder
of the Serjeant-at-Arms, the Speaker Elect becomes Mr.
Speaker, the cry is at once raised, as he passes through the
corridor, " Make way for Mr. Speaker." He then assumes,
in his own room, his State robe and full-bottomed wig, and
coming into the House through his own doorway, ascends
the dais, and, assuming that he has been all alone to the
House of Lords, and that the Commons know nothing of
what has taken place there, he reports to them in solemn
fashion that their privileges have been granted, makes his
acknowledgments to the members, and places himself " at
the service of the House."

The statement just made, that the House of Commons
is supposed to know nothing of what has transpired a few
minutes before, is somewhat important. The fiction is
carried out with care during the proceedings of the Lower
House. The House of Lords is spoken of as " another
place," never by its legal title, and a member of the House
of Commons is not supposed to refer to procedure in " the
other place " except merely as a matter of hearsay. It is
deemed highly important that the privileges of each House
should be kept quite clear and distinct, and still more that
the privileges of the House of Commons should be regarded
as having nothing whatever to do with any procedure that
may take place in the House where the Sovereign sits.

The Sovereign himself may have had his seat, and in
fact frequently does sit, when Prince of Wales, in the
gallery overlooking the House of Commons, and may there
listen to its debates, but once he has ascended the throne,
there is one place in his dominions into which he may never
go, and that is the House of Commons, for fear that his
presence there should exercise any influence, and prevent
the Commons speaking with the utmost possible freedom.
It is rather extraordinary, when one remembers that
throughout her long reign extending over sixty years,
Queen Victoria never once set foot in the House of
Commons. At the same time, the King's name is never
brought into a House of Commons debate, and any member
who unwittingly ventures to suggest that the King has

expressed any opinion respecting anything, would very soon find that the House. of Commons would decline to hear him, and that his words would be drowned in the cry of " Privilege ! Privilege ! "

Why exactly the members for the City of London sit on the Treasury Bench the first day the new House meets, is not quite certain ; there is an allusion to their having done so in a report published in 1568, and they are known to have exercised that right quite early in the time of Elizabeth. It has been said that the privilege arose in order to commemorate the protection given to the Five Members of January 4, 1642, but this is most certainly *not* the case, for the privilege dates back to a much earlier period. In Elizabeth's time, the members for the City of York claimed the same right, in exactly the same way as the Corporation of the City of York claimed certain rights which only belong to the City of London. Whether the York members believed that they had the same right to the Treasury Bench, we are not told, but their claim to occupy that particular seat appears to have lapsed.

Yet another interesting ceremony takes place in the House of Commons, and that is the first reading which is given to a Bill before the King's Speech is read, in order that Parliament may assert its right to act in exactly the way it thinks fit, without reference to the Crown, or to any other authority, and in order that it may show that it has the power to debate anything, that it chooses to consider, whether such a subject is mentioned in the King's Speech or not. Curiously enough, in this particular, the House of Lords acts in similar fashion, because it also gives the first reading to a Bill, and the same Bill in each House is read year by year for the sake of asserting the privilege.

Mr. Michael McDonagh, to whose work all students of the customs of the Houses of Parliament are indebted, and from whose book* I have not scrupled to make the extracts he has been good enough to permit, states that the Bill used in the House of Lords is known as the Select Vestries Bill, and the one in the House of Commons as the Bill for the more effectual Preventing of Clandestine Outlawries. He says that this latter Bill has been preserved in the

* See *Pageant of Parliament*, by M. McDonagh.

drawers of the House of Commons since 1852, and has been in steady use all the time.*

The privileges of the House of Commons are very considerable and it must be remembered that there is no higher authority than Parliament, which redresses its own wrongs, and vindicates its own privileges. The power of its officer who carries the Mace, known as the Serjeant-at-Arms, is vast. He can arrest any person anywhere, can call upon civil, military or police authorities to assist him, can demand the assistance of any person or persons who are near by, and can break into any private residence between sunrise and sunset, but between sunset and sunrise he has no power of arrest, if the person he desires to find is safely within his home.

The members of the House themselves have a right of freedom from arrest while in the House, and in any case cannot be arrested for debt or for political offence, they cannot be suspended or expelled from the House, unless they have been solemnly named by the Speaker and the House has given its consent to the sentence, and then they are passed over to the control of the Serjeant-at-Arms, who has his own prison in the Clock Tower, and can do with his prisoner much as he pleases. Even if condemned to imprisonment they can claim to inform the House in their own seat and to plead their case before the House.

A member once elected to the House of Commons cannot resign his seat, the only method by which he can escape service in the House is by accepting an office of profit under the Crown, and there are offices which as a rule are used when a member desires to resign. He therefore applies to the Chancellor of the Exchequer that he may be appointed to the stewardship of the Chiltern Hundreds, or that he may be appointed steward of East Hendred in Berkshire or of Northstead and Hempholm in Yorkshire. These three positions are declared to be offices of profit under the Crown, and certainly at one time they were so, but now there are no duties connected with them, and there is no salary for the person who holds them. At one time, there was such a salary, and the existence of it rendered necessary the vacation of the seat.

* Other information of great value to me has been placed at my disposal by Mr. Kitto.

The Chiltern Hundreds were Stone, Desborough and Bodenham, and these Hundreds have belonged to the Crown ever since Norman times. They were sequestra'ed under the Commonwealth, but reverted to the Crown on the Restoration. The steward was supposed to protect the Crown against " robbers, rogues and freebooters," and he was to be in possession of the revenues of the stewardship. At one time, Mr. McDonagh tells us, the writ conferring this stewardship always contained the words, " having special trust and confidence in the care and fidelity " of the person to whom the office is given, but since the celebrated Edwin James case of 1861, in which the person who held the Chiltern Hundreds was by no means a careful or a faithful person, these words have been omitted. The office is only supposed to be held for one day, the fact that it is held *ipso facto* vacating the seat. Then the writ is returned to the Chancellor and it can be bestowed the very next day upon someone else.

There were originally more of the offices of profit that could be used by legislators who desired to resign from their seats, for example, the Manor of Shoreham, Sussex, was declared at one time to be an office of profit—the same thing applied to the Manor of Poynings in Sussex, and also to the escheatorships of Munster and Ulster. The two Sussex manors have, however, been sold, by the Crown, to the Lords of the Manor who hold the land round about them, and the two escheatorships were expressly abolished by Act of Parliament.

It is not quite clear whether the two Manors of East Hendred and Hempholm do actually still remain in the possession of the Crown. There has been a dispute about both of them, but there is no practical need for the matter to be brought to an issue, because the stewardships are sufficient for the purpose. If, however, Lord Birkenhead's Law of Property Bill does away with these two stewardships, it is possible that the Crown claim to two of the manors may be revived, in order that it should still be possible to give an opportunity to members who are anxious to vacate their seats.

Of nothing is the House of Commons more tenacious than of the privilege it claims to close its doors in the face of the messenger of the Sovereign, in order that he should request entrance. When the King comes to the Upper House to open his Parliament, the presence of the members of the House of Commons is of course required. The summons takes the form of " a command " when the King is himself upon the throne, it is only " a desire " when the Lords Commissioners represent him, but in either case, Black Rod, retreating backwards before the Lords Commissioners or the Sovereign, as the case may be, makes his way to the House of Commons amidst the cry of " Way for Black Rod," and his passage, according to the regulations of the House, has to be unimpeded, but no sooner is he within reach of the House of Commons, than the doors are closed with a bang in his face and are bolted.

He then knocks three times, the Serjeant-at-Arms, in great surprise, looks out to see who is there, and glances at the Speaker, the Speaker nods, the doors are thrown open, business is at once interrupted, the Speaker rises, the members uncover, Black Rod makes three solemn obeisances to the Speaker, and conveys his message : the Lords Commissioners " request," or the King " commands," and then he retires backwards, bowing, as he leaves, to the Speaker. He carries with him his rod, which is made of ebony, and surmounted by a golden lion rampant, and from it he takes his name. His position is one in the personal gift of the King, and he must be " a gentleman, famous in arms and blood."

There follows the appearance of the Speaker in the Upper House, surrounded by various members who accompany him. He listens to the King's Speech, a copy of it is given to him, and he then returns to his own House, and standing in its presence, with all the members uncovered, he announces to them, what they are not supposed to know, that the King has made a certain speech in another place, and he proceeds to read this speech to the House.

The Speaker's own position is one of the greatest possible dignity. He alone, except the Sovereign, is entitled to hold a Levée. Only he can demand that all those who come to dinner with him wear uniform or Court dress, ordinary evening dress being debarred. There have been difficulties with regard to the Labour members in the House as to what they should wear, and it was found so difficult to alter the regulations concerning the Speaker's dinners, that eventually other arrangements were made, by which a reception instead of a dinner could be given, and the persons attending it were to include those members of the House of Commons who did not feel it in accordance with their principles to wear uniform or Levée dress. To allow any person to dine with the Speaker who was not in the costume which from time immemorial has been the regulation seemed to be almost an impossible thing.

The Speaker is termed the First Commoner of the Realm, and this title he has held since 1688. The House is not properly constituted unless he is present, and in his presence the Mace is always laid upon the table. If the Mace is not there, the House is sitting in Committee, and if suddenly an occasion arises in which it is desirable that a matter be brought before the whole House, the Speaker has to be sent for, the Chairman of Committees retires, and the Mace, which has been resting on its hooks at the side of the table, is removed and placed in position, the Speaker takes his chair, the Committee is over, and the House is again in sitting.

The procedure with regard to the introduction of Bills is again evidence of the desire of the House to retain its privileges. No Bill may be introduced without the leave of the House. It is not at all necessary that the Bill should be printed, it is always introduced in dummy fashion, there is merely a folded paper with the title of the Bill upon it, and a half-sheet of notepaper will do just as well, but leave to introduce the Bill *must* first be asked of the House and formally given. For a first reading the procedure is either purely formal when the Member introducing the Bill hands his dummy to the Clerk, who reads out the title and names a day for the second reading, or the member moves for leave to introduce a Bill and makes a short speech in support of his motion. This may be opposed, and there may then be a division. If the division goes against the member, that is the end. If there is no division, or if he wins on the division, the member introducing the Bill goes to the Bar of the House, and brings his dummy to the table, bowing three times in the process, the Clerk reads the title, and the date for the second reading is named. In both these cases the reading of the title by the Clerk is the actual first reading.

Before either House meets, that interesting search takes

place throughout the entire building, which dates back to the time of the Guy Fawkes plot in 1605. The search is carried out by the Yeomen of the Guard. In the old days, when it was first made, it was necessary for them to carry lanterns, in order that they might see where they were going and detect the presence of the intruder. To the present day, the lanterns are still carried, and the candles in them are lighted, although the whole place is now flooded with the electric light, and there is no need for the feeble light of the lanterns, but the old custom is rigidly adhered to.

After the search has been made, the Yeomen of the Guard are offered some refreshment, cake and wine, and in early days a mounted soldier at once went to the King, to inform him of the result of the search, that the Houses might meet in safety. Now, the Vice-Chamberlain gives the news to the Sovereign by a telegram or a telephone message.

When the House disperses in the evening, the old cry of " Who goes home ? " echoes through the corridors. It is always a cry that awakens much interest, especially on the part of new members or visitors. It dates back to the days when the members were liable to attack and robbery from highwaymen and street robbers, and when it was desirable that they should not go along the lonely streets singly, but that parties of them should unite their forces, and see one another home, and it was also in order that the linkboys, who carried torches, might be summoned to escort the members home. It sounds a little incongruous, when nowadays the members make use of the Tube or of their own motors, and are fairly sure to get home in safety, but the old cry still resounds through the House.

There have been occasions, however, when, for example, a thick fog shrouded London, it has been of some value, and linkboys have even been called in again with torches, not to escort the members home, but to take them across the road, in order that they might find the conveyance that they desired. In this respect, it is important to notice that members of the House of Commons still retain the privilege of having the traffic stopped for them. The police, who get to know them by sight, will hold up any traffic, to admit of a Member of Parliament crossing the road, whether he is walking, or whether he is in his own or a hired conveyance.

No military force is allowed to approach the House of Commons within a certain definite fixed line, a precaution rendered necessary in old days, so that the Army should not fetter the independence of the House, nor bring any influence to bear upon it, or that those who represented the Sovereign, and were supposed to be in control of the Army, should have an opportunity of overawing the representatives of His Majesty's faithful Commons.

The report as to the proceedings of the House of Commons has to be sent to the King every night. It is supposed to come from the Leader of the House ; it used to be sent in the form of a letter, and no one was more punctilious as to the writing of this letter than was Mr. Gladstone. Evening after evening he could be seen sitting in the House of Commons with a pad upon his knee, writing his customary letter to his Sovereign, explaining what had happened in the House with regard to various Bills, and summarising the speeches that had been made. The letter was always written in the curious and somewhat ungrammatical sentences, in which Mr. Gladstone presented his humble duty to his Sovereign, and proceeded to give the needful information.

After a while, the letter was written by someone else in the Government, in order to spare the time of the Premier, but it still always bore the signature of the Premier. Now, the letter is no longer required, and a telegram is sent to the King every night by the Leader of the House, briefly summarising what has happened during the evening. The original letters from the Prime Minister are all, it is stated, preserved in the library at Buckingham Palace, and if that is so, they should form State documents of the highest possible importance.

The members of the Government receive seals of office, when they take their oaths of allegiance to the King, in respect to their official positions. These seals of office are in sets of three, known as the Signet Seal, the Smaller Seal, and the Cachet, but I believe that only one of them is used, and that but seldom. They are, however, the outward and visible signs of the offices that ten of the chief members of the Government hold. There is no seal for the office of Prime Minister. He does not receive from the Sovereign any symbol of that kind in respect to his position.

There are various crimes which a member of the House of Commons in his ignorance may most readily commit, and one of the most serious is to lock a door in the House. This is regarded as about the most terrible thing that a member can do, and it does not matter whether he is a Minister or a Secretary or an ordinary member, if he locks a door in the House of Commons he is brought up before the Committee on Standing Orders, and is severely reprimanded for having done so.

The reason for this strange custom reverts back to the old days of plots against the life or integrity of the House, especially, perhaps, to that most terrible of all plots, the one arranged by Guy Fawkes. The regulation has still been kept in force, and is most tenaciously protected. Every member has a right to go wherever he pleases in the House, no door may be locked against him ; he does not, of course, enter Committee Rooms where he knows Committees are sitting, or consultations are taking place, but if he chooses to go in, he has the absolute right to do so.

There is also a curious regulation as regards a particular part of the House of Commons itself, which is supposed to be actually outside the House, and the member addressing it, must be quite sure that when speaking he stands within the lines which mark the limits of the House. There is a bar or barrier across the end of the House, and a member who is to be reprimanded is brought up to this bar, which is then suddenly drawn out in front of him, and outside of it he remains to receive the reprimand of the Speaker.

To this bar also come the Lord Mayor or the Sheriffs, more usually the Sheriffs, of the City if they have occasion to present any petition to the House. They are entitled to attend in full ceremonial attire, and I am inclined to think that this privilege belongs also to the Sheriffs of other places besides those of the City of London. It is certainly claimed by York. The bar marks the limits of the House, and to put a person outside of the bar of the House is a very serious step.

It is not, however, exactly the same as removing him from the precincts. A person who was not a member, so removed, would also be removed from the precincts, but a Member of Parliament ordered to withdraw must leave the

Debating Chamber and the building, that is, the precincts. A Member of Parliament who is named and suspended, must leave the Chamber and the building, that is, he must leave the precincts.

Another evidence of the tenacity with which the House of Commons guards its own floor, exists in the fact that, although in the House of Lords messengers may wander about in search of any noble Lord for whom there is an appointment, or who is wanted to see a friend or receive a telegram, yet in the House of Commons the messenger may not step on to the floor of the House, and at times has to carry out some curious forms of gymnastic exercise, in order to get at a member without actually stepping on to the forbidden place. The House is particularly sensitive against the intrusion into its midst of any person other than its own members, however well authorised he may be.

When a division is proceeding, a member may speak on a point of order, but if he does so, he must speak seated and covered, and there is often confusion when the member is unable to find his hat and put it on, before he addresses the Speaker, but, were he to rise without it, he would be greeted immediately with cries of " Order, Order ! " Again, no member has an actual right to any particular seat in the House, but the members of the Government have the right to sit on the first benches, those occupied, as already mentioned, by the representatives of the City of London when the House first meets, but, beyond that, a member can only retain his seat by coming in before prayers are said, and putting his hat or card upon that seat.

The House, however, soon recognises that there are certain seats in which certain members prefer to sit, and, as a rule, these seats are retained for them. The rule is not an inflexible one, and another member has just as much right to occupy that seat as the member who is in the habit of sitting in it. There are not actually sufficient seats in the House of Commons for all the members, if they were to attend, but as a matter of fact, it has never been known that they have all attended, and therefore there is no necessity for an enlargement, in order to provide every member with his own seat.

In other Houses of Parliament it is quite different. Many foreign countries allot every member his own definite seat, with very often a locker or a desk at the particular place, in which a member can keep his own papers. In England, it has always been otherwise.

A few more interesting survivals may be briefly referred to. The books issued by the House of Commons are known as Blue-books, and the word Blue-book has become a generic phrase in the English language. The books of course derive their title from the fact that their paper cover is blue, and the interesting circumstance concerning them is that in this colour they date back to 1644.

Archbishop Laud, it will be remembered, was brought to the House of Lords to make a recapitulation of his answers to the charges brought against him. This was on September 2, 1644, and he writes in his Diary thus :

" So soon as I came to the Bar, I saw every Lord present with a new thin book in folio in a blue coat. I heard that morning that Mr. Prynne had printed my Diary, and published it to the world to disgrace me. Some notes of his own are made upon it. The first and the last are two desperate untruths, besides some others. This was the book then in the Lords' hands, and I assured myself that time picked for it that the sight of it might damn me and disenable me to speak. I confess I was a little troubled at it, but when I had gathered up myself, and looked up to God, I went on to the business of the day."

This is believed to be the first mention of a Blue-book, and the habit of having a blue cover on the books issued for the Lords and Commons has been in use ever since.

Another word which constantly recurs with regard to the procedure of the House of Commons is " The Budget," when the proposals concerning the national income and expenditure are laid before the House of Commons by the Chancellor of the Exchequer for assent. The word came from the old French " bougette," a pocket, and the custom was that the papers belonging to the matter about which the Chancellor was to speak were brought to the House in a leathern bag, and laid upon the table, so that to " open the Budget " was to take the papers from the bag, and to read from them the information which it was desired to explain to the House. There is no leathern bag now in use, but the phrase is still retained.

It is odd to notice that we also retain the use of this

word " bag " in connection with ecclesiastical offices. One of the largest fees that has to be paid when a clergyman becomes a Bishop, is that which is charged by what is styled " the Petty Bag Office." The fee is called a " gratification," the official of the Petty Bag Office desires to be " gratified " by the payment of this fee, which comes to nearly fifty pounds, and in this fashion the old word by which the Treasury was spoken of is still retained. I doubt if the Bishop deems it a " gratification."

Again, the names of certain Departments of Government are still called Boards, the Board of Trade and the Board of Admiralty, for example, and the title derives its peculiar fashion from the custom of writing the member's name up upon a board, a habit which is still in use in the Universities.

One of the official duties of the Chancellor of the Exchequer which occurs every year is that of pricking the Sheriffs, although the actual pricking is done by the King himself on the list of persons who have been selected for that position by a Court presided over by the Chancellor of the Exchequer. On this particular occasion, the Chancellor wears his robes of office, one of the very few occasions on which these famous black and gold robes are seen. The habit goes back to the days when there were few persons other than ecclesiastics who were in a position to write, and a mark or a hole made in a piece of parchment was sufficient to denote the name. Even now, the King actually carries out the old arrangement of pricking with a golden bodkin which has a point to it the name of the person who is to hold the office of Sheriff, and the habit is always known as that of pricking the Sheriffs.

It is interesting to notice, with regard to Palatine Counties, alluded to later on, that the Sheriffs for them are not appointed in the ordinary way. They are specifically appointed by the ruler of the Palatinate. The Sheriff for the County of Lancashire is therefore appointed by the Duke of Lancaster, who holds the Duchy, and who happens to be the King, but the writs are in different form to those issued for the other Sheriffs, as the creation is not made by the King in virtue of his Kingship, but in virtue of his possessing the Duchy of Lancaster. To a certain extent, the same thing applies to Cheshire, but not so definitely as in Lancashire.

In Cornwall, a somewhat similar state of affairs exists, because the appointment is in the hands of the Prince of Wales, acting as Duke of Cornwall. For some six hundred years, the Crown was actually unable to appoint a Sheriff for the County of Westmoreland at all, because the privilege of being Sheriff of Westmoreland was a hereditary one in the hands of the Clifford and the Tufton families. The right of being or appointing Sheriffs was given to the Veteriponts by King John. It descended to two heiresses, Idonea and Isabella, and, on the death of Idonea, passed by the marriage of Isabella to the Clifford family. Both Idonea and Isabella are stated to have exercised the rights of Sheriffs in person, an early proof of the ability of a woman before the days of the Sex Disqualification Act to take prominent part in local affairs. In the hands of the Cliffords it remained until late Stuart times, when Lady Anne Clifford, Countess of Dorset, Pembroke and Montgomery, died, leaving only female issue.

This great lady (Lady Anne Clifford) arranged that a distribution of £4 should take place every year adjacent to a pillar which she erected on the roadside near to Brougham Castle. It was to commemorate the time and place where she bade farewell to her mother, when on the way to London, the last occasion upon which she saw her mother. This distribution has taken place ever since the erection of this memorial. The village has neither pauper, public-house nor policeman, and the money, as a rule, goes to the school children.

Lady Anne herself, who has been called the Queen Elizabeth of the North, certainly exercised the right of Sheriff in person, met, received and entertained the Judges of Assize, preceded them into the county, riding on horseback, and on many occasions sat on the Bench with them. When too old to carry out the work in person, she appointed a deputy sheriff to do it for her. She left behind her two daughters, one who married the Earl of Thanet, the other who married Lord Northampton and had by issue a daughter only who herself died without issue, and therefore the right passed to the Tufton family, and was retained down to the days of the eleventh Earl of Thanet, who died in 1849 without issue.

He was supposed to have transferred the rights granted

to his ancestors by King John to the successor to his large estates, but the transference by will to a person who was not heir in blood, was contested, both by his nephew and by the Crown, and it was eventually decided, in lieu of a prolonged lawsuit, that the right, which the Crown had desired for a very long period to repossess, should revert to the State, and that the appointment of Sheriff of Westmoreland should in the future be under the customary regulations.

The heir to the estate received compensation for the transfer of the right, but in the possession of the Tufton family still rests the original Sheriff's seal, and a long series of documents under Great Seal, concerning this extraordinary privilege, which they alone, of all the families in England, possessed.

Finally, let me refer to two habits connected with the religious life of the House of Commons. The bowing to the Chair which takes place when any member passes the Speaker is now an act of courtesy to the Chief Commoner, but in origin goes back much further, because originally there was a chapel called St. Stephen's Chapel, in which, in pre-Reformation days, the Blessed Sacrament was kept, and the members who passed before the altar would, as was customary, bow towards it. The bowing in the House of Commons is definitely stated to have had its origin in this custom. The other point worthy of notice is that the Commons stand at prayer, an unusual custom, but one made imperative by the twentieth canon of the Council of Nice, and which has almost its only example in this habit of His Majesty's faithful Commons.

In considering the procedure of the English Houses of Parliament, I must not omit to mention a far older Parliament, that which forms an amazing survival in the Isle of Man. The high importance of the Manx Legislature consists in the fact that it alone remains an example of the ancient Scandinavian " Thing," the out-of-door parliament, whose origin is lost in the mists of remote antiquity, but which at one time settled the forms of government through the Vikings over the northern parts of Europe. In its turn it probably proceeded direct from the custom of the Druids, who not only worshipped, but promulgated their laws and judged the people in the open air.

In the midst of the British dominions, this ancient habit, brought to Man by its Norwegian conquerors, still remains in all the plenitude of its power, and is the only one of these Scandinavian annual assemblies that has survived.

Manx men still hold their Comitia on the Tynwald Hill, and have retained not only the old name (Thing-hill), but also the substance of its power.

It has two bodies in its Legislature, the Council and the House of Keys. The latter, probably one of the oldest supreme assemblies in the world, if not actually the premier of all, consists of twenty-four members, who were sometimes chosen by the people, and sometimes nominated by the Lord, none being able, however, to sit " without the Lord's will." They are now elected by both male and female owners or occupiers of property, each adult having a vote. There is no property qualification required, and the members can sit for five years.

How the House derives its title is not clear. Some say that the word Key has nothing to do with Manx phrase, and came from the idea on the part of some English-speaking lawyer that in the House existed the power to unlock or solve the difficulties of Manx law, but the more usually accepted derivation is from the Scandinavian word " Keise," meaning " chosen."

Each branch of the Legislature has its own chamber. The Governor presides over the Council, its own elected Speaker over the Keys. The Houses meet separately as occasion requires. The Keys meet when summoned by the Coroner under the Governor's precept, without which they cannot meet. The Council is called together by letter from the Government Secretary who acts as Clerk to the Council. The Keys can adjourn from time to time, but if they adjourn *sine die* they cannot come together again until summoned by the Governor.

The two branches meet in Tynwald (when summoned by the Governor) for administrative purposes, and for the signing of Bills which have been passed in both chambers. The branches vote separately, and the Keys can at any stage of Tynwald retire to their own chamber to consider any question that has arisen. At the end of the meeting, the Governor and Council leave the Tynwald Chamber. The Keys remain to do any necessary business or to adjourn to

any particular day, for Tynwald has brought them into
session.

The procedure respecting Bills to become law is similar
to that of Parliament, but each Bill must be signed by a
clear majority, that is thirteen, of the Keys. The Bill is
then sent up for the Royal assent. When this is given, the
law comes into force *only* on promulgation on Tynwald
Hill.

The regular Court for the promulgation of laws is held
at St. John's on Midsummer day (July 5th, Old Style).
Service is held in the Chapel, and then a procession is formed
to go to the hill about 120 yards off. It is said that this
hill or mound is constructed of soil brought from each
parish (there are seventeen) in the Island. It rises in tiers.
The Governor and Council occupy the top one, the Keys
the next, the clergy the third. The clergy are summoned
presumably that they may be able to inform their people
of the changes in the law. The Court is held in the open
air if the weather is favourable, but if wet or threatening,
a tent is erected over the hill. The church and the Hill
are strewn with green rushes for the occasion. There seems
to have been a custom in some parts of England to strew
the churches dedicated to St. John the Baptist with rushes
on St. John the Baptist's Day—June 24th (Manx Old
Style July 5th)—calling to mind the Baptist's preaching
in the wilderness. Here, however, the rushes are strewn
whenever the Court is held at St. John's—not on July 5th
only.

When the Court has been " fenced " by the Coroner of
the premier sheadings, the six retiring coroners surrender
their wands of office, and the new coroners kneeling before
the Governor are sworn in by the Senior Deemster and
receive their wands from his Excellency.

The several laws to be promulgated are read (now only
in abstract form) in English by the Senior Deemster, and
in Manx by the Senior Coroner, or in case of his not having
sufficient knowledge of the language, by some competent
person appointed by the Governor. At the conclusion of
the promulgation, cheers are given for the Sovereign, the
procession is re-formed, and returns to the Chapel, where
certificates of promulgation are signed by the Governor
and the Speaker, on the original parchment copy of each

Statute. The Court is still in full session. Certain statutory reports are presented, but in recent years it has been the practice to adjourn the Court to an early date, within the week, so as to avoid controversy in a consecrated building. When the adjourned Court has finished its business, the Court is adjourned *sine die*, and as a rule neither branch meets again until about the middle of October.

It is only at the Tynwald at St. John's that the Ancient Sword of State (considered by competent judges to belong to the early part of the thirteenth century) is carried before the Governor.

Manx law has altered very little, and has still several strange peculiarities. Primogeniture extends to females, if there are no males in the direct line; barristers and solicitors are not separate as they are in England, but united in one body, known as Advocates, in similar fashion to that which exists in several of the Colonies : and the ecclesiastical Courts still retain many of the older privileges which in English ecclesiastical courts have disappeared. The summary jurisdiction Courts are known as " Deemster's Courts," and the official who presides over them as the Deemster.*

* For almost the whole of the information concerning Manx law and procedure I am indebted to the Venerable the Archdeacon of Man, who has kindly written out for me his own impressions of Tynwald. I have used them practically intact, and I can hardly express in adequate fashion my gratitude to the Archdeacon for the trouble he has taken and for the invaluable first-hand information with which he has supplied me.

CHAPTER VII

IN THE CITY STREETS

THE visitors to London, and those who stroll about its streets, will often be reminded of events of past history, recalled to memory by words which have survived, and are still in constant use. On the lists of the licensed houses that are dealt with by the magistrates who sit at Holborn, certain houses appear which are not in ordinary ecclesiastical parishes, and such and such a house is said to be within the Liberty of the Savoy, or the Liberty of the Rolls. These divisions constitute parishes of their own, although in one instance the chief ecclesiastical edifice in the district is no longer used for religious purposes.

The Masters of the Rolls, the persons who were entrusted with the custody of the records of the realm, were in the old days generally priests, and often King's Chaplains. It was really only the clergy who were in a position to read and to understand such records. They were often the only persons who *could* read and write, and even when education spread to other sections of the public, the explanation of these archives still remained in the hands of the clergy, and in fact the ecclesiastical courts were responsible for a very large proportion of the deeds themselves.

It was not until Thomas Cromwell was appointed in 1534 that there was any breach of the tradition that clerks only were to be Masters of the Rolls. On the site of the present Rolls Chapel, in the thirteenth century, Henry III had erected a house for the maintenance of converted Jews, who lived there under a Christian Governor, known as Domus Conversorum. This Jewish almshouse, set in what was then called Chancellor's Lane—whence we derive the words Chancery Lane, which is its present title—was broken up in 1377, when the King constituted the new office of Custos Rotulorum, and appointed William Burstal to be the first Master of the Rolls, the house and chapel being given over to him, and annexed to his position.

This chapel continued down to 1617, when a new chapel was built, designed by Inigo Jones, but there still exists an exceedingly fine monument, which belonged to the earlier chapel, and represents Dr. Yonge, who was Master of the Rolls under Henry VIII. This monument is probably the work of Torregiano who was a contemporary of Michael Angelo, and responsible for the work on the superb tomb of Henry VII at Westminster. It is said that part of the cloister of the ancient chapel was transferred, in the early part of the seventeenth century, to the new Inigo Jones building. In the chapel, no doubt, Cardinal Wolsey was often present, as his residence was close by, and in it the Masters and clerks and registrars of the Court of Chancery worshipped, and some of the chief records of the Court were always kept within its walls.

The mediæval part of that original church was destroyed in the seventeenth century, possibly by the Great Fire of London, and later on, some of the windows of the nave also suffered considerable damage. Then came the newly erected Inigo Jones building, and alterations were made to that in 1720 and in 1784, after which as it gradually ceased to be a place of worship, the attendance within its walls being exceedingly small, the remaining records of the Courts of Chancery were transferred to it, and even the seats for the small congregation were made in the form of lockers, so that the building might exercise a double purpose.

In 1856 the interior of the building was again remodelled, and a new ceiling put up, the result of all these repairs and alterations being that towards the end of the nineteenth century there was not a particle of mediæval work left visible, within or without the chapel. When the Public Record Office was extended in 1895, the walls, which had therefore ceased to be important, were pulled down, but a museum, to contain the choicest of the relics, was built upon the old site. In it were incorporated all remains which possessed any historic or artistic value, including the monument just mentioned. Now, the Rolls Chapel, as it is still called, is a museum pure and simple, although in the vaults below it are human remains enclosed in concrete, and there are still memorial tablets on its walls, with three

large monuments and some fragments of a fine chancel
arch of the thirteenth century, so that, as a museum, it is a
place of unique interest, quite apart from the extraordinary importance of the rare historical treasures it now
contains.

The district round about it is still, however, considered
as a separate ecclesiastical division, and is known as the
Liberty of the Rolls, because of the peculiar privileges which
it used to possess, and in consequence it is treated as extra-
parochial, and the memory of its ancient history is retained
in all the legal documents that concern the buildings within
its boundaries.

The Liberty of the Savoy is an even more important
ecclesiastical section, because in it the church, or a portion
of the church, still remains, and the precinct constitutes
a parish by itself. The original Hospital of the Savoy was
built by Simon, Earl of Leicester in 1245, but later on it
was granted by Henry III to Peter of Savoy, from whom
it took its name. He was the Earl of Savoy and Richmond,
son of Thomas, Earl of Savoy, brother to Boniface, Archbishop of Canterbury, and uncle to Queen Eleanor of
Provence, the Consort of King Henry III. When it was
granted to the said Peter of Savoy, it was on the condition
that he should pay yearly at the Exchequer three arrows,
and until the eighteenth century, it is stated, this payment
was still made to the Court of Exchequer, and could probably be demanded even now.

From the Earl of Savoy, the place passed to a religious
house, from whom Queen Eleanor bought it, and presented
it to her second son, the Earl of Lancaster. Within its walls
the King of France was lodged in 1357, when he was brought
to England as a captive by the Black Prince, after Poitiers.
There he was visited by Edward III and his Queen, and he
died in that place in 1364. Later on, the building reverted
again to the Crown, and it was restored and rebuilt by
Henry VII as a hospital for a hundred poor people.

It was dissolved in the time of Edward VI, refounded and
re-endowed by Queen Mary, but fared badly under Elizabeth,
when its revenues were embezzled, and many of its important
possessions disappeared. It still was regarded as part of
the Duchy of Lancaster. In the time of James II there
were Jesuits living in it, and they carried on a school, which

numbered some four hundred pupils, and also conducted a printing press. The schools were dissolved when James II fled from the country, and William III used the building for the residence of numbers of families of poor French Protestants, who were in London at the time, and permitted them to use the church for their place of worship.

By 1755 the place was in a state of ruin, but the precincts still contained the King's printing-press, a prison, a parish church, and three or four other places for religious assemblies, so that Stowe tells us the Dutch, the High Germans, the Lutherans, and the Quakers, as well as the German Calvinists, all met within the same district close up to one another, and there were also harbours for many refugees and poor people, while part of the gardens was used as a burying-ground.

At the beginning of the present century, a great many of the buildings were demolished, when the new approach to Waterloo Bridge was made, and now all that remains of the old buildings is the early sixteenth century chapel known as the chapel of " Saint Mary in the Hospital and of St. John the Baptist in the Savoy." This building was restored by Queen Victoria after a serious fire which had taken place in 1860, in virtue of her position as Lady of the Duchy of Lancaster. There still remains quite an important district round about this chapel, which has separate and definite existence, and is known as His Majesty's Manor and the Liberty of the Savoy.*

Quite recently, the boundaries of this ancient Liberty were beaten ; according to old custom, a jury of sixteen persons being sworn in to see that all the marks which still bear the Provençal red roses, denoting the House of Lancaster, and the three lions rampant of the Duchy, were in order, and headed by the beadle, who carried his silver-mounted staff of office, which has been in use since 1750, the jury went round to assert the rights of one of the oldest jurisdictions in the country. One of the boundaries lies within the vaults of Child's bank, another is on the lawn-tennis court of the Middle Temple, thence the jury passed to New Court, so to the Embankment, to the North stairs leading up to Waterloo Bridge, round to Roman Bath Street, where the old Roman bath still remains, to the

* See also under " Manorial Customs."

Savoy Hotel, to the stage of the Lyceum, and so back to the ancient chapel.

Each juryman was paid by the Duchy for his morning's labour fifteen shillings, and this he received after the ceremony was over. The jury assembled for lunch in the vestry hall of St. Clement Danes, and in the evening the representatives of the Duchy of Lancaster, including the Chancellor, the High Bailiff, the Clerk to the Council of the Duchy, and other notable persons, dined within the precincts at the Savoy Hotel. So was kept up the memory of this interesting district, which has been in the hands of the Sovereigns of England since the early part of the thirteenth century.

The clergyman who holds the position of the Master of the Savoy is still appointed by the Crown. One of his predecessors was a notable man, Antonio de Dominis, who, leaving the Catholic Church, became Dean of Westminster, Master of the Savoy, and was the holder of very strong anti-papal opinions. He returned, however, to Rome at the latter end of his life, and was re-admitted into the Catholic communion.

There are several important persons buried within the Chapel of the Savoy: George, the third Earl of Cumberland; Mrs. Killigrew, the actress, whose father was a Master of the Savoy; George Wither, the poet; the Earl of Feversham, who was in command of King James's troops at Sedgmoor; Gavin Douglas, the poet-bishop of Dunkeld; and Hilton, who in recent days was the Keeper of the Royal Academy.

The most interesting literary association with the Savoy, however, is the fact that Chaucer wrote several of his poems within its walls. It is also famous in the history of the Church of England, because it was the place where the Commissioners met for the revision of the Liturgy in the time of Charles II, when the Nonconformists, Baxter, Calamy and others, were associated with the Bishops and clergy of the Established Church, and constituted what is known as the Savoy Conference.

The most interesting special precinct of that district, however, is the Temple; it has been from remote antiquity the special possession of the Knights Templars, and of the legal bodies their legitimate successors. A part of the

Temple is within the City, but it is the one part of the City where the Lord Mayor has no jurisdiction. He cannot enter the Temple in state, neither he nor the Sheriffs, as such, being allowed entrance within its walls, for the Benchers of both the Inner and the Middle Temple have always retained with pertinacity their rights to manage their own estates, in exactly the same way as the Knights Templars so claimed when they first came into possession of the ground.

On one occasion, a Lord Mayor did attempt to enter the Temple in full state. It was in 1669, and the Lord Mayor was a certain Sir William Turner, who built "the old Mansion House" (73, Cheapside), and resided within it.

He refused to believe that he could be stopped anywhere in the City of London, or that the Benchers of the Temple would be so ill-mannered (as he regarded it), as to refuse him entry into their buildings, when he had been expressly invited to come to dine with them. He therefore announced that he should come with mace and sword in ancient custom.

The Benchers of the Temple protested, and he then declined to come at all. Later on, he changed his mind, and came in state, but the result was a serious riot. He was ordered to lower the City sword, but refused to do so, there was a rush, the sword-bearer was thrown to the ground, and the sword was slightly injured. The City Marshal and the sword-bearer were badly treated, and the Lord Mayor himself had to take refuge against the attack upon himself and his officers carried on by the students of the Inn.

Charles II was informed that a great riot was in progress, and that the Lord Mayor was actually in danger of his life. The City train-bands were called out, and after considerable disturbance, details of which appear in the documents of the day, the Lord Mayor and his party had to return to the Mansion House, very much ruffled, and without the dinner which they had anticipated the pleasure of consuming. Ten years later, a somewhat similar effort took place, and again the Lord Mayor was turned back, but on this particular occasion, there was a fire going on within the precincts of the Temple, and the Lord Mayor stopped the City fire-engine at its entrance, in order to show the full extent of his power within his own district.*

The great Order of the Templars found its home in England in 1128, in the time of Henry I, and its members purchased a very large piece of ground, extending from Fleet Street to the river, and from Whitefriars to Essex House in the Strand. There they put up a vast monastery, with its church, residences for the Prior, Chaplain, Brethren and Knights, a council chamber, a refectory, a barrack, a long range of cloisters and a terrace, which was used for religious meditations, military exercises and the training of chargers. One piece of ground was also kept vacant for tournaments, and to this reference has already been made.† The church was consecrated by Heraclius, Patriarch of Jerusalem, in 1185, and still is the finest of the four round churches in England ; moreover it has attached to it a beautiful Gothic building.

When the Order of the Knights Templars was abolished the control over the estates fell in to the Crown. Edward II granted the Temple to the Earl of Pembroke, who surrendered it in his turn to the Earl of Lancaster, and he transferred it to the persons who were then becoming an organised and collegiate body, the students and professors of law. In the fourteenth century, it was claimed by the Knights Hospitallers, and a great part of the estate, including the house, was transferred to that Order, but the Wat Tyler rebellion interfered with their possession, and their books and deeds, by which they claimed the property, were burnt in public in Fleet Street, when the property appears to have reverted to the legal colleges, whose successors are still in possession of the freehold.

Very little is really known concerning the history of this part of London since it has been in the hands of the lawyers. The revenue of it is probably a very considerable one, but the details concerning it, and the expenditure, are not made public, and it is only those fortunate people who are Benchers of the Temple who know exactly what is the ultimate result. There is no doubt that the management has

* For fuller details see Bell's *More About Unknown London*, a work crowded with curious information, to which I am greatly indebted.

† See Chapter I.

been good since the lawyers have had possession of it, but at the same time, it has been for the advantage of its owners.

A great feature of the Temple is the existence of Middle Temple Hall, built in the time of Elizabeth, and the finest piece of Elizabethan architecture in London. In it, six months after its first appearance at the Globe, Shakespeare's " Twelfth Night " was acted. Probably it is the only building now standing in which Shakespeare himself appeared on the boards, or at least may have been present on the occasion of the acting of his own play. The Inner Temple Hall was almost entirely rebuilt in 1816, but it enshrined several portions of the ancient hall, where the Templars held their Chapters and where they entertained at different times King John, King Henry III, and the Papal Legates.

The entrance to the Middle Temple from Fleet Street is a building erected by Wren in 1684 after the Great Fire, and it occupies the site of a gatehouse which was originally erected by order of Cardinal Wolsey, at the expense of his prisoner, Sir Amias Paulet. Several of the buildings in the Temple belong to Stuart times. It is one of the few places where the ancient custom of summoning the Benchers to their dinner by the sound of a horn is still kept up. The actual horn, which is many centuries old, is still in existence, but it has been cracked, and the horn which is used now only goes back to 1904, and was presented to the Middle Temple by one of its members.

The blowing of the horn is a custom which reverts to the times when the Templars themselves lived in the buildings, and took all their meals in common. It has always been blown at half-past five. It is now blown an hour later, as dinner in the Middle Temple, which has been for a very long period served at six o'clock, is now served at seven. The Warder of the Temple, wearing a silk hat with gold lace round it, leaves the Middle Temple Hall at the time stated, goes to Fountain Court, New Court, Essex Court, Brick Court, Pump Court, Elm Court and Middle Temple Lane, and blows the horn once at each place, and the blast is supposed to be heard in all the courts and by all those in the Inn, and to summon those persons who are to dine at the Middle Hall to their dinner.

The blowing of this horn recalls an interesting bugle call

which still takes place in Cracow, and goes back to the thirteenth century. Every hour of the night a bugle call rings out from the tower of St. Mary's to the four quarters of the city, and is suddenly cut off short in the middle of the final note, commemorating the sack of Cracow in 1243 by Batu Khan with a horde of Mongols. To arouse the inhabitants against their enemies the trumpeter sounded a call to arms, but he was shot in the throat by an arrow, and his last note finished in a gasp.

This perhaps will recall another curious circumstance, that when Sir John Cass, member for the City, founded his school in Aldgate over two hundred and sixty years ago, on the occasion of his signing his will, he suddenly burst a blood-vessel, and the blood covered his quill pen. In commemoration of this fact, every year since that notable event, the four hundred children who attend St. Botolph's Church wear each of them a red quill, so that the event should never be forgotten. The Governors of the school still dine in a room containing all the fittings and furniture of the one in which Sir Christopher Wren used to take his midday meal.

The habit of dining in messes, which is still kept up in the Temple (the mess consisting of four persons), also goes back to the days of the Templars, who sat four together, in order to avoid, it is said, any possibility of quarrelling. It is the duty of a person who is eventually to become a barrister to dine a certain number of times in Hall, and he cannot be called to the Bar unless he has eaten the requisite number of dinners. The fact that he dines in Hall is taken to be proof that he had been attending to his legal training within the boundaries of the Temple.

For a long time, the strictest silence was enjoined at the Inner Temple dinners, the only intercourse between the different members of the messes being confined to an occasion when ordinary courtesy demanded a remark. The dinners now constitute the only legal study of the Temple students, the actual training being carried out in the chambers of the barrister with whom the students are associated, but three years' standing and twelve dinners still have to be declared before a student can be called to the Bar.

The fashion of the loving-cup is kept up in the Temple, as it is in the City Companies, and the Middle and Inner

Temple are both possessed of some very fine silver. The students who are called to the Bar go into the inner room after dinner, and take a glass of wine with the Benchers, and after that, they are recognised as being entitled to plead, but their ceremonial has only just begun on that occasion.

After a barrister has been called, he still pursues the ancient custom of visiting each Court in succession, and is asked by the Judge on the Bench as to whether he proposes to plead. This procession from Court to Court is made by the barristers in full court costume, with the addition of the legal gown, wig and bands, and it is an interesting occasion to see the newly-called members of the Bar making their appearance at the various Courts, and announcing their new position.

Close by the Temple a very old custom is still maintained, the burning of a light in the hall of one of the houses all through the night when everyone else is in bed. The light marks an ancient privilege, and a bygone right of way. It is maintained by the Westminster Council, and not by the tenant of the house. The lamplighter enters at twelve and kindles the light, and on his round in the early morning, he re-enters with a latch-key and extinguishes it. The light is the remaining symbol of a right of way formerly enjoyed by residents in that small street, giving them the power of proceeding to a spring of water in the basement of the particular house, which was at one time their sole water supply.

One of the most ancient churches of that neighbourhood is the one known as St. Clement Danes, because it occupies a site connected with the Danish invasion. It is said that King Harold and other Danes were buried on that site. It has also been stated that a number of Danes who had pillaged the Abbey of Chertsey, were slain on that place and buried there. A third story is to the effect that, when the Danes were driven out of England, a certain number of them were left behind, because they had married English women, and they were ordered to take up their residence in that particular district of London, and there it was that they built their church. Whatever may be the actual reason, it is quite certain that the church has always had a certain association in its name with the Danes, and that it covers the site of an ancient chapel of St. Clement's, which had existed from the time of the Conquest till that of the Reformation, and was always supposed to cover the grave of Harold. The Church now occupies a prominent position in the Strand on an island site. The name of the church is familiar to children, by reason of the old rhyme known as " Oranges and lemons," which brings in an allusion to its bells. Recently the ancient habit of giving away oranges and lemons to the children of the parish has been revived, when the old bells, which were silenced since 1913, were restored in time to ring in the Peace. These bells had for generations pealed for many a victory, and greeted many a new Lord Mayor, and tens of thousands of children have repeated the old rhymes :—

> " Oranges and lemons,"
> Say the bells of St. Clement's.
> " You owe me five farthings,"
> Say the bells of St. Martin's,

and so on.

It has been suggested that the connection of oranges with St. Clement Danes is an inaccurate one, and that the rhyme took its origin from the church of St. Clement's, Eastcheap, because in that neighbourhood there was a market, and oranges and lemons were exposed for sale in the neighbourhood of that church, when they were unloaded from the docks close at hand, but the idea is surely heterodox, because for a very long time the rhyme has been closely associated with the church in the Strand.

The boundaries of the parish of St. Clement Danes have been perambulated for many generations, the ceremony being known as " beating the bounds." In pre-Reformation days there was a long and important religious procession and, at the conclusion of the day's labour, a feast, but at the time of the Reformation all these processions were put down, and this one disappeared for a period. In the seventh year of Elizabeth, however (1565), although the regulation against religious processions remained in force, processions that were concerned with boundary beating were revived, and this one amongst the number.

There is still in existence an ancient hammer, dated 1573, which has been in use in the parish for nearly three hundred and fifty years, and another, nearly as old, dated 1598. These hammers, mounted with silver, and bearing upon them the Tudor rose, with the letters " E.R." and the anchor of St. Clement Danes, were used to keep order at the time of the feast, and are still used for the same purpose.

Recently the ceremony of beating the bounds has been revived with all its accustomed interest, and careful examination is made for the sign of the anchor, the mark of the boundaries of the parish. Part of the parish boundary coincides with that of the Liberty of the Savoy, and so the beating starts within the vaults of Child's Bank, then to Thanet House, passing through the Outer Temple to Essex Court and New Court, and so on to the Middle Temple lawn, obtaining special permission of the Benchers of the Temple to go over the ground of the Temple to inspect the boundary mark. The procession is ushered into this notable Inn of Court by the chief porter of the Middle Temple, in full uniform, and he sees that it passes with proper decorum in and out of the precincts under his control. Thence the procession passes in two boatloads to the middle of the river, where the parish boundary ends, returning to the Hotel Cecil, to the stage of the Lyceum, King's College and Strand Lane, Lincoln's Inn, New Square, and so on back to the church. At Lincoln's Inn, again, special permission had to be obtained, because this ancient Inn, like those of the Temple, retains its own privileges, and debars all processions from entering upon its grounds, except under special permission.

Of the seventy boundary marks that used to exist, only twenty-five, however, could be found in 1922. Many of them had disappeared when old houses had been destroyed and new roads laid out. Each boundary mark was carefully tapped by one of the choirboys with his wand, in order that he should be aware of its existence. The customary protest was made at the doors of the Temple and Lincoln's Inn, because there was always a certain amount of doubt whether a rector and parish officials in the execution of this important duty may be barred out. The Inns of Court have insisted upon their rights, which go back to remote antiquity, and in consequence their permission is always asked, although the protest is made. The permission is not invariably granted ; some twenty-six years ago the procession was stopped from entering Lincoln's Inn, and had to go round the boundaries of the Inn, instead of passing actually through its premises.

On the last occasion when the boundaries were beaten there was no such difficulty, and after the bounds had been carefully beaten the old custom of the Box Supper was revived, curious old tobacco boxes and snuff boxes were put on the table, the ancient hammers were in use, and as far as possible the atmosphere that had belonged to the ceremony for generations was revived.

Close by, in this same quarter of London, there used to stand an ancient Catholic church, called the Sardinian Chapel, originally attached to the residence of the Sardinian Ambassador, and in the days when Catholics were forbidden to have chapels of their own, a building to which very large numbers of the Catholics in England went to hear Mass. The actual building itself was very much injured in the Gordon Riots in 1780, and then was rebuilt, almost on the same site. Some few years ago it disappeared entirely, in connection with some alterations that took place in that part of the world, and another church in Kingsway, dedicated, as was this one, to St. Anselm and St. Cecilia, took its place.

One of the peculiar interests connected with the old church was that for a very long time it was the scene of an ancient and impressive custom upon the opening of a legal term, called the Red Mass, and this ceremony now takes place at the Cathedral instead of in Lincoln's Inn Fields. Actually, Mass was said on that particular old site for nearly two hundred and fifty years, and it was in the approach to that church that the celebrated deadlock took place between the carriages of the French and Spanish Ambassadors, both meeting in the crowded street, and neither Ambassador being prepared to give way to the other. On that occasion a crowd gathered very rapidly, and the people took the part of the representative diplomatists to such an extent that, eventually, both Ambassadors descended from their carriages, and walked to the chapel side by side.

The Red Mass was so called from the vestments that were worn on that occasion. It is what is known as a Mass of the Holy Ghost, and is in order to ask the assistance of the

Holy Spirit upon the legal procedure about to commence. Red is the Pentecostal colour, and the emblem of the Ineffable Wisdom as well as of the Apostolic gift of tongues, and the flowers on the altar, upon that occasion, are chosen of this wonderful and stately colour. The ceremony, even during the time of Catholic difficulties, was never allowed entirely to disappear, and it is now as magnificent as it has always been, and is attended by such of the judges and barristers who belong to the ancient faith, and who all come to it in legal attire.

Another interesting ceremony the City possesses is that known as the Trial of the Pyx. The King's treasure used to be kept in a chapel at Westminster Abbey, still known as the Chapel of the Pyx, the word itself coming from the Latin " pyxis," a box, which has almost its exact equivalent in Greek. At one time the door of this room bore seven locks, and keys were kept, not only by the Sovereign and the Lord Chancellor, but by the Abbot of Westminster, so that there were great occasions when the door had to be opened, and any of the King's treasure removed. It is said that some of the bits of skin that appear on the inside of the present door are human skin, and that, in connection with one great robbery of the Pyx, the horrible punishment of flaying alive was performed on some unfortunate person supposed to have been concerned in the robbery. The little low, vaulted room, supported on short stumpy pillars, can still be seen by the curious visitor twice in the week, and it contains an altar supposed to be the earliest now in the Abbey.

The ceremony of testing the quality of the gold used in the currency is still, however, known as the Trial of the Pyx. It takes place in Goldsmiths' Hall; the assayers and chemists are in attendance, with the needful apparatus by means of which it can be proved whether the coinage is up to the accepted standard or not, and after the examination has taken place, and the public notice been put in *The Times* to the effect that the standard is a true and accurate one, equivalent to the quality of the gold that should be used, the officials concerned in this annual event dine together.

The very streets of London remind one of ancient custom. For example, Cannon Street has nothing whatever to do with military warfare, it has taken its name from Candlewick, the word which is still preserved in the title of the ward in the City of which Cannon Street forms a part. There were two Companies connected with the manufacture of candles, the Tallow Chandlers and the Wax Chandlers. They both still exist, and the Tallow Chandlers have a delightful Hall in Gresham Street. Chandlers in the old days were important persons, the cost of candles being very considerable. Stowe, referring to the books of the Earl of Lancaster, speaks about a charge of nearly forty pounds for 2,390 pounds of tallow candles for the household and of 1,870 Paris candles for the use of my Lord and his family. As money in those days was worth some eight times what it is now, this was a very substantial item.

The first will in the English language is referred to in deeds preserved in Durham Cathedral archives. It is the will of a chandler, who bequeathed candles to various churches, and some important ones that were over nine feet high to the cathedral at York. Electric light and gas have not altogether driven away the use of candles, and one would hope that they may never succeed in doing so, because there is something very mellow and restful in candle-light. There are many of our current phrases that refer to the use of candles, before there was any other arrangement for lighting, such as when we say " The game is not worth the candle," or " Burning the candle at both ends," or "Holding the candle to the Devil," and we of course refer to extinguishing the light of the candle when the phrase is used in which a person says, " That puts the tin hat on it."

The custom of ringing the curfew bell is still kept up in London in Gray's Inn, Lincoln's Inn and the Tower of London. It occurs in the provinces in many places ; for instance, it is still rung at Alnwick, Offchurch, Kirkby Stephen, Richmond in Yorkshire, and Bury St. Edmunds. It used to be rung in many important towns, but there are still quite a number of smaller ones where this warning bell can yet be heard. The only place, I believe, where it has never ceased to ring is at Wallingford. I am assured that, from 1066 down to the present time, the bell has never ceased to be rung in the evening. The old custom was to ring it first at nine, and then at ten, and by the latter time all lights were put out entirely.

Perhaps it may be well to mention amongst London customs that go back for some time the fact that the Chief Magistrate of the Metropolitan Police Courts, and his principal clerk, drive down to Ascot Racecourse for the days of the racing, to hold a court for the instant punishment of any offenders. In all probability, Sir Chartres Biron does not actually drive down in the present day, but takes the less formal method of going by rail or motor, but he and his chief clerk, Mr. Gaskell, do attend during the races, and the habit is one which has gone on for at least a hundred years, if not from an earlier date still. Certainly, in the last part of George III's time, or in the early part of George IV's, there was some disturbance at Ascot, and the King, who was present, was so angry at the delay which ensued in punishing the offender that he ordered that a London magistrate (if possible the Chief London Magistrate), should in future attend at the racecourse, with a clerk, so that no such delay should again ensue.

There is a small guard-room on the Grand Stand, and the habit is still kept up of the attendance of the magistrate, although, as a matter of fact, the work that he has to do now is almost non-existent, but he is there, in case of any disturbance, so that his services might be called upon if required.

CHAPTER VIII

MANORIAL COURTS AND CURIOUS TENURES

THERE are probably more survivals from ancient times in connection with the manorial courts than with any other authority in the country, but if the postponed operations of the Law of Property Act come into force, some ancient customs connected with the copyhold tenure of land will fall out of existence. It will be unfortunate, because these courts have existed from remote times and enshrine many important rights connected with land which are in danger of being forgotten. The courts are divided into three groups, the Court Baron and the Court Customary and the Court Leet.

There was an Act passed in the time of Edward I, which recognised a broad divergence between them and declared that the Courts Baron exercised strict manorial rights. A Court Baron, which is not a court of Record, is incident to every Manor and was ordained, as well for the maintenance of the services and duties stipulated for by Lords of Manors on their granting out lands to others in fee, as also for the purpose of determining actions of a personal nature, as debt or trespass or detinue of goods where the debt or damage was under forty shillings, such actions lying not only between the tenants of the manor, but also against strangers coming within the manor. Freehold tenants alone were suitors to this Court and the same persons were the judges. For this reason two freehold tenants at least must be present to act as judges, as freemen could only be tried by their peers ; and if one only should be present, he had no peer and therefore must have appealed to the lord paramount. The Lord of the Manor is Chancellor in his own Court. However, apart from purely Manorial matters, all the jurisdiction of the Court Baron in other matters was taken away by the County Courts Acts, 1867.

The Customary Court is for the copyhold tenants of a Manor. At this court, the copyholders in attendance form the jury and are called the " homage," while the Lord or his Steward is the judge.

The most interesting of the Courts is perhaps the Court Leet which was a court of record, depended for its jurisdiction upon Royal franchise and need have little, if any, connection with a manor. There has been a great deal of dispute over the meaning of the word " Leet," which in early Norman documents appears as " lete." There is a phrase in use in the country-side, speaking of a place where cross-roads meet, as a " two-way " or a " three-way leet," and the name of the court has been assumed to have come from the old English word " laetan," to let, from which this word " leet " is derived.

Some later authorities have suggested two other origins for the word, one a connection with the word " lathe," which is still used in the counties of Kent and Suffolk, to represent a section of the land which encloses several hundreds, and another, which refers it to the old Danish " leith," a court of judiciary assembled, a word which still lingers in the Scandinavian tongues, when one speaks of a division of the country specially arranged for military purposes.

In Scotland it has quite another use : it there meant a list of persons who are nominated for election to a particular office, and is, like so many other old Scottish words, derived distinctly from French, and in this case from the French word " élite," elected. It is generally now used in the phrase " short leet," which is the selection made out of a large number of applicants for a post, from whom the final choice is made.

The Court Leet is really one of the highest and most ancient tribunals of the Common Law, and is even, in some documents, termed " The King's Court," for its ordinance has been ascribed to King Alfred. It can inquire into such offences as murder, manslaughter, arson, rape, or in regard to any offence that has been regarded as felony in Common Law, and concerning which it certifies to the King's Justices. It also has the power to inquire into difficulties with regard to weights and measures, and it did so, until quite lately, in St. Giles's, Bloomsbury, and in Stepney. It still possesses such powers in Westminster, and it is a Court of Record.

One of the most interesting is that held by the City of London over the Manor of the " village " of Southwark, a Lordship granted in the time of Edward III. There are actually three Manors, and the High Steward, who is the City Recorder, holds Courts in each with time-honoured ceremonials, juries, prothonotaries, fines and presentments.

The needful summons to any of the above mentioned Courts is still as a rule given in ancient form. This announces that the Lord of the Manor has appointed to hold a Court Baron, or a Customary Court, or a Court Leet, as the case may be, on such and such a day, and the tenants are requested to make their personal appearance " To do their Suit and Service, to pay their Arrears of Quit Rent and Reliefs to the Lord of the same Manor, for all such Lands and Tenements as they hold of the same Manor, according to the Laws and the Customs of the Manor aforesaid." They are also, as a rule, summoned " to bring with them a true particular of all such Lands and Tenements as they hold of the same Manor, together with the number of Acres, and Boundaries of the same, to the end that the same may be duly enrolled, otherwise a Distress," so the notice states, " will be taken upon their Lands and Tenements, if they neglect this Summons." The notice is sent out by the steward of the manor.

The courts are generally initiated by the steward reading a document, worded in strange, old-fashioned, formal manner, which declares the opening of the court, and is preceded by the usual Norman phrase " Oyez, Oyez," which has been corrupted into the words " O yes, O yes," If in connection with a fair, it bids all persons there assembled to preserve His Majesty's Peace without offering any violence, and without making any Raid or Rout or illegal assembly, and without drawing any weapons or spilling any blood, and it demands that every business person having connection with the fair shall declare himself to the steward, and that, if any trouble should arise between buyer and seller, the people are to repair to the Court of Piepowder,* and have justice done, according to the equity of the case.

If it is just an ordinary manorial court, the steward or the bailiff gives notice that whoever owes " suit or service "

* See Chapter IX.

must appear, or will be fined, and when the court is opened, he calls upon all the persons who owe " suit or service," to draw near, to make their attendance, to answer to their names, and to " save their amercements," the latter word meaning simply their fines. Then follows the election of the foreman of the jury, who is sworn in the ordinary way, and as a rule the statement by which he is requested to make his oath runs something like that used in an ordinary court of law, but is more ample in its phraseology.

He has to inquire into such things as are given him in charge, and to make true presentments thereof. He undertakes to keep secret the King's counsel, his own, and that of his fellows, and he promises to present no person out of " envy, hatred or malice," nor to spare any man, nor conceal anything out of " love, fear, favour or affection," or " for any hope of reward or gain, but to the best of his knowledge, and according to any information he may receive," he presents " the truth, the whole truth, and nothing but the truth."

Then the jury inquire into the state of the ditches, the watercourses, the sheep-dips and what are known as the sinkholes ; they speak of any rents or services withheld from the Lord of the Manor ; they refer to the fact whether there exists a pair of stocks or a pound, and whether they are kept in proper repair ; and they announce that no person whose estate does not warrant such an action may use game or sporting dogs.

There follows the attendance and swearing in of any new tenant to the manor, announcements of the death of any deceased tenant, and of the succession of their heirs, and then there are certain dues paid to the Lord of the Manor, which vary in different manors, and according to different rolls, sometimes being but a few pence, and sometimes a quit rent for very much larger sums.

There are declarations as to peculiar tenures, one person having, as is the case in Berkshire, to present two white chickens ; another, as is the case in Kent, having to undertake to go over with the Lord of the Manor whenever he shall cross the sea, and various other strange regulations, fee farm rents, as they are called, to which some reference is made in another part of this chapter.

After the election of the constable of the manor, which

follows, he takes his oath truly to serve the King and the Lord of the Leet, or the Lord of the Division or Manor, the word " manor " of course simply coming from the Latin phrase, which implies to remain or to dwell or to stay, and which has an almost exact equivalent in Greek. In some manorial courts, there is the appointment of persons who taste the ale and who test the quality of the bread, the ale-tasters and the bread-conners, and these are still regularly appointed in the City of London, and in other courts.

In the West of England, the courts have to do with questions concerning the mining industry, the opening and closing of roads, the granting of licences, ancient ferries, or with the relinquishing of such ferries. Occasionally, this work is not carried on by the manorial court, but by a special court summoned for the purpose acting under the authority of what is known as a writ " ad quod damnum " which issues from the Attorney-General, and decides whether it is to the prejudice of the Crown that any licence should be granted or any privilege relinquished. These writs " ad quod damnum " can also be granted by Lords of the Manor, and the investigation then proceeds on similar lines, to see whether the manor is damaged or prejudiced in any way by the existence or by the relinquishment of any rights appertaining to it.

At the conclusion of the ceremony, the whole court is dismissed, and the bailiff cries out that, if any person who hath appeared at the court have anything further to say, he shall be heard, but otherwise all manner of persons are " hereby discharged of their attendance at this court " until obliged to attend again on a new summons. The usual fashion is for the ceremonial of the day to end in a substantial lunch or dinner, at which the healths of the Sovereign and the Lord of the Manor are drunk, and so the procedure has gone on from Norman times. One of the courts, for example, which has recently ceased to exist, the Gillingham Court Leet, is known to have been established in 1070, but its purpose disappeared when Gillingham was incorporated in 1902, and there seems to be no reason for its continuance, save the feeling of regret that any court which lasted in England for eight hundred and fifty years should finally disappear.

The Courts Baron and Customary in the Barony of Burgh were held at Burgh-by-Sands in 1923 for the last time. They date back to the time of the Norman settlement. When the Baronies of Cumberland were carved out by Randulph de Meshines, the particular one to which the Court had reference came down through the Morvilles, Multons, Dacres and Howards down to the Lowthers, and the Manor now belongs to the present Earl of Lonsdale.

A Court Leet, view of Frank-pledge and Court Baron of an old Manor, dating back before the Conquest, and recorded in Domesday Book, was held quite lately at East Hendred, near Steventon. The occasion was unique, because there has been no Court held for nearly forty years, the last occasion being when the late Mr. John Allin was the Lord of the Manor. Since that date the affairs of the Court appear to have been allowed to lapse into ancient history, and therefore when the new Lord of the Manor recently convened a Court, the copyholders, tenants and villagers (or villeins) woke up and determined to do their best on the occasion.

According to Domesday Book the King's Manor appears to have a history back even to the times of the Saxon King Edward the Confessor. Its official recital in the Domesday Book is as follows : " The King holds Henret in demesne. King Edward held it. It was then rated for four hides and a half, it is now not rated at all. There is land for five ploughs. In demesne are 2 ploughs and 8 villeins and 13 boors with 2 ploughs and there are 2 serfs, a mill of 42 shillings and 4 acres of meadow. Henry held a hide there which belonged to the King's farm. Godric held it. The King bestowed it on Godric's wife for feeding his hounds."

According to " Dugdale " this estate which at the Norman Survey belonged to the Earl of Evreux was given by him to the then Priory of Noion in Normandy. After the suppression of these alien Priories in 1414 during the reign of Henry V, this Manor was given by his successor, Henry VI, to the Carthusian Monastery of Jesus of Bethlehem at Sheen.

In " Magna Britt," Vol. I, p. 173, at the British Museum Library, it is stated :

By his Charter, third year of reign of Henry VI, he granted to the Monks a weekly market and two fairs yearly, also exempted them from certain taxes and impositions and likewise gave them the liberty of Frank-pledge with the privilege of a Pillory and Tombrel, and also the privilege of erecting a gallows for malefactors.

On the dissolution of the Monasteries, 1536–9, this Manor fell to the Crown and hence obtained the name of " The King's Manor." During the Commonwealth the Manor was sold to a Commoner, but at the date of the Restoration King Charles II resumed possession and it remained a Royal Manor until King George IV sold it in 1823.

Formerly a great woollen and cloth trade flourished at East Hendred, which was an important market-town. The ancient Parish Church was formerly attached to this Manor and contains many monuments and brasses to persons described as " Pannarius " and " Lanarius," that is, merchants in cloth and wool.

The customs of the Manor are that on the death of a copyhold tenant or surrender a fine of one year's rent is payable, and a heriot of the best good is due when the copyhold tenant dies on the premises unless he has made a surrender to the use of his will, in which case a heriot of sixteenpence is due, being the heriot which is payable when the copyholder dies off the premises and a like heriot is due and payable on every surrender.

The Lord of the Manor has the right of appointing his own Steward.

The Court was held on the Wheatsheaf in East Hendred, in the ancient Court Room where the Courts were formerly held hundreds of years ago. Precisely at high noon the Steward of the Manor, accompanied by the Bailiff and the Court Cryer, entered the Court Room, and the Court was opened according to ancient custom with the Cryer's proclamation, " Oyez ! Oyez ! Oyez ! " followed by the old rites and ceremonies handed down by oral tradition from time immemorial. The Court Leet was first opened, and the Jury listened to a charge from the Steward in the old phraseology of ages ago as to what their duties were, and the Jury were dismissed to their labour of questing or finding out and " presenting " any treason, bloodshed or felony which ought to be presented to the notice of the Lord of the Manor or to the King's Judges. Of course, in such a peaceful village as East Hendred nothing could be found to warrant such a presentment, and thereupon the view of Frank-pledge was taken whereby each and every tenant became mutual bail or pledge for the good behaviour of his neighbours to the Lord of the Manor and the King of the Realm.

The Court Baron, which followed immediately the closing of the Court Leet, was more for the small copyhold tenants to decide questions between the Lord and his tenants and between tenant and tenant. Apparently this must be a very happy, contented Manor ; the Jury could not find any complaints to enter on their presentment, unless it was that the Court was not held frequently enough. But there was not a single disputatious point raised that required judicial investigation.

Now was the time for the Court Baron to assert their ancient rights and privileges of appointing certain officers of the Manor, which they did unanimously. One of the officers was the ale-conner or ale-taster, whose duty was to test or taste the ales sold in the village, so that nothing should be sold obnoxious or likely to be injurious to the health of the Lord's tenants, or hurtful to man's stomach. The Court ale-testing cup was presented to him in ancient form.

The Bailiff then performed his duties by collecting the quit-rents, which he did without difficulty, as the tenants came up to the table and appeared eager to render their dues to the Lord of the Manor. The Court was then closed with the ancient salute and ceremonial, and the quaint proceedings brought to a happy conclusion.*

A similar Court Baron and Customary Court Demissions took place in Penrith some little time ago (says the *Penrith Observer*), in connection with the lands of the Lords of the Manor of Stainton, and was conducted by the Steward to the Manor, Mr. William Little, who was then in his ninety-second year. He said that he was afraid that Court would be the final one, as in the course of the next year the tenure would become freehold.

It is not to be thought that these courts are unpopular : such is by no means the case. The people of the country-side attend them with great regularity, and are much

* I am indebted to the *Berkshire Chronicle* for much of above information.

attached to the old method of holding them. They take part with great solemnity in all the ceremonials connected with the court. They are willing to acknowledge the privileges that belong to the Lords of the Manor, and to pay the rents that it may be necessary to demand. It is only occasionally that some of the more unusual demands cause any feeling in the matter, but as a rule, so conservative are the people of England, and so attached to ancient customs, that they are quite ready to pay such fees as the Lord of the Manor can prove he has the right to charge for infringements, or for the inception of a new tenant, or on the death of a tenant.*

I have known a case when a heriot (which is the right of the Lord of the Manor to a chattel, a sum of money, or very often, in early manors, the best beast of a copyhold tenant) was required, an effort was made to remove from the stables a noted race-horse, in order that it should not be seized, and I have heard a case, somewhat similar, in which all the animals, save an ancient donkey, were removed from the premises ; but even in this latter case a compromise was speedily arrived at, the donkey being left more as a joke than by the way of a serious offer, and the Lord of the Manor was paid the sum which he demanded as the heriot, instead of the best beast being taken.

* I am permitted by the Lord of several manors in Sussex to quote from a letter recently received from one of his tenants, in which he expresses a certain amount of surprise at receiving the notice for the payment of a fine on admission, inasmuch as the previous Lord of the Manor had not taken special care to collect such a fine, and he states : " I do not consider myself mug enough to pay one and a half year's rent on my few poverty-stricken acres. Also I do not make any offer as for admitting me to them, for I have been in possession for two years, and I am sticking." He then goes on, with reference to the Lord of the Manor, to say : " Undoubtedly he expects something, therefore, as a sporting offer, if he likes to turn in all future claims against the estate (I am at present bursting with generosity), I will pay ten pounds, which, if judiciously placed on the winner of the Derby, should bring him wealth beyond the dreams of avarice." This is not the manner in which the tenants usually write, but the correspondence has an amusing character, and it is therefore thought well just to quote this " sporting offer." Needless to say, the Lord of the Manor did not accept the offer, it would have been far too serious to relinquish all claims for this amount, and I am equally sure that, if the offer had been accepted, the money would not have been laid out in the manner suggested.

A great deal, of course, depends upon the Lord of the Manor and the terms upon which he remains with his tenants, but as a rule there is a very friendly spirit between the lord and the tenants, and the attachment of the English agriculturist to the ancient habit and custom is so complete, that he does not dream of opposing his lord, and in that which his father and grandfather and those who preceded him have accepted he just as readily acquiesces.

One of the most important of all the Courts Leet is the Court of the Liberty of the Savoy. It consists of a steward and eight burgesses, and a jury for the year of sixteen persons is annually elected at the Court. The finding of the jury is conclusive, although they hear no evidence and examine no witnesses. It is a survival, according to Mr. Justice Stephens, of the stage in English history at which ordeal and purgation had fallen into disuse, and no exact substitute for them had been discovered. It can deal with any complaint regarding an unsafe house or a disorderly resident, and the complaint need not be in writing, but may be made verbally. A pronouncement, however, has to be in writing, and signed by each member of the jury. The punishment is a fine, four of the jury can settle the amount of that fine, and the money goes to the expenses of the court of the Liberty.

In the Shetland Isles, it is still the custom to summon a jury by sending round a stick passed on from house to house by the persons who are in the habit of serving on these juries. The stick has a cross upon it, if the matter is ecclesiastical, and it has a burnt end, if it relates to a fire. There are other symbols used upon it, which tell the juryman what is likely to be the subject of the complaint, and these symbols go back to days when it was only the clergy who could read and write, and when symbolism was in general use.

Another ceremony, which still exists in connection with these Court Leets, is known as the " Leet Ales," the giving away of ale, or the arrangement of a parish merry-making or feast, in connection with the holding of the court, and here it may be well to point out that we still keep up the reference to this custom when we speak of a " bridal " party, as that is really the " bride-ale " or the bride-feast. At the Universities, there are still festivals known as College

Ales, Audit Ales, and Church Ales, and in many parishes, there still remain, either on the occasion of meeting the court, or at some other time, the Parish Ales. The parish ale conner, or ale taster, was in old days a very important person, but since ale and beer have become excisable commodities, his importance has waned very considerably.

Then, in connection with the same courts, and at other times in parishes, there remain the customs of doles, which are many centuries old. One of the most important is that which is retained at Tichborne in Hampshire, and by reason of the fact that the Tichborne family has always remained true to the ancient faith, the ceremonial attending the distribution of the dole is ecclesiastical, and there is a special service, when the parish priest blesses the flour which is distributed, and sprinkling the money with holy water, censes it, offering up certain prayers that God would bless, to the benefit of those who were to receive them, the doles to be distributed.

The origin of this particular dole is said to go back to a certain Lady Tichborne, who requested of her husband the means to establish a gift of bread, to be given to all poor persons who might ask for it, on the Feast of the Annunciation. At the time that she asked for this favour she was very ill, and her husband, when he promised her that she might have such land as she could crawl round in the neighbourhood of his estate, while a certain torch was burning, imagined that she would be able only to secure a very small property, but by an extraordinary access of strength, she crawled round a piece of land which contains an area of twenty-three acres, and this land has always retained the name of " The Crawls " to this very day. The income derived from the rent of this is applied for the dole, and has been so applied for eight hundred years, for tradition has it that, were the distribution omitted, the prosperity of the family would immediately cease, and the family itself become extinct from the failure of an heir male. This is one of the most remarkable doles still existing in England.

The Tichborne Dole now consists of twelve sacks of flour, and gallons of flour are doled out to the various tenants, one for each adult and half a gallon for each child. The flour is blessed by the priest before it is distributed, and it

is given away on Lady Day. The dole has now been
distributed for over eight hundred years.

Another dole is the gift made at the Hospital of St. Cross,
Winchester, to every stranger who comes, of a drink of
ale and a piece of bread. These gifts in the old days were
given to every wayfarer at the doors of the greater monasteries, and were a source of considerable comfort to
the tramps on the highway. They still continue in the
monasteries that are the successors of the older houses, and
at the monastery of Coalville near Leicester, and at the great
Carthusian house of Cowfold in Sussex, doles of bread are
given away, as they were in ancient days, to the persons who
stand in need of them, and ask for this assistance at the door
of the monastery.

Sunday by Sunday doles of bread are still given in several
churches. Near to Hull, fish, we believe, is given away ;
in Clavering in Essex, bread, and also in Newmarket, and
perhaps, also, at a place called Farnham in Buckinghamshire. There are also doles of money given to widows, who
have to pick up the money from a certain lady's grave,
in the parish churchyard of St. Bartholomew the Great
in Smithfield, the widows having been present at Divine
service just before. Similar doles exist in various places
in the City of London, where poor women have to attend
church on certain days in order to receive a dole from a
charity arranged on their behalf generations before. Bread
is given away on Whit-Sunday in Liverpool Street in connection with one of the Bishopsgate churches, and Christ's
Hospital boys receive raisins and new pennies, under similar
strange arrangements, while there are doles of this kind
existing almost all over England.

In Dundee, I am informed, there are still a few ancient
tenements the tenants of which are entertained when they
attend to pay their rents ; each person getting a meat pie
and a bottle of ale, the custom having been kept for a very
long time.

Captain J. W. Dixon reminds me of the charity at Roches-
ter in Kent, which still provides free board and lodging to
a certain number of mendicants, provided they are not
" rogues nor proctors "—the latter meaning professional
mendicants.

Mr. Henry Upton mentions that there is a dole in existence

in Dublin, created under the will of Lord Newtown-Butler in 1723. The bread is put on shelves in two cases, one on either side of the chancel of St. Anne's Church, Dawson Street, and under one of the cases is the following inscription : " The Right Honble Theophilus Lord Newtown, of Newtown Butler, bequeathed to the poor of St. Anne's parish for ever 13 pounds per annum, to be distributed in bread at five shillings each week. 1723."

Every Sunday, he says, the fresh supply of bread is put in the cases, and it is distributed during some part of the day.

Some of the ancient tenures by which land is held are of importance, and are still most carefully carried out. A few of them do not belong to very remote antiquity. For example, on Waterloo Day (June 18) the Duke of Wellington solemnly presents to the Crown a small tricolour flag, as rent for the estate of Strathfieldsaye, granted to his great ancestor by the nation, under this arrangement, and the flag is annually placed over the bust of the Iron Duke in the Guard Room at Windsor Castle, where it remains until the following year, when the new one takes its place. This is known as a tenure of Grand Serjeantry.

There is some land in Leicestershire which is held by the ancient tenure of the presentation of a garland and three roses : there is an estate in another part of England, the rent of which is a herring pie, and yet another pays its rent by means of the presentation of a faulchion—a military weapon now entirely obsolete—which typifies the power by which the Lord of the Manor could demand the assistance of his tenant in military adventures. In order to hold certain estates a horn has to be wound—a man has to wind it, that is, to put wind into it, and to sound it. In several places red roses are paid as rent for land, and in many cases pepper, which in Tudor times was a precious commodity, is presented for rent.

A Yorkshire estate carried the obligation to deliver to the landlord three quarterns of pepper every year, and one in Sussex still pays a rent of 1 lb. of black pepper annually. The rent of one Scottish estate held under the Crown is the presentation of a snowball in June. This is not by any means an easy rent to pay, but it has been demanded quite recently, and it happened by a fortunate occurrence that the weather was sufficiently cold for a snowball to be presented of natural and not of artificial snow, although, as a rule, nowadays, the aid of chemistry has to be called in to help, if the tenure is demanded in ordinary summer weather.

There is an estate in Yorkshire which is held under very much the same tenure. The holder is called upon to pay as rent a red rose at Christmas and a snowball at Midsummer, the two objects being mentioned in order to render the payment of the rent as difficult as possible ; but the owner of the land has no particular trouble with regard to either, because he grows the roses under glass, and declares that the snow never disappears until August from certain well-protected hollows on the moor just above his house, and in consequence he can always get sufficient to make a ball, the size of which the deeds do not mention. It is stated in the immediate neighbourhood that sometimes the snowball has not exceeded the size of a pea.

The town of Banbury retains certain privileges on the part of its Corporation, for which it has to pay the Bishop of the diocese. The rent originally was a hundred and forty hens and thirteen hundred eggs, which had to be sent in at intervals to the Bishop during the year. I believe now this ancient rental is commuted into a money gift. Other estates are held under the peculiarities of having to make certain gifts to the King if ever he comes on the estate. In one, if he visits the town in winter, he is to be given three eels, but if he comes in the summer, the payment to be made is two great white geese. The town of Yarmouth, I hear, still sends the King a herring pie, the old custom being to send a hundred herrings, which had to be made up into twenty-four small pasties.

In one manor in Kent the tenant had to render a pound of black pepper every year (since commuted for a money payment). This payment is in respect of some land which was once an island surrounded by the sea. No doubt the original tenant was a seafaring man trading to the East, and the Lord of the manor in fixing the annual payment had this in mind, and made his tenant pay in an Eastern spice he required, and, at that time, very difficult to obtain.

A red rose is presented to the King as a quit rent when he

passes through the Glen Ormiston estates. Mr. M. G. Thorburn paid the rent in 1923, using the following formula : " As owner of the lands of Glen Ormiston, which I hold in free blench farm fee and hold for ever, to pay to Your Majesty and Royal Successors one Red Rose, if asked. Your Majesty has been pleased to ask it, and I here present it."

The Duke of Atholl in similar fashion presents a white rose by way of rent, and the owner of Grendon, Buckinghamshire, a bunch of roses.

The Munros of Foulis must, when required, furnish the Sovereign with a bucketful of snow.

Certain lands at Aylesbury are held under the tenure of providing as quit rent straw for the King's bed, whenever he shall visit that neighbourhood.

There are two estates, not very far from London, which were conveyed, not for the ordinary time of ninety-nine years nor for the still longer period of nine hundred and ninety-nine, but as regards one of them it was to be held by the man and his heirs " until the world's rotten." As regards the other estate, a bequest of land was to stand good " so long as grass doth grow and water doth flow." These were curious methods of providing for perpetuity.

I believe that a few years ago, a lease which had been granted for nine hundred and ninety-nine years fell in, and that this constitutes the only instance known of such a circumstance. If I am rightly informed, it concerned a piece of cathedral property, and I think that the cathedral was Ely, and that a piece of land which had been granted nearly a thousand years ago, by the then possessors of the ecclesiastical land round about the Cathedral, fell in to those who are their present successors. There have been, of course, many instances of the falling in of leases granted for ninety-nine years, or leases granted for a term of lives, but I am not aware of any other case in which a nine hundred and ninety-nine years' lease has come to an end, and the fact has been recorded.

A cottage on the Hampton Lodge estate in Surrey was demised for a thousand years, by a lease dated the 29th of September in the 31st year of the reign of Queen Elizabeth, at the yearly rent of one red rose. The rent has never been paid by the vendor of the estate, who sold it in 1923, nor, so far as they could discover, by any other persons in recent times, but the cottage has to be regarded as leasehold property held at this yearly rent for the residue of the term of a thousand years, and not as freehold. It can, of course, be enlarged into freehold, but its historic tenure has always been retained.

Land was conveyed at times in strange fashion. For example, some Yorkshire property was transferred with a straw, the handing over the straw representing the corn land that was being transferred. If it had been a grassy meadow, a turf or a sod would have been handed over when the purchase took place, and timber is conveyed even now when a purchase is made, by breaking off a small piece and passing it to the new owner.

There was a reference a little while ago to the transference of some land in Westmoreland in 1607 in which a lady handed to her son, as a token of passing over her property to him, a powder horn, which in this particular instance, she called " a powder tumbler," showing that it was a horn which would not stand upright. The transference was simply typical of the household effects, amongst which, no doubt, there were drinking vessels made of a similar material.

A little while ago, two small manors were offered for sale, and it was specially announced that the possessor of one of them, that of Newton Bushel, had the right to wear a cocked hat, to have a mace carried before him, to hold a Court Leet, and to appoint a portreeve, a drover and an ale-taster. These seemed, however, to be almost the only privileges appertaining to that particular manor, and in consequence it fetched a very small sum at auction, the man who paid £31 being now the possessor of all these privileges, as well as of a large box of old deeds.

Preston is a home for many of the stranger habits connected with local life, and at the historic town in Lancashire every twenty years a procession takes place which is known as the Guild Merchant. On that occasion ordinances are enumerated, and privileges that used to be of vast import-ance to the freemen of the town, are described ; while the Guild Merchant, in all the functions of its ceremonial, represents the development of the town of Preston, from remote antiquity down to the present day. Preston was one of the first towns in England to possess self-government, and held certain important liberties, by an early charter, in which the burgesses themselves were declared the owners of their town, so that the privileges that belonged to these days are expressed and perpetuated in this elaborate pageant, which, it is said, has never ceased to be held at intervals of about twenty years since 1328 and in full force since 1542.

It is in connection with manors and tenures that one or two strange habits with regard to the descent of land still hold good. In many parts of Wales, in the North and in the ancient kingdom of Kent, there are estates where the land does not descend from the father to his son, and primogeniture does not come into operation at all. The land descends from the father to all the sons in equal proportion, according to the old right, known as gavel-kind, the word being derived from an early German phrase, meaning " to go to all the kin," or " the children," although by some scholars it has been taken to come from a Welsh or a Saxon word meaning a common tenure.

Then, another curious descent of land is known as " Borough English," and this is the custom where the youngest son inherits instead of the eldest. It is claimed as of Saxon origin, and in force in many places where the Norman system of descent was not permitted to be exercised, the people tenaciously holding to the older method, hence its name. It still exists with regard to land at Chiswick and Fulham, and there are portions of certain manors in the outskirts of London, especially at Hackney, which still descend according to Borough English, and not in the ordinary manner.

It casts the inheritance upon the youngest as the one least able to support himself and more likely to be left destitute of any other support. Its origin is connected with the amazing Jus primæ noctis or Droit du Seigneur, which is actually still mentioned in the deeds of certain manors in England, but which has had no actual existence since mediæval times.

There is, again, the custom of escheat, whereby if a person dies intestate and without heirs his freeholds become the property of his lord, and the escheat is usually with a small reservation in favour of the Crown, in the documents spoken of as "feudal Lord Paramount," but there are circumstances in which the Lord of the Manor claims his escheat of all the land.

Colonel Chichester-Constable is still styled Lord Paramount of Holderness and this title has been in the same family since the time of Philip and Mary, the present owner being the forty-fourth in direct succession. He appoints the Coroner at Hull and has very important seigniorial rights on the sea coast and on the banks of the Humber, and extensive manorial rights also.

Yet another manorial custom exists in many remote villages, where frankpledge is brought into existence. There has been, perchance, some difficulty and controversy between neighbours, some dispute as to water-courses or land, and the steward of the manor binds the neighbours over to be responsible for one another's conduct. It is the security given by a group of franklins, or free men, and it is termed frankpledge for that reason, the neighbours entering into a covenant that they will keep the peace, and that they will see that each person in the group does so, they being jointly responsible for any infringement of this pledge.

A Westmoreland manorial custom applies to estates subject to the law of "free bench" by which, on the day of her marriage, a wife became entitled to a free table upon the death of her husband, and this was represented by half the income of the estates free of all control and restraint as to marriage. It was declared in 1923, in the case of Thompson v. Burra, that the widow was entitled in her absolute discretion to elect whether she would stand possessed of the right she had secured to her over the property on her wedding day, without any restraint whatever, or whether she would give that up, and rest content with the annuity and the restraint as to widowhood, and as to residence at the Hall, which her husband's will imposed, he not having been aware of the fact that the estate he was dealing with was subject to this unusual law. Fourteen days were given to the widow to prepare her decision, and it was stated that this decision would affect many manorial properties in Westmoreland, in addition to the one respecting which it was brought into notice.

Some other strange privileges remain in connection with land. Many people have a right to cord wood and make faggots in connection with the holding of a particular piece of land, and that privilege has to be retained, and specially referred to, whenever the land is sold. This privilege is in force, I believe, in Mitcham. In other cases, there is the right to turn out sheep and beasts on the common ; in some instances there is the right to have a balk, that is to say, a strip of land outside the boundary of the particular field, which does not belong to the Lord of the Manor, or to the owner of the field, " but which is used by the owner of the field for turning his plough, and which cannot be taken into the adjacent land."

Sometimes a strip of land, bounding an ancient park or forest, is known as a freeboard, and its existence has to be recognised. It is the extent of a deer's leap, and its purpose is to enable the Lord of the Manor to " take the deer he happened to shoot as they leapt over his fence on to his neighbour's land." There are woods which are still known as the Deerleap Woods, and these were originally narrow strips of land, adjacent to places where deer were retained.

There are many instances of the owner of the land having a right to take turf from adjacent lands ; there are privileges of sending out cows on to an adjacent common, and one of the most notable of the privileges is that by which strips of land may be retained at the sides of the roads ; although treated as parts of the manor, they may not be sold or taken into the adjacent fields. These strips of land add enormously to the pleasant effect of the road, bordering it very often with stretches of turf, and with land on which there are footpaths, but in recent days they have frequently been the subjects of lawsuits.

I well remember one such case in Surrey. In this a very strenuous effort was made, by a new Lord of the Manor, to take into the adjacent fields what he regarded as absolutely waste land, from which he was deriving no income. The contest between him and his neighbours was a long and severe one, but he was defeated in the end, and the grassy strips which lay between his hedges and the main road, and which added enormously to the amenities of that road, had to be left as they were, greatly, I know, to his anger.

Manors also possess Admiralty rights if they adjoin the sea-coast, rights as to wreckage-harbours, piers and foreshores—all curious survivals.

In connection with Admiralty rights, it might be mentioned that there is still carried before the President of the Admiralty Court, who has the supreme jurisdiction, a silver oar, which has engraved round the rim of it the name of the Marshal of the Admiralty who was in control in the time of Elizabeth, and this oar, with the Tudor name upon it, still hangs in front of the President's desk when he adjudicates in court.

The village stocks come under the jurisdiction of the manorial courts, and there are many of these stocks still existing in England. The last that remained in London were in Portugal Street. They stood almost opposite to the building now occupied by the premises of Messrs. George Bell & Sons, the publishers, and were removed in 1826, when the street was widened. The last use of the stocks, so far as one has been able to trace, belongs to a period of between 1870 and 1880, when the stocks were used, it is said, at Newbury, Newbold-on-Avon and Weymouth, and there are stocks still to be seen in villages close by London, as for example at Abinger and Shalford in Surrey, at Horsham in Sussex, at Roydon, Kelvedon, Havering-atte-Bower, near Tring, near to Barnet, near to Buntingford, at Lynton in Devon, Oakham, and in various other places.

The pillory, which was also under the control of the manorial court, is an instrument of punishment far less easy to find. I have seen one at Saffron Walden, which for a while was fastened close to the ground, under the misapprehension that it formed part of some stocks, and I believe that I was the first to point out that it was a far more important thing as part of a pillory, and it is now exhibited in its proper position.

The pillory was used in London down to 1830, in which year a pillory stood outside the Old Bailey, and the punishment itself was only abolished in 1837. There are, however, some pillories still existing, and in one or two villages in England the quintain also still remains, a form of amusement very popular in the early days of fairs, and which took its origin from the tournaments, and corresponded to some extent with the tilt. We still retain the name of the Tiltyard in London, the place where the knights used to exercise their prowess by running at the tilt.

CHAPTER IX

MANORIAL CUSTOMS, FAIRS AND COURTS OF PIEPOWDER

ONE of the most interesting manorial customs still retained is that which takes place in Warwickshire at Knightlow Cross on Knightlow Hill, situate about midway between Coventry and Dunchurch, on what was once a famous coach road from London to Holyhead.

It is known as the Collection of Wroth Silver, and appertains to the Duke of Buccleuch and Queensberry, who is the Lord of the Manor. The formal notice of the ceremony is given in the local papers when the persons from whom the payment is to be made are summoned to appear at Knightlow Cross, Ryton-on-Dunsmore, on Martinmas Eve, before sunrise, that is to say, at about seven o'clock in the morning. The steward takes his stand facing the east, close to a remarkable square hollow stone, all that now remains of an ancient wayside cross, which originally stood there. The stone is about thirty inches square, and has the hole in the centre for the shaft. The steward reads the charter, and cites a certain number of parishes to appear before him, by their representatives, to pay the money that is due.

There are eight parishes summoned to the payment of a penny each, six for three-halfpence each, seven for twopence-halfpenny each, five for fourpence each, one for a shilling, one for two shillings and twopence, and one for two shillings and threepence-halfpenny, and the person paying used in old days to go thrice round the cross, say " Wroth Silver " and place the money in the hole of the cross. Now he throws it into the stone, repeating the words " Wroth Silver," and as each separate amount called for is thrown in, the money is removed by the Bailiff of the Court Leet and the Court Baron, who always attends the ceremony.

For non-payment of these fees, there is a fine of twenty shillings for every penny not forthcoming, or else the forfeiture of a white bull with red nose and ears of the same colour, and this particular forfeiture was once demanded during the last century, a wild white bull having been required by the agent of the late Lord John Scott, who then held the manor, but it was found impossible, although the bull was presented, to obtain one that answered exactly to the description in the charter.

Probably the fine or forfeiture gives us the key to the meaning of this exceedingly ancient ceremony. It is said to have existed for over a thousand years, and it was probably first inaugurated when, owing to the vast stretches of forest, moor and fen, public highways, with the exception of Roman roads, were unknown, and there was grievous inconvenience on the part of persons who desired to move cattle from one part of the country to the other.

The word " wroth " has been derived by some archæologists from the Anglo-Saxon " worth," a roadway, or by others from " weorth," a word which in certain cases means a field, but is also used to represent a price or a value, and by others again it is derived from " rother heyder," cattle money, and hence it is regarded as a sort of payment or toll for passing over certain roads. Whatever may be the origin of this curious word, it is quite clear that the payment, which in ancient days represented a considerable sum, was made in connection with privileges regarded as very valuable, and this is proved by so heavy a fine being enforced in cases of non-payment.

There was an effort made in 1685 to do away with the custom, but it was decided by the Court that the then Lord of the Manor had a full right to the privileges which had been referred to in a deed of Inspeximus granted by Charles the First to his ancestor, Sir Francis Leigh. Probably the origin of it goes well back into Saxon times, and may even belong to a period anterior to that, and it evidently concerns ancient rights of bringing cattle to and from various villages by roads which extended through this particular manor. It is practically for rights of way for cattle.

There used to be similar collections in the New Forest, where it was referred to as cattle money, but these Hampshire manors belonged to the Crown, and the privileges have been discontinued, probably because the expense of keeping them up was greater than the result obtained, while in the Hundreds of Knightlow, the various lords of the manor have been careful to keep in force this curious and ancient custom, and still to maintain it with all its original ceremonial.

After the money has been paid, the various representatives of the different parishes sit down to a substantial breakfast, provided by the Lord of the Manor, and on the removal of the cloth, the guests are furnished with hot rum and milk, together with pipes and tobacco, and then certain persons are admitted into the manor, and various toasts proposed and accepted. The breakfast takes place at an inn in the village of Stretton on Dunsmore, which bears the appropriate sign of the Dun Cow.

The white bull, the fine for non-payment, should belong of course to the wild cattle of early days, which were white. There are still at Chillingham Park, at Cadzow Castle and at Vaynol Park herds of the ancient white cattle of Britain, those at Chillingham belonging to the Earl of Tankerville, at Cadzow to the Duke of Hamilton, and at Vaynol to Sir Charles Assheton-Smith. There was at one time a similar herd at Chartley Castle, but the animals that remained of that herd were sold to the Duke of Bedford and transferred to Woburn Abbey.*

There is probably no town in England more tenacious of its ancient customs and of the privileges connected therewith, than is Hungerford. It is a striking example of self-government on ancient lines, because it has always been governed by a Constable who has associated with him a Bailiff, a Portreeve, and a body of commoners called feoffees. The Constable is the chief magistrate, Lord of the Manor, and coroner, and no one can occupy that position until he has previously filled the office of Bailiff and Portreeve. In 1573, the inhabitants stated, in a complaint that they made to the Earl of Pembroke, that for over three hundred years they had held these privileges by charter under the Great Seal. The list of Constables is practically complete from 1550, but the earlier books are missing. The Bailiff

* I am indebted for the foregoing information to Mr. R. T. Simpson, and to material obtained from his book on the Collection of Wroth Silver, now out of print, published in Rugby in 1910.

is the person who collects the tolls and summons the jurors. On his retirement he becomes Portreeve and collects the quit rents, and he is then in succession for Constable.

The Constable and other officers have always been elected on Hock Tuesday, the Monday and Tuesday following the second Sunday after Easter. The word " Hock " is said to be derived from a word " hocken," signifying to seize, and on that day there are certain privileges attached to the inhabitants by which they can bind those of the opposite sex, and hold them until they purchase their release by a small sum of money, and this local privilege is supposed to commemorate the slaughter of the Danes by Ethelred in 1002. The events, however, that the Hocktide ceremonials celebrate are the two notable privileges that belong to the inhabitants of Hungerford, the rights of the use of their common, and the rights of free fishing in the river Kennet. These fishing rights were granted by John of Gaunt, Earl of Richmond, fourth son of Edward III, who, by right of his wife, possessed the manor of Hungerford, and an ancient bugle horn is still preserved in the place, said to have been given when the grant was made. It is of brass, has a black-letter inscription upon it, the word " Hungerford " and the badge of the House of Lancaster, the star issuing from the crescent, which now forms the arms of Hungerford. The inscription is as follows :—

JOHN A GAVN DID GIVE AND GRANT THE RIATT OF
FISHING TO HUNGERFORD TOVNE FROM ELDRED
STVB TO IRISH STILL EXCEPTING SOM SEVERAL MILL POUND
JEHOSOPHAT LVCAS WAS CUNSTABL

The seventeenth-century horn, preserved at the Town Hall, bears the date of 1634, and this is blown annually to summon the tenants at the Manorial Court ; it has been used ever since that date, and is still in use.

The free fishing rights were nearly lost in 1569, but the inhabitants made a strenuous protest, and an order was issued by Queen Elizabeth in 1574 that they should have and enjoy their ancient rights. The common privileges came to them, as far as can be ascertained, in 1613, under a charter of James I.

The Hocktide festivities are exceedingly interesting, two tithing men parading the town on Hock Tuesday, each carrying a staff ornamented with flowers, surmounted by an orange, and decked with blue ribbon. These are called "tuttimen," from a West Country word "tutty"—a flower or a nosegay, and they are entitled to demand a penny a head for every person in the town, for services rendered during the past year, and if the fee is refused, all the females in the house must submit to be kissed by them. On the following Friday, the Court Baron is held, at which the officers are sworn in, and every resident in the borough above fourteen years of age must attend on that occasion or be fined a penny; and the holders of two other ancient offices, the Constable and the Hayward of the Tithing of Sandon-Fee, are also elected, and sworn in. A banquet is served in the evening, in honour of the new Constable and Bailiff, and a toast is drunk in solemn silence to the immortal memory of John of Gaunt. A breakfast on the following morning terminates the Hocktide revelry. There are processions of children during the day, and one child is elected to represent the Queen of the festivities, and is decorated with an ornament resembling the badge of the town, while the whole place gives itself up, on such occasions, to great excitement. The supper which takes place on the Friday in Easter week is known as the Macaroni Supper, and it is held at the John of Gaunt, or Lancaster Arms, which is town property. The fare consists of macaroni, Welsh rarebit, watercress salad, and punch, and the punch is made from an old Hungerford recipe. Hock Tuesday is the following Tuesday, and is known as Hockney Day, or more generally as Tutti Day.

The privileges which the town holds are very important, and they have been commemorated for many centuries in this interesting fashion ; as the Hungerford children sing :

> " The ancient market-place has heard
>   For half a thousand years,
> The summons of the mighty horn,
>   Time-honoured Lancaster's.
> The Tuttimen have trimmed the poles
>   With blossoms fresh and gay,
> And kissed the merry, bashful maids,
>   On Hock Day holiday."

The value of the fishing in the Kennet is well known to

all fishermen, and in another of the Hungerford songs the
children sing :

> " And be it known throughout the land
> That Kennet trout are best,
> While sport and labour intertwined
> Are good, must be confessed."

Hungerford men still also elect Water Bailiffs to see to
the right of fishing, Keepers of the Keys having custody of
the Seal, Ale Tasters and Searchers and Sealers of Leather.*
The Sandon-Fee Court Baron, alluded to above, still functions and has its jury, Steward and two Tything-men,
as it has always had. It also claims head pence which
are collected by Overseers and go to the payment of the
Hayward.

This Court meets annually alternately at the Angel and
the Salisbury Arms in Hungerford, and the fees paid by
tenants who turn out cattle on the marsh are used to provide
the luncheon for the officials and jury.

The Forest of Savernake is held by Lord Ailesbury upon
tenure of blowing a horn to welcome the King, should
he ever visit the estate. The horn is a magnificent ivory
one adorned with silver bands, and belongs to the period
of Henry II, given, it is stated, when the first grant of the
Forest was made. George III is said to have playfully
reminded the then Lord Ailesbury, on the occasion of a
visit, that, not having been welcomed by a blast of this
horn, he had forfeited his right to the Forest. Lord Ailesbury thereupon sent for the horn, and proceeded to wind
it, producing a very feeble blast, which the King called
gruesome, but with which he was pleased to consider the
tenure had been duly paid.

Hornblowing is also an important ceremony at Ripon.
In ancient times the chief official of the City from 1400 was
styled the Wakeman. He was the Guardian of the People,
and amongst his duties had to sound a horn every night at
nine at the four corners of the cross in the market-place.

The arms of Ripon represent a horn, and when in 1604
the last Wakeman was appointed first Mayor of Ripon, the
hornblowing duties were placed in the hands of a new

* See *The History of Hungerford*, by Money, 1894, kindly placed
at my disposal with various special illustrations and important
information by Mr. Caleb Camburn, M.B.E., of that town.

official, known as the Mayor's Hornblower. Such an official
still has a place in the city life and a horn of 1690 is even
yet in occasional use. The old custom of blowing at nine
o'clock at the four quarters of the compass is continued,
and the horn is also blown at the door of the Mayor's
house.

A remarkable Baldric or Belt belongs to Ripon, on which
are a fine and unique series of silver badges, commemorating,
from the sixteenth century, the early Wakemen, and bearing their arms and merchant marks. This Belt was repaired in the time of Charles II, and attached to it is the
ancient horn of the City, a fine new one presented in 1864
being now used for the horn-blowing ceremony. There
are five notable days observed in Ripon still called Horn
Days, Candlemas, Easter Monday, Wednesday in Rogation
Week, the Sunday after Lammas (the feast of St. Wilfrid),
and St. Stephen. On all these the Horn and Belt are
worn by the Wakeman. The City motto is "Except
Ye Lord keep Ye Cittie Ye Wakeman waketh in vain."
The original Wakeman was said to have been named
Horner, and to have borne three Horns on his shield, and
from him the City took its arms.

A very interesting and ancient court is that which still
meets in the New Forest, its Court-house being known as
the King's House, and situate at Lyndhurst. It is called
the Court of Swainmote, but is generally known to the
people about the district as the Verderers Court, because
it is presided over by seven Verderers, six of whom are
elected by the commoners, and one is nominated by the
Government.

These judges are not necessarily justices of the peace,
but are invested while sitting in court with powers almost
exactly the same as those possessed by justices, and they
have complete powers of jurisdiction over offences that
belong to the forest.

There are rights and privileges concerning pasturage, turbery (that is to say, the digging of turf and peat), estrovers
(that is the picking up of wood that has dropped), and also
concerning the consumption of beech mast by the pigs kept
by different commoners, while offences against the common
of pasture, the common of mast, or against turbery, and
other similar crimes, are dealt with in this court, and have

always been within its jurisdiction. It dates back to a time earlier than that of William Rufus.

The persons who make the charges against the culprits are termed " agisters," and there are no police in the Court, as the police have no authority with regard to forest offences.

One of the most curious regulations which this Court has to deal with is that concerning turfs, because the cottagers are privileged to have so many turves, according to the size of their fire-place, and if the old open fire-places for the consumption of turves are done away with or altered, then, *ipso facto*, the rights of turbery cease. The large fire-places are entitled to so many cords, that is to say, small cart-loads of turves, and, owing to this curious regulation concerning the size of the fire-place, one can often see in many houses in the New Forest modern improvements that have been made in the living rooms, while the fire-places have not been reduced in size, and are still left square and in their original condition, in order to protect the very highly valued privilege of turbery.

It may be of interest when mentioning fire-places to remark that in Gilsland, near the Northumberland border, are lonely farmhouses, where, it is said, the kitchen fires, fed solely with turf or peat, have not been allowed to go out for at least two hundred years.

One house, it is stated, has been occupied and possessed by a succession of members of the same family for six hundred years !

This Court also deals with some of the game offences, and here it is interesting to remember that the domestic rabbit is practically an exotic in England. There were no rabbits in the England of Anglo-Saxon times, although the creature was well known in Spain from very early days. It was introduced into England by the Normans, and both the word " rabbit " and the word " coney " are Norman-French in their origin. Our British ancestors could have known nothing of the rabbit, now one of our most common animals.

Why the Normans introduced it we cannot of course tell, probably as an article of food, but it quickly settled down in this country, and has become so accustomed to the place, that we forget it was not of English origin. It has always been found in Spain.

In some manors there have been very strange customs kept up. For instance, at Caistor, in Lincolnshire, there was retained until the middle of the nineteenth century a most singular service. The owner of Brigg held certain lands subject to the performance, on Palm Sunday of every year, of the ceremony of cracking a whip in the church, and while the clergyman was reading the first lesson, the tenant cracked the whip three distinct times in the church porch, and then folded it up. As soon as the second lesson was commenced, he went up to the clergyman, presented the whip to him, held it over his head, and waved it three times, holding it in that position during the reading of the lesson.

The whip had a purse tied at the end of it, which was supposed to contain thirty pieces of silver; it had also four pieces of elm attached to it, representing the Gospels. The three cracks were typical of St. Peter's denial of his Lord, and the waving of the whip over the clergyman's head was supposed to be an act of homage to the Blessed Trinity. The whip was known as the gad-whip, the word being derived from the same phrase as the word goad, meaning a prick; a gad-fly was a pricking or stinging fly, a gad-whip was a whip for goading on, or gadding, or stinging cattle.

The origin of the ceremonial went back to exceedingly remote times, and is said to have been connected with a penance imposed upon some tenant for an act of murder. There was, however, a strong opinion against this custom being carried out during Divine Service, and Sir Culling Eardley-Smith, who was the last Lord of the Manor to insist upon the performance of the service, petitioned the House of Lords that it might be done away with. The House appears to have had no power to interfere with this manorial custom, and then the Bishop of Lincoln was appealed to, and he too stated that the power did not rest with him. The ceremony therefore continued down to 1846, when it was allowed quietly to drop out of existence, and it has not since been revived.

It is, however, still in the power of one of the Lords of the adjacent Manors to demand that this ceremony should be performed, or, in the event of its being neglected, the Lord of the Manor of Broughton must pay a penalty to the Lord of the Manor of Hundon. Probably even now the penalty could be enforced, and if the necessary books concerning the old right were brought into court it would be seen that they confirm the absolute right of the lord to demand the penalty.

A falchion, a curious weapon, has still to be presented by the Lord of the Manor of Sockburn to the new Bishop of Durham, when he enters upon his diocese, and a similar one by the Lord of the Manor of Pollard's Land, when he takes up his residence at Auckland Castle. It is stated that the Sockburn presentation has not been made since April, 1826, when Dr. Van Mildert, the last Prince Bishop, demanded it. Other Bishops have not demanded the presentations, but at any moment the demand could be made.

In respect to Durham Cathedral, there is also still held a claim for sanctuary, and to the person who claims sanctuary a gown of black cloth is given, bearing upon it the cross of St. Cuthbert. Whether this claim could now be supported is not very clear.

It is said also that curfew bell does not ring in Durham on Saturday, because one Saturday a ringer of very evil character went into the tower, and before he could ring the bell, was carried off to Hell by the Devil, and that, in memory of this shocking occurrence, curfew has been silent ever since on Saturday.

In one of the Yorkshire manorial Courts the jury are still called upon to deal with rights and privileges which bear strange old-fashioned names. There are carrs, ings, garths, clooases, hags, boddums, yakkers, plaans, pinders, pinfolds, turfing, bracken, ling, hoofing-places and plantings. The pinders are places where things may be impounded, the ling is in use for brooms, or, as the Yorkshireman generally terms them, besoms.

Fairs are a fruitful source of ancient habit and custom, although they have ceased to be as important as they once were. Their origin can be traced back to Roman and Anglo-Saxon time, and for many generations in England they were the mainstay of the distributing trade and often in country districts the only means by which household requisites could be obtained. The traders attending them were secure from competition, special regulations being made covering every detail of the fair life, and with the great liability to disturbance and quarrelling, the establishment in these fairs of what are called Courts of Piepowder came to pass.

These courts derive, it is said, their curious name from the dusty feet of the suitors. An alien merchant was called in Normandy " Pied Poudreux," and we have words in English from very much the same derivation, " pedler," the man who vends his goods where he can, travelling from place to place, a " dusty-foot " as some old English phrases still term him, and by which pedlars are even now spoken of in Scottish law. Justice was done in these courts immediately, according to the law of the land and the custom of the town, to either rich or poor, and to all who were on foot in the fair, and it was done as quickly as the dust could fall from the feet. This very ancient court existed in London down to 1850, but in that year, St. Bartholomew's fair, to which it was attached and which had existed for hundreds of years, disappeared.

There were still Courts of Piepowder, however, at Sturbridge Fair, at Cambridge, at Modbury, and at the Bridge Fair at Peterborough. Certainly such courts existed down to the last few years, and to the best of my knowledge the Peterborough one still exists, even if others have disappeared. The documents and books relative to such courts are carefully preserved at Yarmouth, Boston, Hull and Winchester. The Winchester court was a notable one, it took its origin in the time of Edward IV, or rather, it was specially authorised by that King, and an exceptional privilege and grant was made in respect to it by Bishop William of Wayneflete, and even such modern Bishops as Trelawney, Hoadley and North personally opened the fair and the court, North in particular keeping up all the old customs connected with it, and claiming the various fines and tolls that belonged to it.

The court belonged to the Lord of the fair or his steward, it had absolute authority over all the commercial complaints, and " an offender might be taken," says Henry Morley, " a jury of similar traders empannelled on the spot, the offence heard on the spot, and the man would be commencing his punishment, all within an hour."

There are, I am assured, two Courts of Piepowder actually

still in existence. One is in Bristol, and it is held in connection with a still older court called a Tolzey Court, which dates by tradition from Saxon times, and sits on every Monday in the year. Its chief official is called the Protonotary. Many of the powers of this court date back to the time of King John, when Bristol Castle was a Royal residence, and it still has powers over dues to be collected from foreigners, and over questions of disputes and government, where the cause of action arises within the City of Bristol. Its steward is regarded as a Royal officer. The Piepowder Court is a branch of the Tolzey, and is held every year in the open street called the Old Market, before one of the Tolzey stewards. It sits for fourteen clear days from September 29, during which time the Tolzey Court of the Guildhall is suspended, and when it is dissolved, the proceedings are adjourned into the Tolzey.

The other court is, I am told, held at Hemel Hempstead, once a year, and its work is in connection with the management of the tolls, the buildings and the stallages.

One Court of Piepowder is of immortal memory, that described in glowing language by John Bunyan in *The Pilgrim's Progress*, where he speaks of Vanity Fair.

The Lord of the fair was the freeholder of the ground on which the fair was held. At his Court of Piepowder, Christian and Faithful had offended against the customs of the fair, and the regulations of the trading guild ; they were taken to the court, the jury was empannelled, evidence given by the different witnesses, sentence was pronounced, execution carried out, and poor Faithful was burned at the stake, in the very precincts of the fair. The description by the Bedfordshire tinker of this court of summary jurisdiction is a wonderful one, exact in every minor detail, and gives a vivid picture of his own time.

The Court of Piepowder in Bristol, which retains the old name of the Tolzey Court, takes it from " tol," the old form of spelling the word toll, and the tolls for that court, and for those at Berwick, at Guildford and Dungannon and Ely, until the present day, were taken in kind, a pint of corn from each sack, for example, at Berwick, an egg in every thirty at another place, the tongue of an ox at another.

At Ely, the ancient proclamation is made in ancient form and in the name of the Bishop of the diocese, commanding that " all vagabonds, idle and misbehaving persons, all cheaters, cozeners, rogues, steady beggars and shifters do depart out of this fair immediately after this proclamation of the Bishop, upon pain of imprisonment and further correction by the Court in the fair (that is to say, the Court of Piepowder), that his Majesty's good subjects may be the more quiet, and that the King's peace may be the better upheld."

In Newcastle, it is the Mayor and Sheriff who proclaim the opening of the fair, and the existence of the Court of Piepowder. In Modbury, South Devon, it is the Portreeve, at Guildford it was the Mayor, and the Guildford Court goes back to November 23, 1285. The charter for the Surrey capital commands that the Mayor and good men of that town and their successors shall " for ever hold a Piepowder Court from hour to hour, during the fair, and all things that belongeth to the same Court shall be carried on within the town aforesaid for ever."

The name of one of the old fairs near London is commemorated in the title given to a fashionable West-End district, including Curzon Street and Hertford Street, still known as Mayfair, from the ancient fair that used to be held on that ground in the early days of May.

Abroad, these fairs still continue with something of the same ceremonial as is the case in London. That at Beaucaire claims to be at least seven hundred years old, and is still an important market for remarkable and extraordinary fabrics. Germany claims that Leipsic is older still, it was originally a fair for all kinds of merchandise, notably for furs and books ; it is now known almost exclusively for the sale of books. The greatest and oldest of all fairs is probably the one at Nijni-Novgorod, which continued until recent years its customary existence, spread over an enormous space of ground, and visited by many thousands of buyers. It was the great opportunity for the purchase of Eastern things, brought there in vast quantities, and thence distributed throughout Europe. Whether or not it exists at the present time cannot be stated.

A very ancient fair is that which takes place at Corby, and this is the only one, I believe, that retains in actual use the old punishment of putting persons into the stocks. Every twenty years there takes place at Corby, near to

Kettering, what is known as the Charter Fair, according to a privilege granted to the place by Queen Elizabeth. The entrances to the village are then barricaded by gates, a toll is demanded from every person who seeks admission, and those who refuse to pay it can be taken to the stocks, and many do still undergo punishment on refusing to pay the substantial toll which can be demanded for entrance to the village at that particular time. Men are carried to the stocks on a pole, borne by two strong men, and women who refuse to pay it are carried in chairs, and the charter, which is still solemnly proclaimed at each entrance to the village, gives the power of imprisonment for a certain brief time if the toll is not paid.

Helston, in Cornwall, has possessed a fair from time immemorial, and in connection with it there survives what is known as the Furry Dance. This Furry Dance has been described as the most interesting observance of antiquity remaining in Cornwall, and it is stated by one writer, Mr. Polwhele, that there is hardly any custom existing in England that is of greater antiquity than it, with the exception, of course, of the coronation of the Kings, and of the payment of quit rent by the Corporation of the City of London, to which reference has been already made.

The strange old word " Furry " is probably derived actually from " feria," a fair or jubilee, but it has been suggested by several writers on Cornish customs that this dance belongs to a far more remote period than the days of the fairs and probably had its origin in a Roman festival. In 242 B.C. a celebrated courtesan named Flora bequeathed her entire fortune to the people of Rome, that they might annually, in May, celebrate her memory by singing, dancing, and drinking, and the revels became known as the Floralia. After some considerable period, the authorities of Rome are said to have exalted Flora as goddess of flowers, fruit and herbs. It is quite possible that the Furry Dance or Fery Dance of Helston may represent the Floralia of Roman days, and have been introduced into this country by the Romans. Whatever may have been its origin, the custom which is now carried on at Helston only, but which in earlier times was celebrated at Penryn on May 3, and at the Lizard on May 1, goes back to such a remote period that there is no remaining evidence of its origin. It is declared to have been always in existence, and by the people of Helston it is said to have been instituted in memory of a fight which took place between St. Michael, the patron saint of the place, and Satan, when the Devil is stated to have dropped in the streets a huge block of granite which he had brought from hell. This remained in the town until 1783, when it was broken up for building materials.

In the Domesday Survey the borough is called "Helleston," and the inhabitants insist that the legend just mentioned gave rise to the origin of the name of the place. It is one of the oldest of the Cornish boroughs, and from the time of Edward I had the privilege of sending two members to the Houses of Parliament.

The dance takes place in the streets, and commences very early in the morning, continuing all day, the dancers going in and out the various houses, and drawing into their midst the persons who are visiting the town at that time. Sir William Treloar, who was Lord Mayor of London in 1906-7, was given the freedom of Helston, by reason of the fact that his ancestors had come from that place, and on May 8 he attended there in full state, and took part in this Furry Dance. He declared that there was a certain amount of dignity about the proceedings, but that the fun began about four o'clock in the morning, when the trumpets roused everyone, and he described how he himself danced through Helston Highway, in and out of the various houses, until he was thoroughly tired out.

Crowds of people go down to Helston to witness this interesting survival. A curious old song is repeated by the dancers while they are engaged in the ceremony, with reference to Robin Hood and Little John, and to the coming of the Spaniards, one of the stanzas running thus :—

" Whereas those Spaniards that make so great a boast-O
　They shall eat the grey goose feathers and we shall eat the roast-O,
　　In every land-O
　　The land that e'er we go,
　With halantow, Jolly rumble-O,"

and so on.

There is a curious custom which still attaches to the Manor of Oakham, by which a horse-shoe is claimed from every Peer who for the first time passes through the town. There is a long and important series of these horse-shoes, varying in size, exhibited in the Guildhall, which is actually the Norman hall of Oakham Castle. The Castle was founded by Henry II, and the manor in his time came into the hands of Walchelin de Ferrers, and subsequently passed, through many owners, to the Duchy of Buckingham, from whence it descended to the Earls of Winchelsea and then to the Finch family.

The custom or right at Oakham is to stop the horses or carriage, until a sum of money is given, and if the person so stopped does not comply, a shoe is taken off his horse.

It is probable that the levying of this strange tax was one of the means the De Ferrers employed for testifying to their power as Lords of the Manor, and it is possible that the fact of their bearing six horse-shoes in their own coat of arms gives us information concerning the reason for the levy. It is questionable whether it could now be enforced, but, so far as is known, there is only one case in which a Peer refused either to pay or to give a horse-shoe, and the case was taken to law. It concerned the Earl of Lincoln, and the episode is referred to in Speed.

The owners of about a hundred and sixty of the horse-shoes exhibited on the various walls of Oakham Castle are known and the names are inscribed upon them. The horse-shoe said to have been given by Queen Elizabeth has, however, a very doubtful connection with that sovereign.

The building is a beautiful example of Norman architecture and is still used as the Assize Court and Magistrates' Court. The horse-shoes with their coronets of varying size form a remarkable and not unpleasing form of decoration.

Perhaps the premier place with regard to ancient families would be claimed by the Shirleys of Ettington in Warwickshire. There is evidence to prove that they are the direct descendants of a thane who held Etendone in the time of Edward the Confessor, and therefore the estate has belonged to the same family for more than nine hundred years. It is probably the only one in the kingdom that can show so uninterrupted a succession. There are, however, two estates in Scotland the owners of which can make similar claims.

CHAPTER X

THE COURTS OF LAW

A LLUSION has already been made in these pages
to various legal customs, notably to those concerned with manorial law, but there are other
curious legal survivals worthy of consideration.

Originally, all civil and criminal jurisdiction belonged to
the King's Privy Council, and one degree of it still adheres
to that body. If the Sovereign establishes courts of justice
beyond the realm by prerogative, the appeal lies to the
Sovereign as to the fountain of justice and hence to the
Privy Council and *not* to the courts of justice. This appeal
has grown by analogy from the position of the Channel
Islands, because they were not bound by Acts of Parliament,
and appeals did not lie to the Parliament from their courts,
but to the successor of the Dukes of Normandy and to his
council. So it comes about that causes of final appeal
from places beyond the sea do not lie with the House of
Lords, as they would were they English causes, but with
the Privy Council.

In this connection it should be noticed that every Privy
Councillor is, *ipso facto*, in the Commission of the Peace for
every county in England, and is still entitled to sit upon any
Bench at which he may desire to be present. Privy Councillors are still constitutionally empowered to inquire into all
offences against the King, and to commit the offenders to
safe custody, although, as a matter of fact, they send such
offenders to the ordinary magistrates in the usual way.

It is interesting evidence of how tenacious we, in England
are, of powers given at a remote period, and of how little
change there has been with regard to the main lines upon
which the Courts of Common Law are based, that at the
present day a judge who goes on circuit sits under three
distinct commissions. He has the Commission of General
Gaol Delivery, by which he clears the prison of all persons

awaiting trial. He has the Commission of Oyer and Ter-
miner, the old Norman-French phrase, by virtue of which
he tries the criminal cases for which the grand jury have
found a true bill, but he has, besides that, what is known
as the Commission of Assize, and this particular power he
obtains from the second Statute of Westminster, passed in
1275, an exceedingly important charter of liberty, drawn
up, not in Latin but in Norman-French, and which, in its
original language, is still quoted in this commission. It is
almost equivalent to a code of law, dealing with criminal
offences, has never been superseded, and all our circuit
judges still sit under the powers given them in the thirteenth
century, while the document giving them these powers
quotes the Norman-French phraseology in use at the time
when the Statute was passed.

Almost every court of justice, whether it be a superior
court, a Court of Quarter Sessions, or a Court of Summary
Jurisdiction, is still opened in England with a proclamation,
which starts with the two Norman-French words " Oyez,
Oyez," and therefore the memory of the Conquest and of
the use of the Norman-French introduced at that time,
has been retained in England for well nigh a thousand years,
and is used all over the country, and almost day by day.
This is, perhaps, the most complete of all the ancient
survivals that remain in the country.

Certain courts of law are still known as the Courts of
King's Bench, although the judges are given a more convenient seat than the wooden bench upon which they were
wont to sit, but the word " Bench " is still applied to
magistrates sitting in session, because originally they all sat
on one long, narrow bench. In front of it, some little dis-
tance down the court, was a wooden barrier, called a bar,
which separated the superior from the lower pleaders ; the
more important barristers sat within the bar, and were
termed Inner Barristers, and those who were less important
were without the barrier, and were termed Outer Barristers,
a phrase which still continues in the local word " utter,"
and certain proceedings in the Law Courts are still declared
to be " in banco," the phrase having reference in the same way
to the bench on which the judges sat. When the courts sat
" in banco " the judges occupied their respective benches.

Another curious habit connected with the Courts of Law

is that concerning the " Box Days," which are two days in spring and autumn and one day at Christmas, during vacations, in which petitions may be filed. The phrase goes back some three hundred years, and is still in regular use. It arose from the fact that each judge at one time had a private box, with a slit in it, in which informations might be placed on the Box Days, and the judge would then examine the papers quietly, when he had the opportunity of opening the box.

The very word Court takes us back to a remote period, for a court was originally a sheepfold, and the people who possessed the district called Latium before it actually became Rome used to establish enclosures with hurdles in which to place their sheep, which they called cors, and a collection of these cors was called a cohors, and then a further group became the centre of a hamlet or a town, and later on, of a fortified place, gradually of a Royal residence, and eventually, of the legal establishment of which the King was the head, so the Court. We call Lincoln's Inn, Gray's Inn, and other similar societies of lawyers, Inns of Court, because originally they were held in the court of the King's Palace, which was the place for dispensing justice and punishing crimes committed against the power of the Sovereign, and the Inns have still retained that title to the present day. We have a very different use of the word Court remaining when we speak of Court plaster. This takes us back to the time of Charles I, when little patches of plaster were applied by the Court ladies to their faces.

There are many very interesting survivals in connection with the Law Courts. Evidence of the clerical origin of the lawyers still survives in the circular orifice in the centre of the judge's wig, all that remains of the monastic and clerical tonsure. The cap which the judge assumes when he passes sentence of death is just a part of his ordinary full-dress costume, and is placed on his head in order that when he is executing the most serious part of his duties, the condemnation to death; he may be in full robes. The judges wear their black caps also on the occasion when they receive the Lord Mayor.

The sign of covering the head when condemnation is being carried out is also a very ancient sign of mourning, and takes us back to remote antiquity, because Demosthenes speaks of covering his head when he was insulted by the populace, and in Holy Writ we frequently hear of the head being covered on such occasions. David, we read, had his head covered, Haman, covered his head, and Jews of the present day cover their heads when in the synagogue, or when taking the oath in a court of justice and as a sign of reverence.

Evidence of the ecclesiastical origin of the courts consists in the fact that on the great Saints' days the full dress or ceremonial robes of the courts are still worn. The reason for the divergence in the costumes in the different courts is, that when a judge wears red, he sits as representing the sovereign power, but when he wears black, in the *nisi prius* courts, he is only an official settling disputes. The act of kissing the Book by witnesses derives from the fact that from the mouth come the statements that the witness will be making, evidence that we still keep up when we use the word adore, or oral, orison, osculate, peroration, orator or oracle— all of which come from the root word which became " os," the mouth. " Inexorable " we obtain from the same source.

One or two phrases heard quite recently in a court may be alluded to. The witness was told he was " begging the question," assuming as a fact the very thing he intended to prove, and in that phrase we have one that goes back to the days of Aristotle. The English sentence is just a translation of the Latin phrase *petitio principii*. On another occasion, speaking of a punishment that the man had undergone, the counsel spoke of it as " Lydford law," or as " Coupar law," the two phrases meaning exactly the same. In Lydford Castle offenders were confined in a horrible dungeon before they were brought up for trial, and the same sort of procedure took place at Coupar Angus, and hence to punish first and try afterwards is known either as Coupar law or Lydford law.

We still speak of prisoners standing in a " dock," the word coming from an old Flemish word, " docke," which means a cage, and in ancient days the dock was an actual cage, made of iron and protected by horrible spikes, which formed a sort of *chevaux de frise* about it, and gave it a very formidable appearance. It is now a much simpler kind of gallery in which the person stands, but there is a movement on foot that it should be simplified even more, because, according to English principles, a man is innocent until he has been proved to be guilty, and in American courts the formal dock has been wholly abandoned and a chair is in use, while in this country many persons desire that a similar course should be adopted.

The constable, who is so prominent a person in a court of law, is strictly speaking a peace officer, the phrase being originally applied to the one who was the head of the stable, the count of the stable, and the word is derived by way of Norman-French from the same root as that from which we get many other expressions in English. The word "iter," a journey, comes from "ire," to go, and we still talk of justices "in eyre," referring to a circuit, and the actual word "circuit" itself in reference to the judges means a "going round." We speak also of "itinerant" judges, and derive also the words "ambition"—which was originally going round to solicit votes, or seeking for preferment—and exit, and initiation, and transit, all from the same original source.

The "barrister," of course, takes his name from that bar within which he is called, but it is interesting to remember there is still a fold at the back of his gown that represents the original pocket into which his fees were dropped, when a man plucked him behind by the gown and dropped in his fee, the counsel not being supposed to be able to see it, and even now he cannot sue for his fee; it is an honorarium made to him for his services, and is in consequence handed in before he undertakes the pleading. If he chooses to retain it, and not carry out the obligation which accepting it has involved, there is no power that can bring him to book for such an offence.

A phrase which is often heard in the Law Courts, when the question of a marriage settlement comes before the judges, is that of "pin-money," and that phrase goes back to very early days. It arose as one of the attempts to do away with the theory that the wife was a mere chattel and incapable of being the owner of anything. A husband therefore would "bind himself, by settlements, to give his bride, year by year, a sum of money which she would have a right to spend entirely independently of his control," and this, which was for her dress, and for the ornaments connected therewith, was called "pin-money." The word itself takes us back to the fourteenth century, when pins were first introduced into use. They were eagerly purchased by women, at the fairs and stalls, with money given them for that specific purpose by their husbands.

It is important to remember that this pin-money, if it is arranged by a marriage settlement, has to be spent, and in the manner indicated. It is a fund that must be spent during married life, as the legal phrase says, " by the intercession and advice, and at the instance of her husband." Pin-money cannot be given away to anybody else. No creditor has any power against pin-money, and cannot enforce any rights, and if any sum is saved out of pin-money, by its not being spent, it does not belong to the wife, but to her husband, and pin-money is the only money of which she is legally possessed, and with which she can do absolutely as she pleases, provided it is spent by herself, and on herself.

It is still considered that the husband has an interest in his wife's maintaining an appearance suitable to the position which he occupies. She has no right to make any saving out of the household allowance. If she does, that saving is not hers, she is merely a trustee for it to her husband, and if she spends it on other purposes, she is a fraudulent trustee, but pin-money, as it is still called, is hers absolutely.

The power of the coroner, a very ancient one and granted him in the time of Edward I, to inquire into all cases of suspicious death, has sometimes had a rather curious consequence. In 1901, there was an action against the London and North-Western Railway for damages for negligence in the carriage of a Peruvian mummy, broken in transit from South America. No steps, it was stated, could be taken in adjudication upon the action, until a coroner's inquest had been held upon the body. The verdict was quoted in *The Times* thus : " That the woman was found dead at the railway goods station on April 15th, and did die, some date unknown, in some foreign country, probably South America, from some cause unknown. No proofs of a violent death are found. The body has been dried and buried in some foreign manner . . . and the jurors are satisfied that the body does not show any recent crime in this country, and that the deceased was unknown, and about twenty-five years of age."

Inasmuch as the body was probably many thousands of

years old, the verdict is somewhat amusing, but until that
verdict was made, the ordinary law courts considered that
they were unable to move, and after it had been made,
they were able to decide the question of the damages to
which the owner of the mummy was entitled.

The oldest ecclesiastical court in the Kingdom is still
known as the Court of Arches, and takes its name from
the fact that it originally met in what is now called Bow
Church, the building which was originally known as St. Mary
de Arcubus, and which took its name from the stone arches
in its crypt. The church has, since the Great Fire, ceased
to be used as the meeting-place of an ecclesiastical court, but
it still enjoys the distinction of being the building used for
the confirmation of the election of Bishops, over which the
Vicar-General of the Province of Canterbury still presides.

An ancient and local maritime court that has survived
the Municipal Corporation Act of 1835 is the Admiralty
Court of the Cinque Ports. This goes back earlier than
1300, and is still in existence, and meets whenever it is
necessary for it to do so.

The other Court of the Cinque Ports, the Court of
Shepway, is acknowledged in the Royal charters which
date from the twelfth century, when the men of Hastings
were to have the same privileges " as the charter of Henry
our Father gives them," and to enjoy the franchise they
had in the time of Edward the Confessor. Hythe, was
given the privilege it had in the time of Edward the Confessor, William I, William II, and Henry, and Sandwich the
same. The Charter which gave the men of Rye and
Winchelsea their special privileges at the Court of Shepway
was signed by Richard at Messina on March 27th, 1190,
when he was on his way to the Holy Land for the Crusades.

The Court of Shepway was summoned in 1923, when
the Shepway Cross at Lympne was dedicated.

A strange old habit is retained in the London Quarter
Sessions. On its County days there always appears, at
the end of the Agenda, an order that additional rates, under
the Army Discipline and Regulation Act, should be made
for the use of carriages and animals, for removing the
regimental baggage and stores of His Majesty's forces. This
is only an ancient custom. No rates are actually made,
the clause is read out and passed, the rates stand, as they

have always stood, but the proceedings of Quarter Sessions would not be complete unless this particular clause appeared in a note of its proceedings.

On the occasion of the recent presentation of two wild ducks to the King, by way of feudal tenure, the Chief Magistrate of Jersey, who was clad in extraordinary and magnificent robes, addressed his Majesty thus : " This, Sir, is Your Majesty's Court of Heritage, it is the oldest Land Court in the West of Europe. It has been here in an unbroken record. Is it Your Majesty's pleasure that the Seigneurs pay their customary homage ? " and then followed the homage to which I have just referred.

It may be interesting, however, to refer to a court which claims to be far older than any which exists in the Channel Islands, and which still carries out its jurisdiction in its ancient form. This is the Water Court of Valencia, which has complete jurisdiction over the water-courses that were arranged by the Moors, when they were in possession of Spain, and which play so important a part in the agricultural work of that particular province. The arrangement is for the water to be turned on to different plantations in succession, and there are strictly regulated orders of precedence on the part of the growers round about Valencia, and very stringent regulations concerning the length of time that the water should flow in their channels, to fructify the land, and as to keeping up these channels, and attending to their boundaries, and of the regulations that concern them.

The Water Court meets once a week, out of doors, just in front of one of the doors of the Cathedral. The officiating judges are selected by the agriculturists of Valencia from their own people, and they, and those who come before the court, all attend in their ordinary costume, the chief judge only wearing any symbol of office. They sit on curious velvet-covered settees, they keep no minutes or notes of their transactions, and once their decision is given there is no appeal from it. They have sat once a week continuously, ever since the days of the Moors, and all questions concerning the use of water in agriculture in the Province of Valencia come under their jurisdiction.

They have absolute control of the arrangements, can forbid any recalcitrant grower the use of the water, or can reduce the time during which he has that use, and can fine him in kind (though not in money) if he has been found guilty of an offence against the water laws. The arguments that take place are sometimes prolonged, but there is no adjournment of any case, and little delay in announcing the decision, while, whatever it may be, it is accepted implicity, and at once obeyed. I have watched this court in its procedure with great interest. It claims to be the oldest in Europe, and maintains that it is the only court whose decrees are implicitly obeyed, and against whose orders there is no appeal.

The court is known as the Tribunal of the Waters. It sits at eleven o'clock every Thursday at La Puerta de los Apostoles, which is the gate of the Cathedral. The judges are seven, chosen by each other, out of the yeomen and irrigators of the Huerta, and the complaints respecting irrigation are settled in very summary fashion. No advocates are allowed, no oaths taken, no records kept. Moreover, the language employed in the court is the old dialect of Valencia, and when the case is over, the judges consult together, before they give their decision, from which as I have said there is no appeal. The tribunal is known from records kept in Valencia to have been in existence since 961. Many efforts have been made on the part of local officials in the place to suppress it. Fortunately they have been without success, and it still meets in exactly the same way, and for exactly the same purpose, as it has always met.

The irrigation over which it has supreme power consists of eight great canals, together with smaller veins, and with an enormous network of minute channels, and for these three divisions, the original Arabian names are still retained. The main trunk is still called the " Canna Mulcannal," the smaller veins the " Atquia," which the Spaniard pronounces " Acequias," and the still smaller ones with their dams, are known to the peasants as the " Sudd," grouped by the Spaniards into " Azudas." The object is to secure a fair distribution of water, so that nobody's land can be left dry, and nobody's over-flooded, and the arrangement of the canals is most admirable, working exceedingly well, and giving fertility and wealth to the district. It is of course understood that the apportionment of the water has always been, and will always be, a source of solicitude, and at times of some contention.

CHAPTER XI

BISHOPS AND CLERGY

I HAVE already had occasion to draw attention, in the chapter on the House of Lords, to certain peculiar survivals concerning the Bishops and their position that still continue, but there are many other anomalies in ecclesiastical matters equally worthy of consideration. Comparatively few recognise that the old pre-Reformation name for the Blessed Virgin, that of Our Lady, is still retained in the Prayer-book Calendar. Although in many instances she is termed the Blessed Virgin, yet in one the old phrase remains. There are probably still fewer who realise why the Church of England differs in the nomenclature she applies to the majority of Sundays in the year, when she calls them " Sundays after Trinity " instead of " Sundays after Pentecost," according to Catholic fashion. The change arose from the fact that St. Thomas à Becket was consecrated on Trinity Sunday, June 3, 1162, in Canterbury Cathedral, having been ordained Priest the day before, and to mark the complete change that had taken place in his life, he thereafter counted the Sundays that follow the day of his consecration according to their relationship to Trinity Sunday, and the practice that he adopted has been accepted by the Anglican Communion ever since he was canonised.

Another curious point in connection with St. Thomas à Becket should be marked, the fact that he became so popular as a saint that altars were dedicated to him in a large number of English churches, and that his name was associated with those of the Blessed Virgin and St. Michael, as a saint of such importance that his intercession could well be invoked after the intercession of the Archangel had been sought. Then, again, after 1538, when St. Thomas was declared a traitor by Henry VIII, images and pictures of him in churches were removed, the use of his name in prayers was forbidden, and his altars passed without a name for a while, being known simply as "the side altar" or "the other altar."

Important evidence of this has quite recently been discovered in the muniment room at Queen's College, Oxford, where, in connection with the preparation of a book on Weyhill, a village which is near to the Pilgrim's Way, it has been found that an altar was definitely dedicated to St. Thomas, and that, in an inventory of the church goods, dated 1540, just after the declaration already referred to, it is only alluded to as "the other altar" although the High Altar and the Lady are specifically named.

A very interesting link with pre-Reformation days is represented by the remarkable power resident in the Archbishop of Canterbury, in virtue of his being the perpetual Legate, *Legatus Natus*, to the Pope. He still has the right to grant degrees, such degrees being before the breach with Rome, degrees in the University attached to the Papal Court; but now recognised as degrees in the University to which the then Archbishop happens to belong. They are, however, granted distinctly in virtue of his Legatine power, although no Archbishop of Canterbury has been a Papal Legate since the days of Cardinal Pole. His special commission was cancelled in 1557 by Paul IV, although he was allowed, as Archbishop of Canterbury, to retain the style of *Legatus Natus*. It is also still possible to obtain a faculty from the Archbishop of Canterbury for the special privilege of eating flesh during Lent. The privilege of granting this was given to the Archbishop in the time of Henry VIII (25, Cap. 21), and confirmed by Charles I. It has been so granted within comparatively recent days, and the original Tudor faculty seal is still in use on the document.

To Lent we owe, of course, two words now in modern use, noon and collation. On the fasting days, but one meal could be taken by those who strictly adhered to the regulations, and that was in the evening after Vespers. Gradually the practice crept in of having this meal at the hour of None (3 p.m.), but the hour of None could be taken by the hungry to mean not so much three o'clock, as the hour at which the office of None was recited, and it then was reasoned that this office could be recited as soon as the office of Sect was ended at midday. So it became the custom to recite None at midday, as or near to midday as possible, and the None hour became the Noon hour.

From one Noon to the next was a very long interval, and the Church permitted water or other liquid to be taken in the evening. The drink, when first sanctioned in the ninth century, was taken at the hour when the *collationes* or conferences were being read aloud in the monasteries, and consequently when a portion of solid food (which to-day is restricted to eight ounces) was permitted as a part of the Lenten diet, the name " collation " was retained, and is in general use at the present day.

The Bishop's apron is, of course, all that remains of the original cassock which the Bishop wore. The word should be " a naperon," which has been converted by a blunder into " an apron." An almost identical error consists of the use of the word " adder " for a " nadder." The word should be " nadder," as it is derived from the Anglo-Saxon word " naedre," meaning a snake, and the same word, with various slight changes, appears in similar form in various other languages ; in English, " a nadder " became, by corruption, " an adder."

The word " napron " comes, as will readily be seen, from the word " nappe," the French word for a kind of cloth. The word " nap " is still written when alluding to the rough surface of cloth, and from the French word " naperon," " napkin " comes. Its origin is clearly seen in our word " napery," which means the linen for the table, but it is not so commonly remembered that we have the word " map " in exactly the same way. It was originally a napkin, then some painted cloth, and so a cloth representing the world, the " Mappa Mundi," and eventually the word " Map."

The peculiarity of the Bishops' hats with their strange cords and ties takes us back to the days when they rode on horseback about their dioceses, and when their hats were liable to be blown off, and were tied down by cords, and it is the remains of these cords we see still in use. The gaiters of course have the same origin.

There was considerable controversy in early mediæval times in England about the exemption of persons in Holy Orders from the usual working of the criminal law. This was known as " benefit of clergy," and came into existence at the time of the Conquest. There is no trace of it in Anglo-Saxon times. At one time it was declared that, by the law of God, all clergy were exempt from temporal punishment, and we still possess an interesting survival of this law in the privilege of the resident members of the Universities of Oxford and Cambridge to be tried for misdemeanors, not in the ordinary law courts, or before the magistrates, but in the Vice-Chancellor's court.

The election of Bishops still retains some pre-Reformation features. In old days, the mode of election of a Bishop was for the King to send to the Chapter a " congé d'eslire "— permission to elect, and the election was then confirmed by the Pope, the Bishop-elect taking the oath to Him, paying the fees, and making the profession of obedience to the Metropolitan, and then the King gave a formal consent, and returned to the Bishop the temporalities of the see, which had reverted to the Crown on the vacancy. Now the " congé d'élire," as it is now spelled, is still issued for the Chapter to elect, but it contains the name of the person who is to be elected, while in some instances the document requiring the Archbishop to consecrate the elected person still retains the statement that he is to receive " such benedictions and ceremonies and other things requisite," but there is no need " to obtain a bull for the purpose from Rome."

The privilege of the Chapter of Canterbury, which goes back to remote times, is still retained in the fact that no consecration of a Bishop of the southern province may take place out of Canterbury Cathedral, except by special permission of the Dean and Chapter of Canterbury. The oath of allegiance to the King is still taken, and in ancient form, but the only " spiritualities " which the King on that occasion conveys to the Bishops are now the emoluments from ecclesiastical sources, such as the tithes, because those are the sole spiritualities which are vested in the King, and can be transferred to the Bishop by him. This is in contrast to those temporalities which would be income from manors and the like.

All Bishops of the original diocese of Canterbury who are elected by the Dean and Chapter have to be confirmed by the Vicar-general, sitting in Bow Church. This procedure

has existed for some four hundred years, and the confirmation of Dr. Woods to the See of Winchester in 1923, translated from the See of Peterborough, took place in ancient
form, the Vicar-general giving his final decree confirming
the Bishop in the formula that has always been in use.

A distinct and very unusual ecclesiastical privilege
remains in the diocese of Man, which, by the way, differs in
many respects from the other English dioceses. Its Chapter
does not receive a " congé d'élire " on the vacancy of the
see ; its Vicar-general had extensive jurisdiction, and affilia-
tion cases on the Island are still decided by him in virtue
of his ancient power, while the power of making canons for
the regulation of the Church still rests in the power of the
Convocation of the island, which meets annually. The see
is generally known as that of " Sodor and Man," the origin
of the first word being that the islands on the coast were
divided into two groups, the Northern Islands, Shetland,
Orkney, Fair Island, and some of the more remote islands
constituting the northern group ; and others from Lewis
extending right down to the Isle of Man, forming the
southern group, and the phrase for describing the southern
group was Suthr-Eyar, and this passed into the form Sodor,
which was the original name of the see. The title Sodor
and Man did not come into official use until the seventeenth
century, and was due to entire forgetfulness of the fact that
Man was part of Sodor, though, as a matter of fact, when the
new title was introduced, it was the only part of the Southern
Islands with which the Bishop of the diocese was actually
connected.

We have in process of time entirely reversed the original
meaning of the word " curate." He was the person who
had the cure of the souls in the parish, and we now apply
it to the assistant clergyman, who more strictly should be
called the vicar, and the reason it was so applied was that
the cure of the parish has been entrusted to the person
who is the clerical stipendiary, and so he was termed the
curate. "The parson" is simply "the person"—the parish
" persona " ; the " vicar " is really he who did the work
of the parish on behalf of another, and is now applied to the
parson of a parish who is not in receipt of the great tithes,
where the tithes belong to a layman.

The original name for the clergyman was " clerk," and

when we speak now of a " clerical error," that is to say, an error made in spelling or in writing by a person who is now termed a clerk, we are really using a word originally only applied to the clergy, as they were the persons who could read and write, and very often the only persons in the district who had that ability. The fact that the word " curate " is misapplied makes it all the more serious that the persons who are now called curates possess no vote for the election of proctors.

Up till 1429, all curates were free from arrest. As regards the celibacy of the clergy, it is interesting to notice that down to 1610 all children born of clergy were regarded as illegitimate, and for nearly a hundred years later than that, it was declared that within certain peculiars, originally subject to monastic administration, the illegitimacy of the children of the clergymen was still so regarded by law. I believe it was not until the beginning of the eighteenth century that clergymen's children born at St. Alban's, Bury St. Edmund's and Glastonbury, were recognised as legitimate, and prior to that time, special regulations and declarations had to be made in order to bring the birth of these children within the limits of the ordinary law. It is not that the children born in these places were actually illegitimate, but that through some oversight the old regulations connected with a celibate clergy had never been repealed.

Another survival of an ancient monastic privilege was retained by the town of Bury St. Edmund's until the very middle of the nineteenth century. The monastery was originally exempt, both from episcopal and archidiaconal authority, and the wills of its burgesses were proved before the sacrist of the monastery. After 1539, it still remained exempt from the jurisdiction of the Archdeacon of Sudbury, and the wills of Bury St. Edmund's people had to be proved before a special commissary of the Bishop of Norwich, and then, in 1844, this strange old survival was finally swept away by an order of the Privy Council, which declared that the town was a part of the Archdeaconry of Sudbury and so passed the privilege of the Abbey.

The clergy were, in pre-Reformation days, supposed to be represented by the Bishops or the Abbots who sat in the Upper House, and hence it came about that no clergyman, whether rector, vicar or curate, even now can sit in the Lower

House. There have been clergymen, certainly, who have sat in the House of Commons, but they have been persons who have relinquished their Orders, and are considered laymen. Priests of the Church of Rome and clergy of the Church of England can sit in the Upper House, e.g., the late Lord Petre was in Orders and so is the present Marquess of Normanby.

A curious pre-Reformation habit is still kept up in Hereford Cathedral, where the two sexes to this day sit apart, the men on one side of the nave, and the women on the other. I believe this is the only English Cathedral in which the custom, to be noticed in Catholic churches, is still perpetuated.

There are still three deaneries in England which are Archiepiscopal Peculiars. They arose from the right of the Archbishops to execute jurisdiction where their cities or palaces were situate. The Archbishop of Canterbury had many palaces, and in respect to some of them, he appointed commissioners, who were termed Deans, and the Deans of Bocking, Hadleigh and Stamford still retain their title and costume, although their position at the present day is not much more, save in dignity and title, than that of an ordinary parish clergyman.

Till within the past few years, a remote church in Surrey, known now as St. Martha's, but originally as the Church of the Holy Martyrs, was not regarded as part of the parish in which it stands, and the appointment of a clergyman at Chilworth did not involve superintendence of this little church. The power to appoint a clergyman to this church was still vested in the layman who held the estates, and who always appointed the Rector of Chilworth to the position, but he was able to carry on such ritual as he chose at St. Martha's, and was subject to no comments on the part of his Bishop. By a recent Act, the privileges of this and many other Peculiars were abolished.

There is still, however, a strange quiet corner in London, known as Ely Place, strictly speaking, a part of the Diocese of Ely, and still not recognised as part of the Diocese of London. The domestic chapel of the Bishops of Ely stands in Ely Place, and the episcopal mitre and arms are to be seen close by. Whether the Bishop of Ely now exercises any jurisdiction over this quiet corner is doubtful, but in any case it is quite certain that the Bishop of London does not, and it is probably, for ecclesiastical purposes, outside the limits of *any* diocese. It is closed at night by its own gates, and the persons who reside within it keep up their own watchman, who still goes round, night by night, and calls out the hours and the state of the weather, according to ancient mode. In this respect it is, I believe, unique in London.

It should also be remembered that Ely Place was part of the garden that surrounded the town house of the Bishop of Ely, and, as such, was regarded as a Liberty and a Sanctuary, entirely outside the control of the Mayor and Commonalty of the City of London, and even a place where the King's writs for certain offences had no effect. It is for that reason that it now enjoys its curious civic isolation and autonomy. It is still extra-parochial, and is governed by Commissioners who are elected directly by the house-holders within its precincts. These Commissioners levy the only rates that are paid, and they are concerned with the employment and payment of the watchman, who wears quaint and picturesque uniform.

There are moreover, many other places that recall the religious life of the City, such as Ave Maria Lane, Paternoster Row, Creed Lane, and Amen Corner, all of these having reference to the existence of shops for the manufacture or sale of ecclesiastical ornaments, especially rosaries, round about St. Paul's.

The word " marry " we obtain from the same source as that which gives us the words " masculine," " male " and " marital," all of them connected with the word " maritus," a husband. One of the curious words that has arisen in that sense is the word " mallard," which we apply to a wild drake. It practically means nothing more than a male, and the phrase is repeated twice, because the suffix " ard " was particularly applied to words signifying the male gender. There is also another form of the word " marry " in the form of an ejaculation, but in that case, it is from another source, it means " By Mary," in the same way as " Zounds " refers to the wounds of Christ, an ancient phrase ; " Gadsdeath," to " God's Death," and " Gad-zooks " to " God's Wounds," while " Odsbodikins " came from very much the same source, having reference to the

Wounds of the Body ; the word " Gad " in all these strange phrases being simply a familiar form of the word " God."

It is curious to remember that we have derived two words, " roam " and " canter," from the pilgrimages which took place to Rome, and from the manner in which the horseman accommodated himself to the rough road on the way to Canterbury. We have assumed the use of the word canter as applied to a particular pace on the part of a horse. Saunter in like manner comes from pilgrimage times, being derived from Sainte Terre (Holy Ground).

The " pall " or " pallium " sent as an emblem of authority from Rome to the Archbishops, and without which they were unable to exercise their supreme functions, still appears in the coats of arms of the Archbishops of Canterbury and York, a strange " Y "-shaped object, denoting the piece of wool with its pins to fasten it, still sent from Rome to Catholic Archbishops, and constituting the sign of their supremacy. The coronet which the Bishop of Durham bears round about his mitre reminds us of the Palatinate which he originally possessed, and which gave him almost princely powers. His diocese and his palatinate were not coterminous, so that his powers as Bishop Palatine extended far beyond the boundaries of the diocese. Durham was practically in the position of a " buffer state " between England and Scotland, and over it the Bishop ruled almost as a King. The Bishop of Durham is said to hold office by " Divine Providence," the same phrase being used with regard to the Archbishop of Canterbury. All other Bishops, including the Archbishop of York, only hold their position by " Divine permission." The power was diminished in 1536, but the Palatinate was not finally annexed to the Crown till 1836. The coronet is now the only evidence of its early existence. There were two other Palatine Counties in England, Chester and Lancaster, in which the person who was in supreme command, and who was known as the Count Palatine, exercised a royal authority, just as supreme as though he had been the regal tenant of the palace itself. The remains of this interesting jurisdiction exist by reason of the fact that the County of Lancaster is still a Palatine County, under special control of the King, who is Duke of Lancaster, and the Earldom of Chester is the particular perquisite of the heir to the Throne. Thus is kept up the memory of the unusual position held by these two counties in old days.*

There is a curious survival of the use of this word " Palatine " still remaining in Chichester, where there is a street called Pallant Street, denoting a particular district within the city with four main streets which formed at one time a peculiar under the special jurisdiction of the Bishop.

It is not everyone who recognises that the windows of King's College refer to the various decades of the Rosary, nor is it generally known that the Oxford Calendar has certain special features it has always preserved. The Translation of St. Thomas à Becket, for example, appears on it under date July 7. Moreover, the Prayer-book that was issued in Oxford is an exact and faithful copy of what is known as the " sealed prayer-book," the one which accompanied the Act of Uniformity, whereas I believe I am right in saying that the one in Cambridge is not absolutely identical with it. There was a division of opinion between the two Universities at the time, and that division is still continued by some very slight and very unimportant variations between the two books printed at the two Universities.

In Cornwall, at Altarnum (the Altar of St. Nonna), there still remains in the church an altar which stands right away from the chancel, and which, from its position, proves that it was one of those where the priest stood the whole time facing the congregation, instead of, as he stands at present, with his back to the congregation. The survival of this position still remains in the four great basilicas in Rome, the Papal churches at whose high altars none but the Pope can celebrate, and in St. Peter's, St. John Lateran, St. Mary Major, and the Cathedral of St. Peter and St. Paul, the altar is placed between the clergy and the congregation, and the Pope, when he officiates, faces the people the whole time, and does not turn round to give the *Dominus vobiscum* or his blessing at the end. The Rev. S. J. Rowlands tells me that in the ancient church of Deerhurst, near Tewkesbury, the pew-like sittings remain around the east wall, thus presenting the table aspect of the service, and this is a relic of the time of the Commonwealth, when the Elders were accustomed to sit facing the flock. It is said that a

---

* To the appointment of the Sheriffs for these counties allusion has already been made.

similar arrangement is in force at Stanton Harold, close to the seat of Lord Ferrers.

The appearance of a stranger at harvest is gladly recognised in many districts. Food and drink is at once placed before him, if he comes to the harvest without the knowledge of any person round about. He represents a visit from Our Lord to see what will be the result of the harvest, and it is stated that it is sure to be successful if a stranger suddenly comes in while it is being reaped. In another part of England there is precisely the opposite theory, and a stranger is hooted off the field, and there he is said to represent Satan, and may do the harvest harm.

The custom persists in Scotland, where, if a stranger appears on the harvest field, he is seized, and unless he pays a ransom, is dashed up and down, and thrown upon the sheaves. The customary phrase applied to him is that he is a " Benjie," a word used in other connections to signify an Evil Spirit.

The name of the Devil is introduced in very much the same way in natural things, not so much in plants as in parts of the country, the Devil's Punchbowl, the Devil's Jumps, the Devil's Hollows, the Devil's Hills, the Devil's Rocks, and so on, are well known. The very common phrase that occurs on most people's lips, " Who the dickens are you ? " or " What the dickens are you doing ? " a phrase which we find in Shakespeare, is derived from a reference to Satan, whom country people still associate with the appellation of " Old Nick," and from which this expression is derived. It has nothing whatever to do with the name of the author of the *Pickwick Papers*.

The use of the Sign of the Cross occurs in many country districts, where all idea of its religious importance has passed away, but the most general use is on the hot cross buns that are eaten on Good Friday. The word " bun " itself we are said to take from an old Greek word " bous," which represented a sacred cake offered to the gods in their temples. There are many strange superstitions still retained in connection with the bun that has the cross upon it ; some people believe it can never grow mouldy, others hang up the buns in order to keep off witches, or to protect the house from fire ; and in some villages a piece of a hot cross bun, however dry or stale it may be, is yet declared to be an invaluable cure for diarrhœa.

Mr. Wallis tells me that in the East and North Ridings of Yorkshire many of the villagers make what are known as witch-cakes. They are of dough, and cut to represent a rough conventional design of the rising sun. They are generally hung up behind the cottage door. It is not easy to obtain any information respecting the origin of the custom.

In connection with the cross on the hot cross buns, I well remember, as a child, seeing a very old servant marking the sign of the cross on the dough, whenever she prepared it, stating that, unless she did so, the dough would never rise. There was no one, in my experience, less sympathetic with Catholic practices than this particular person, who was a Calvinistic Baptist of the very straitest sort, but she never omitted this ceremony, which she said she had been taught by her grandparents, and she was quite sure that an accident would happen to the dough if it was omitted. I have also a very clear recollection of her once being taken ill in the kitchen at the time that she was making the dough, and the final work having to be left to another servant. The dough was utterly spoilt, and the old servant said that it was not owing at all to her own illness, or to the carelessness of the other girl, but entirely to the fact that the sign of the cross had not been marked upon it.

Another interesting survival of the use of the Sign of the Cross is mentioned by Sir James Yoxall. " I can myself remember," he says, " a Methodist mother in Israel removing her wedding ring, and using it to stroke, in crosswise fashion, a stye on the eye, as a certain cure."

The Rev. S. J. Rowlands reminds me that in Liverpool a custom obtained every Good Friday of making an effigy of Judas Iscariot, with a sack stuffed with straw, and states that a similar effigy is held out from the bowsprit of Spanish ships, if they come into Liverpool on Good Friday, and afterwards burnt. I may add that the same custom exists in Seville, where the effigy is flogged before it is burnt, and there is great excitement amongst the assembled people when the burning takes place, and considerable noise in the way of cheering and hooting, while the people dance round the fire.

One of the religious survivals to be noticed is that which occurs on July 25, when the passer-by is recommended by the boy in the street to subscribe to his grotto, "pray remember the grotto" being the phrase. Sometimes August 5 is the day that is kept, that being the feast of St. James the Great, which, in the Old Style, was commemorated on July 25, because in pre-Reformation days it was customary on that day to visit the shrine of St. James, and it is still the great day of pilgrimages at Santiago de Compostella, one of the most notable shrines in Europe. Probably to no place in the world has there been so vast a succession of pilgrimages as to Santiago, hundreds of thousands coming from all parts of Europe to that place, and in pre-Reformation times it was regarded as so important that a visit should be made to Compostella, that the declaration the visit had been made was put amongst the deeds of the estate, and unless it was found amongst such papers, the owner of the estate was regarded as a man who had no proper sense of his religious duties. In fact, at one time, there was an attempt to make it *necessary* that the " Compostella," as it was called, should be produced, if the property was to pass down in succession from father to son. This happened not only in Spain but even in England. The English people were just as tenacious of the importance of this pilgrimage to Spain as were other people, and tens of thousands of Englishmen and Englishwomen made the pilgrimage. For hundreds of years, representations of the shrine of St. James used, however, to be erected in the streets and churches, in order that those who could not make the long pilgrimage should perform their devotions before the shrine of St. James in their own parish, and people were reminded in the highways of their duty on that particular day. Children at the present time prepare a little grotto, light it up with a candle, and ask for a contribution just as their ancestors did in times past for the larger shrines that were erected both in the streets and in the churches.

The scallop shell* was taken as the emblem of this

* To this custom Sir Walter Raleigh makes allusion when he sings :
" Give me my scallop shell of quiet,
My staff of faith to walk upon,
My scrip of joy, immortal diet,
My bottle of salvation,
My gown of glory, hope's true gage ;
And thus I'll take my pilgrimage."

pilgrimage, and pilgrims used to produce one as evidence that they had been to Santiago. Exactly why this shell was so adopted cannot now be stated for certainty. It has been said that the shell was very abundant on the sea-shore near to Vigo and the other ports at which the pilgrims used to disembark, but whatever was the reason the shell became the emblem of St. James, and as a survival we find that an oyster shell is still used by the boys in the street as a collecting bowl.

At marriages it is odd that we still keep up the use of a bride-cake, because it is the survival from a particular kind of cake used in Roman times amongst the highest members of the patrician families. It was only those who were patricians who were entitled to have their marriage per-formed before the Pontifex Maximus, and upon that occasion they partook of a symbolic cake. Hence we derive our habit, and the use of the bride-cake really implies that the persons are of importance and well-born, although now it is used by all classes of society.

The Jews keep up the old idea of living in a tent by means of the canopy they use on the occasion of a wedding. The bride and bridegroom still receive their friends at the door of the tent, that is at the entrance to the canopy which is held up over them.

Probably no book so completely enshrines ancient sur-vivals as the Roman Missal. It is full of strange and fascinating relics of past antiquity, and its Apostolic origin is demonstrated by the fact that there are distinct traces of Judaism in the earlier part of it, indicating that the Apostles followed the Jewish form of service up to a certain point, when they gathered together to break bread, and then introduced the sacred elements of the Eucharist, which were only participated in by the faithful. A careful con-sideration, however, of all these points, is beyond the scope of this volume.

I may also mention that the Carthusian Order founded in the eleventh century, the only one of the Orders that has never been reformed and in the opinion of its monks needs no reform; is a veritable museum of old manners, habits and customs, hardly one of its original regulations having ever been changed or amended. It knows nothing of services introduced in later ages, its ritual being severe and archaic, having a closer and more intimate connection with the rite of Apostolic times than has any other ritual in the Church. Its simplicity marks its remote antiquity.

There was a curious survival in Edward VI's Prayer-book, handed down from the pre-Reformation Mass-book, and which still is retained in the Roman use. It was in connection with the Friday after the fourth Sunday in Lent. Originally, in early Christian days, the gathering of the people on that particular day was at the Church of St. Eusebius, which happened to be then the chief Christian cemetery, and in consequence, the celebration had necessarily the character of a Mass for the Dead. In place of the Epistle for that day, the lesson was read from the Book of Kings, narrating how the Prophet Elijah raised the son of the widow from the dead, and the Gospel was the resurrection of Lazarus. Both these lessons, the Epistle and the Gospel, were retained for a time in the English Prayer-book. There is now no special service for that particular Friday, and in consequence, they have disappeared.

Even in our use of colour in ecclesiastical matters, for exterior decoration, we go back to days of antiquity. There was an edict in the time of Henry VIII which stated that the clocks and the " planettes with dialles " were to be " enamelled blew and the signs upon them gilte." This is recorded in the Harleian MSS., and a writer, commenting upon it, pointed out that blue and gold were the colours named in the Book of Exodus that were to be used in making the vestments for Aaron and for his sons, and for the girdle of the ephod. William Salmon, in a work he published in 1678, called *Polygrafice*, says that Faith was always represented in white, bearing a cup of gold, and " Eternity in blue, seeded with golden stars." This use of blue and gold has been brought to the notice of passers-by quite recently, because the faces of the clock of St. Clement Danes, Strand, have just been repainted, as they were in old days, blue and gold, in similar fashion to the clock dials which appear on many church towers in old country towns.

CHAPTER XII

ECCLESIASTICAL CEREMONIES AND SURVIVALS OF OLD RELIGIOUS USE

THE most important survival of old monastic privileges which still remains in the present day is the right retained by the Abbey of Westminster, which is not subject to archi-episcopal visitation. Whenever the Archbishop of Canterbury or the Bishop of London enter Westminster Abbey, a protest is still solemnly made by the Dean of Westminster that in so entering the Archbishop or Bishop do not claim any jurisdiction over the building or the persons connected therewith.*

This special exemption from episcopal jurisdiction found, says Canon Westlake,† its first formal expression in a deed which belongs to Westminster Abbey, dated 1222, but it is clear, he states, from the wording of this grant, that the exemption belonged to an even earlier period than the beginning of the thirteenth century. There is curious evidence of the monastic origin of the Abbey in the fact that no ladies are ever allowed to sit in the stalls. The stalls are, of course, the seats occupied in Benedictine times by the monks. After the Reformation, they were expressly reserved for members of the collegiate body and their officers. There were then twelve Prebendaries, there are now only five. Many of the seats are not now occupied by the Cathedral officials, and male worshippers are occasionally allowed to fill them, but no women are ever permitted to sit in these stalls, and if by chance they take

* While these pages were passing through the Press, I noticed a reference to this very question in the Private Diaries of Sir Algernon West. Speaking about the funeral of Mr. Gladstone, he writes that "the Prince of Wales wished the Bishop of London to say a few words after the funeral, but the Dean refused absolutely, saying 'No Bishop has any jurisdiction in Westminster Abbey.' So the idea had to be given up."

† See his *Guide* to the Abbey.

172

their seats upon them, they are requested to leave, as while there they are committing a breach of a very long-standing tradition.

Another strange circumstance in connection with Westminster Abbey is the fact that the Earl Marshal at the time of Coronation still takes over, as he did from the Benedictine Abbot of the old days, the entire control of the Abbey, and for a while all ecclesiastical power is suspended. The Earl Marshal is then the only person who has the right to permit entrance to the Abbey, and in his hands rests its entire administration and every detail concerning its services, and the arrangements made for the coming ceremony. The Dean, in solemn fashion, hands over the key of the Abbey to the Earl Marshal of England, and it is returned to the Dean after the Coronation. During the time for the preparation for the Coronation and the actual ceremony, the Earl Marshal is in absolutely supreme command.

Perhaps the most interesting of the ancient ceremonies retained in the Church of England is that in connection with the distribution of Maundy money, which takes place annually in the Abbey. The last Sovereign in England who actually washed the feet of poor men on Maundy Thursday was James II, but this ceremony, in commemoration of the act of Our Lord, is still carried out in Catholic countries, and was, until recently, one of the notable events of Holy Week in Vienna, when the Emperor of Austria took the chief part in it. It still takes place in Spain with its accustomed ceremonial, but in England the day is commemorated only by the distribution of the silver currency, struck specially for that occasion, and given away to a certain number of poor men and poor women, who have been selected as suitable recipients for the bounty.

English sovereigns have always attached great importance to this ceremonial. Elizabeth observed the day with specially lavish bounty, and there is a remarkable miniature in existence, representing her distribution of Maundy money. Charles I and Anne also distributed the Maundy money with specially imposing and stately ceremonial, and to-day, linen scarves or towels are worn by all the officials connected with the Royal Almonry, and by the children of the Royal Almonry, who also take part in the ceremonial. These are of course typical of the towel which Our Lord girded about Himself, when He washed the disciples' feet.

The ceremonial is one of the few occasions when the public see the Yeomen of the Guard in their full uniform, the oldest military body in the kingdom, whose record dates back to 1485, and who still wear, with proud distinction, the Tudor crown ornament which commemorates their original appointment.

The gold embroidered cross-belt worn by the Yeomen of the Guard was originally the buff service cross-belt used to support the heavy butt of the arquebus and afterwards of the matchlock.   The belt still actually contains the massive swivel for attachment to a firearm no longer in use.   The Yeomen of the Guard were made a permanent institution by Henry VII, and they form not only the oldest Royal body-guard, but the oldest military corps now existing in this or in any other country.

Those who are to take part in the Maundy ceremony carry with them bunches of flowers and foliage, reminiscent of the day when the Yeomen of the Laundry performed a preliminary ablution of the feet of the beggars, with ceremonial herbs; prior to the washing of the feet by the Sovereign.

The money is borne into the Abbey by one of the Yeomen, who carries on his head a splendid silver-gilt dish, and the strings of the purses, red and white, with which originally they were bound to the girdle of the persons who used them, hang over the borders of the dish, with curious effect.   The number of pennies given away corresponds with the age of the King, the recipients, as well as the pence in the white purses, equalling years of the King's age.   The money consists of pieces of the value of four-pence, threepence, twopence and a penny, the total number of pence agreeing with the number of the years of the King's age, and the coins are current coin of the realm, although specially struck for the purpose.   I am inclined to think that there might be some difficulty if one of these pennies was presented as the fare in an ordinary omnibus, because of its exceedingly small size, and the chances are that the 'bus conductor would not recognise it as current coin, but it is really so, and but for its size, the coin would pass readily from hand to hand.

As a matter of fact, however, the little group of silver coins has a higher value than its intrinsic importance, and collectors are always eager to add it to their collections. The red purse should contain within it a pound, in gold, and thirty shillings, an allowance in lieu of provisions formerly given in kind ; it does not in these later days contain gold coins, but the distribution is made in paper. In addition to this Maundy money, there are three other sums of money distributed on the same day, known as the Minor Bounty, the Discretionary Bounty and the Royal Gate alms, and these, in accordance with ancient usage, are distributed at the Royal Almonry Office, to some " . . . hundred aged, disabled and meritorious persons, who have been personally recommended by the clergy of selected parishes," throughout the different dioceses of England and Wales.

Gate Alms no doubt derived its name from the money that was given to those beggars who clustered round the gates of the Royal Palaces, and the duties of the King's Almoner, with regard to poor people, are expressly laid down in some papers belonging to the time of Edward I, where it is stated that he was to collect and distribute the fragments from the Royal table, and give away the King's cast-off robes, but it is particularly noted that he was not to do so either to " players, minstrels or flatterers."

Cardinal Wolsey, when first he kept his Maundy cele-bration, or, in the old phrase, " made his Maund " (the word coming of course from the word " mandatum," and being carried out in obedience to Our Lord's commands), did so at Peterborough ; and on the occasion in 1530, gave three white and three red herrings to each recipient of his alms. It is to his benefaction that the Almonry owes its present seal. On this seal is represented a great three-masted ship, *Henri Grace de Dieu*, in full sail. This im-portant vessel was built by Wolsey in 1512 and presented by him to Henry VIII, and when he was the King's Almoner he had it represented on the seal he used for the documents in connection with the ceremony, and this seal still exists, and is in actual use, at the present day.

The great monastries all had their almoners, and also some of the chief noblemen, and the office still survives and is used in various ancient hospitals, and in some few other places.

It is of interest to notice that the Lord High Almoner and his assistant, the Sub-almoner, remove the ceremonial copes which they wear when they enter in the processions of the Maundy, and gird themselves with linen towels before they make the presentation. The ceremony must have been far more imposing in the old days, when the Sovereign himself took prominent part in it, but it is still an exceedingly interesting and picturesque one, and one of the most important survivals of an ancient religious observance. In Monte Cassino, in Italy, it is carried out with great elaboration, and the recipients there are still actual pilgrims, but, in addition to the washing of feet, they are given a big loaf of bread, and a piece of money, and are then taken in to the large refectory, and have a substantial meal. Similar procedure takes place in many other Catholic monasteries throughout Europe.

The word " penny " itself is a curious survival. It does not really mean a coin, but a token or pledge, and it comes from exactly the same word as that from which we derive the word " pawn," while we also take from it such words as " panel," " pane," "counterpane" (the counterpart of a deed, *not* a quilt), and " panicle." The readiest pledge that one would leave in pawn was a piece of cloth, hence the Latin " panna," a piece of cloth, and the Spanish word " paños " for clothes. The original panel was a piece of cloth, or patch, and so we obtain the word which now applies to a pane of glass, and we take the word penny from the same phrase, its literal sense being a little pledge, a token, and hence a coin. In its spelling in the early versions as " peny," we see, in easier fashion, from whence the word was derived.

Dancing in church has passed away from being an English ecclesiastical custom, although the dancing in the street still continues in more than one place in Cornwall, but the dance in honour of the Blessed Sacrament still takes place in Seville at Christmas and the Feast of Corpus Christi, and through the octave of that feast, when certain choir-boys perform their stately measures before the High Altar, wearing the old costume of plumed hats, and rich silken dress worn by the pages at the time of Philip III.

It is said that many episcopal dignitaries in Spain were afraid that this old rite might degenerate into frivolity, and were also concerned at the large number of tourists who came to Spain at certain times of the year, especially for the feasts of Corpus Christi and the Immaculate Conception, to see this strange sight. Accordingly the Holy See was petitioned that a decree should be issued abolishing it. The people of Seville were deeply concerned, however, and passionately protested against the abolition of a custom to which, as a proud possession of their city for many hundreds of years, they were much attached. A compromise was brought about at Rome, to the effect that, as long as the costumes then being worn by the pages could be utilised, the custom might continue, but when these costumes were worn out, they were not to be replaced, gradually the number of dancers was to be diminished, and eventually the dance was to die out. The clergy and people of the Cathedral of Seville have, however, been so careful in repairing the costumes, and in putting in patches where necessary, in order that the bulk of the fabric should still remain, that there seems little chance of the dance ever being abolished ; the costumes bid fair to wear for ever, they are so carefully examined and so well mended and repaired.

A somewhat similar dance takes place on the feast of St. Willibrod at Echternach Abbey, and there the procession, dancing, goes all round the town, and then enters the Abbey, and the more solemn part of the performance takes place immediately before the High Altar. In this case, also, it is witnessed by thousands of people, who crowd into the town for the purpose of viewing it. Both customs go back to the days when dancing was a sign of honour and distinction. David danced before the ark.

At Painswick, in Gloucestershire, there is an interesting festival called " Clipping," which appears to be a direct survival of the Roman festival of the Wolf-god, the Lupercalia. This festival, as has been pointed out by Mr. Seddon in his paper on the subject, was marked by a dance round the altar, by the sacrifice of young dogs, and by the fact that the children dressed themselves in the skins of goats, and rushed down the streets of the town, with thongs of goat-skin in their hands.

To-day the Painswick children encircle their church, have

on the special day what they call their " puppy-dog pies,"
and rush down the street shouting the words " High gates,"
which Mr. Seddon is inclined to derive from the Greek
" Aig-aïtis," signifying an affection for a goat. The festival
is kept on what was originally the Feast of the Nativity of
the Blessed Virgin, according to the old calendar, and it
would appear that it is the direct descendant of that which
was kept at Painswick before it was Christianised, and links
up the feast of the Lupercalia, which was changed by Pope
Galasius in 494 into the Feast of the Purification of the
Blessed Virgin, with several of its ancient habits still
remaining.

There exists an even more interesting ceremony in connection with the parish of Brockworth, about four miles
from Painswick and six from Gloucester. Near the place
is a hill called Cooper's Hill, and annually, on Whit Monday, there takes place a cheese-rolling festival, called the
Wake. At the top of the hill is a tall mast, under which,
on this occasion, the villagers dance, and the more staid
inhabitants of the district, including the Squire, usually
participate in this festivity. The cheeses are started rolling
down the hill by the parish Squire, and the young men of
the village race furiously down the bluff after them ; the
one who first seizes the cheese, keeps it. The mast under
which the dancing takes place is decorated with flowers
and ribbons for this occasion, and the feeling in the village
is that its communal rights of grazing on the adjacent
common would be lost if the dancing and the cheese-rolling
did not take place. It has nothing to do with Maypole
dancing, because the mast is too high to admit of the
ordinary ribbon attachment, and it is three miles from the
village and some seven hundred feet higher than the village
green. Archæologists believe that the ceremony has an
intimate connection with ancient Druidical rites, which were
concerned with the rolling of discs downhill from a high
place, flanked by a pole or a mast which was of itself an
object of superstition. At one time there was a fire erected
under the mast, which makes the evidence in favour of
Druidic or Phœnician origin still stronger.

At St. Benet's Church, Cambridge, the men who attend
Church of England services at Easter time are paid for their
attendance. John Meere willed two houses in the parish in

1558 for the preaching of an English sermon one day in the Easter holidays, upon the duty of obedience of pupils to their masters, and all the men who are present are paid for their attendance.

A curious ceremony takes place at Blidworth, in Nottinghamshire, when the clergyman rocks, in an ancient cradle, at the altar rails of the church, the youngest male baby in the parish. The ceremony is a survival of the old miracle play, and of the special scene which represented the Presentation of the Child Christ in the Temple. It is known as " The Rocking."

Curious and interesting survivals of the days when England was called the Heritage of Our Lady, and the common objects of the country-side received names in accordance with the ideas of the people, remain in the familiar names that are still given to many flowers ; many both of the garden and the field having been dedicated to the Virgin. The plant that is called, in some parts of England, the Kingcup, is frequently styled the Marygold, and we have the Madonna lily and the Lady lily, also having reference to the Blessed Virgin. There are many other flowers, moreover, that recall exactly the same ideas—the campanula by many country people is still spoken of as Our Lady's looking-glass—the cowslip as Our Lady's bunch of keys—foxgloves were the Virgin's gloves, and the same name is also applied to Canterbury bells—the harebell is known as Our Lady's thimble—a little orchid is called Our Lady's tresses—a yellow lotus known as Our Lady's fingers —the cuckoo pint bears the name of Ladysmock, the yellow and white flowers of a plant of the same order as the wood-ruff, are called Lady's bedstraw—the calceolaria has the name of Lady's slipper—the black bryony is sometimes called Solomon's Seal and sometimes Our Lady's Seal—the ribbon grass has the name of Our Lady's garters, the ground ivy in Italy always has the name of L'erba della Madonna, the maidenhair fern has reference to the same devotion, and there are several flowers that are pink and blue that are called Mary and Joseph flowers. One of the milkworts is known as Our Lady's milkwort—the wild clematis, known as Traveller's Joy and Old Man's Beard, is called in one part of England Virgin's Bower. The lily of the valley has been known as the Purification Flower, and there are others that recall exactly the same special devotion. With regard to the Passion Flower, to which we still give its ancient name, it contains, according to the country-side, many pieces of sacred symbolism. The leaves are thus said to represent the spear that pierced Christ's side, the tendrils the cords that bound Him or the whips that scourged Him, the petals, which are ten, are ten of the Apostles—Judas and Peter, who betrayed and denied Him, being absent—the pillar in the centre is the Cross, or the pillar at which the scourging took place, the stamens the hammers, the style, the nails. The inner circle round the pillar represents the crown of thorns, the white in the flower is the emblem of purity, the blue the type of Heaven, and the scent is said to represent that of incense, and so, in that way, the flower stands for a complete series of symbols connected with Our Lord's Passion. The Aspen is declared to have its habit of trembling from the fact that it grew near to the Cross, the bird known as the Crossbill is declared to have obtained the peculiar form of its bill through its efforts to pull out the nails that bound Our Lord to the Cross, in which it was assisted by the Goldfinch, which still bears on its bill the marks of the Holy Blood, and in some old-fashioned districts the wood of the Cross is declared to have been the hawthorn, and hence it is regarded as an unlucky thing to bring even the bloom of the hawthorn inside the house.

The legend connected with the Crown Imperial, or *fritillaria imperialis*, especially with regard to what are known as the " tears " that are to be found on its pendent petals, belongs to pre-Reformation days, and is very interesting. The plant is said to have grown in the Garden of Gethsemane and to have been particularly favoured by Christ, but in those days it bore its flowers erect from under its leafy crown, and its petals were white as snow. On the night of the Agony, it is said, while all the other flowers of the garden bowed their heads as Our Lord passed by, the fritillaria, in its pride, remained erect. It had always been praised and admired, and it expected that its pride would continue. It received from Our Lord a gentle word of expostulation as He passed it by, and the blush of shame came to its snowy petals, for in humility it hung its head, and it was then that the tears welled forth from its eyes, and are still to be seen within its pendent blooms.

What a curious thing it is that we so completely miscall the Jerusalem artichoke, and that we even misinterpret the original of the word artichoke itself. We derive the word from an Arab name for the plant, and this came through the Spanish into the Italian language, and becoming " articioceo " became " artichoke " in English, and has nothing to do with " choke " and nothing to do with " heart " or with the Latin " hortus," a garden, while the French word " artichaut " has nothing whatever to do with " chaud," hot, or " chou," cabbage, and the use of the word " Jerusalem " is simply a corruption of the Italian " girasole," so applied to the sunflower artichoke from its habit of turning towards the sun.

The oldest society of bellringers which still remains in London was established in 1637, and was the immediate successor of a far older guild, which had been in existence for a long time. When first established, the Society used to ring the bells at St. Martin's Vintry, and on that being burned down, it transferred its work to the neighbouring church of St. Michael Paternoster Royal, situate upon College Hill. This street in the City of London derived its name from the existence of a college of the Holy Spirit and St. Mary, founded by Whittington, and dissolved by Henry VIII. It was what was known in later days as a God's House. It had almshouses and a hospital connected with it for the use of thirteen poor men, the number commemorating the twelve Apostles and their Master, and from the Church of St. Michael the Society of Bellringers took the name of The College Youths, and under that name this particular group of bellringers still remains.

At Higham Ferrers there are two bells rung at seven in the morning and seven in the evening, which are called the Tantony Bells. They are so called, it is stated, because they used to be rung to call home the swineherd with his charges, and St. Anthony was the patron of swineherds and swine. The first bell is the time at which gleaners in the cornfields are allowed to begin, and no gleaning is allowed after the second bell.

It is rather interesting, in connexion with ecclesiastical matters, to notice that there exists, in the eye of the law, a body called the " English Presbyterian Divines in and about the Cities of London and Westminster," and yet that the existence of this body is practically unknown to the great majority of the adherents of the Presbyterian Church, not only in London, but throughout the country. Moreover, this body possesses an ancient right of presenting addresses to the King, and it makes full use of this privilege whenever a fitting opportunity occurs. Representatives of this organisation were amongst those who presented addresses of congratulation to the King quite recently, on the occasion of Princess Mary's wedding. The remarkable part, however, about this organisation is, that the divines who took part in the ceremony are *not* Presbyterians at all, but are Unitarians. They do not represent the Presbyterian organisation, but they have inherited by virtue of an Act, passed in 1844, called the Dissenters' Chapels Act, all the property, prerogatives and rights of the ancient community whose name they perpetuate. Chief amongst these privileges is the right of direct access to the King. It dates back to the time of Charles II, when the English Presbyterians petitioned the sovereign that they should have a right of access to him, in order that they might protest against what they were pleased to regard as Roman Catholic agression. The right of access was granted to them by charter, the existence of which is accepted by the Great Officers of State, and the privilege of access was reaffirmed as lately as 1836, when the organisation had already declared its adherence to the Unitarian Communion. In many instances, however, the divines who appear before the King under this extraordinary title are the direct descendents of the original Presbyterians whose privilege they hold, and the minister who headed the deputation on the last occasion was a descendant in a direct line of seven ministers, the first of whom was a Presbyterian, although he himself, and all the brethren who accompanied him, are now Unitarians. Under somewhat the same privileges they now control Dr. Williams' Lending Library in Gordon Square which did originally appertain to them.

One of the most interesting survivals in connection with religious life, still exists in Willesden. The place was famous for the shrine of the Black Image of Our Ladye of Willesden, to which pilgrimages were made from all parts of the country. The wealth of the shrine attracted the attention of Thomas Cromwell, who ordered the image to be removed to Chelsea and burnt, and also levied a fine of 28s. 6d. upon the parish for ever, to be paid to the Crown, for being in possession of what was called " an idolatrous image." In Queen Anne's reign this charge was transferred to Queen Anne's Bounty, and one pound is still paid, so the Rev. J. Dixon, Vicar of Willesden Church informs me, as the annual fine. As a matter of fact, it is stated that the original black statue was never destroyed, although it was declared that it was burnt. It had been removed over-night, and quite another figure resembling it substituted for it. There is a statue of Our Lady now preserved in the Cistercian Monastery at Coalville in Leicestershire, which is declared to be the actual original at one time at Willesden. There is a wooden statue now in Willesden Church, which was presented by certain parishioners quite recently, and represents, to some extent, the original one.

The habit that exists, especially at country funerals, of looking into the grave at the conclusion of a funeral, is declared by the Rev. F. C. Finch to go back to the time before coffins came into ordinary use, when the mourners took a last look at the shrouded body of the deceased person, and he goes on to state that in the Anglican prayer-book it is still directed that the earth be cast upon the " body," not the coffin.

A football is still kicked down the High Street at Atherstone on Shrove Tuesday, although the game is actually illegal in the streets, and this custom, which is said to date back some seven hundred years, is also connected by local antiquaries with the performance of a miracle play.

The use of the cross remains in Hereford in two quite different connections. There is a hospital called the Red Cross, which was founded in 1614, and the persons inhabiting it were to be dressed in red cloth, lined with red baize, but the White Cross district and the White Cross Road, derive their names from a white stone cross which marks the site in the city where the market was held in 1660, while the Plague was raging within the boundaries of the place.

CHAPTER XIII

ODD HABITS AND WAYS IN COUNTRY LIFE

THE bearing of rushes in country villages, which still exists, especially round about the Lake district, is partly an ecclesiastical and partly a domestic custom. It has to do with the days when rushes were used as carpeting on the earthen floor, especially when quantities of sweet-scented rushes were needed in churches, because of the difficulties that arose from inter-mural burial, and the North-country folk, especially of Cumberland and Westmoreland, hold most tenaciously to the custom which some say goes back even to Roman times.

The children now carry large bunches of rushes and flowers into the church on the rush-bearing festival, many of the girls themselves being adorned with flowers and moss, and carrying between them a homespun linen sheet, richly decorated with flowers and filled to the brim with rushes. There are strange objects made of these plants, a rush serpent is represented on a pole, David's harp has rushes for its strings, the Hand of St. Oswald is represented in rushes, with his name and his date ; Moses is presented lying in a rush basket, and there are crosses, triangles and innumerable ecclesiastical symbols, all reminiscent of the days of mystery plays and Passion plays, made with rushes and flowers, and carried into the church, amidst a scene of great excitement on the part of the villagers.

The church also is strewn with rushes, special floral objects, notably crowns of flowers, are stood about in different parts of it, under its arches or close to its columns, and a service is conducted by the clergy of the parish dealing with the festival, and then away go the children for sports or for tea, and the customary reward given to each child connected with the ceremonial is a large slab of gingerbread. The day of the Rush-bearing is the most important in the place, and in many of the villages is kept on August 5th, the feast-day of St. Oswald, a Saint who has a particular importance in the district. In Grasmere and Warcop especially, the ceremony is a very notable one, and attracts attention from crowds of people round about, who come to view the curious customs of the people.

There is one building in London which is still floored with rushes by a habit that has survived, although the rushes now are woven into a kind of matting, but Innholders' Hall has never had carpets laid down in it, and has always been floored with rushes, according to ancient custom, and very particular are the members of the Court of the Innholders that the custom should be still carefully kept up.

Perhaps the most curious ceremony in connection with the bearing of rushes is one which occurs at Killin in Perthshire every Christmas. The church is dedicated to a well-known Gaelic saint, St. Fillan, and preserved near by it are a number of stones, large and small, worn smooth by the action of water, which are reputed to have been used by the saint, in faith cures, on the members of his congregation, as well as in curing sprains and other ills in cattle. The saint appears to have adopted some of the modern methods of massage, and to have used the stones for stroking the places that needed the cure.

Considerable importance is attached to these stones, and they are housed safely in a grated niche in the inner side of the eastern gable of an old meal mill, which is now used for handloom weaving and belongs to the Marquess of Breadalbane. Every Christmas, in accordance with an ancient tradition, these stones are put upon a fresh bed of " water-carried straws, and rushes uncut by the hand of man," and these rushes, which are torn, rather than cut, are taken to the niche, and the stones are placed upon them. The ceremony has been kept up, it is said, ever since remote times long preceding the Reformation.

Another very ancient custom is carried on at Barton-on-Humber in Yorkshire, where at Easter-time children indulge in what is known as egg-rolling, rolling eggs upon a rough ground in a particular lane, until the shells are broken, and this custom is said to arise from an ancient ceremony which took place in the mystery play of the day, and represented the rolling away of the stone of the Holy Sepulchre.

Egg-rolling also takes place at Preston on Easter Monday. The eggs are coloured, and afterwards eaten. The idea is associated with the renewal of life at Easter, symbolised by the egg, and the colour and joy of Nature's reawakening, symbolised by the colour. In Christian days, it is said that the egg-rolling had a connection typifying the rolling away of the stone from the Sepulchre. Every possible colour appears on the eggs, and some forty thousand people sometimes take part in the carnival.

A similar habit appertains to Scotland, where certainly in one village in Fifeshire there is a particular sand hillock known as " the Elders Brae " and used for rolling the eggs.

There are strange local fashions still retained in different towns, as for example the wearing of the oak-apple on May 29th, and the punishment by stinging nettles of those who dare to appear without the oak leaf,* which happens in many places, and the annual announcement in Berwick that the inhabitants had better retire within the walls of their town for fear of the Scottish invaders.

There are actually no suburbs to Berwick-on-Tweed ; it occupied a dangerous and difficult position between the two countries, being subject to attack on both sides, and the safety of the people was enforced when they kept within their walls. Even now Acts of Parliament that apply to England and Scotland specially mention the town of Berwick-upon-Tweed, as belonging to neither country, and specifically referred to, in order that the Act in question may affect the inhabitants of it.

Haggis is always specially brought from Scotland into England for the St. Andrew's Day festivities, and as the train crosses the Tweed at Berwick, a portion of the haggis is thrown into the river. The story is that when Mary Queen of Scots made her memorably rough sea journey from France to Scotland, she was offered, to her disgust, some of this dish, and indignantly ordered it to be thrown into the sea. She so resented its smell and flavour that she declared that haggis should never be allowed out of Scotland.

* Professor Reid tells me that he remembers when a boy that the engines that came into Fenchurch Street Station on Oakapple Day were all decorated with oak leaves.

When any Scotchman brings haggis out of Scotland with him, he always throws a morsel into the border river as he passes.

One of the most odd of ancient village customs is that which is still carried on at Biddendon in Kent. There were two maids, Elisa and Mary Chulkhurst, who were born some eight hundred years ago, joined together at the hips and shoulders. They lived together in this state for thirty-four years, when one of them was taken ill and died, and the survivor was at once most strongly advised to be separated from her sister by dissection. She absolutely refused, saying, "As we came together, we will also go together," and about six hours after her sister's death, she also was taken ill and died. In accordance with the regulations laid down in her will, the rent of a piece of land is used for the annual distribution of cakes of bread to strangers on Easter Monday, and of loaves with cheese, which are given away on the same day to the poor of the parish, and all these cakes and rolls bear the impress upon them, a strange archaic device, representing the two Biddendon maids.

A dancing festivity in a certain village has been revived within recent years because a certain Mr. John Mill, who for thirty years was collector at the port of St. Ives in Cornwall, made a will, by which he settled for ever upon the Mayor and residents an annuity of ten pounds, and ordered that every five years certain curious gifts should be made. These were as follows :—Five pounds equally divided was to be given to ten girls, who were not to be over ten years old, and who were to dance round his tomb for a quarter of an hour, and afterwards sing the Old Hundredth.

One pound was to be given to the fiddler who was to play on that occasion, two pounds were to be given to two widows, who were not to be less than sixty-four years old, and were to accompany the girls as chaperons. One pound was to be paid out for white ribbon for the girls, the women and the fiddler to wear. Five pounds was to be paid to the best netter of fishing nets in the village, and five pounds to the man and his wife, over sixty, who had reared to the age of ten and upwards the largest number of legitimate children, without receiving parish relief.

At the distribution last year, one of the widows was

eighty-three, and she had danced round the tomb on two previous occasions. It was difficult to decide upon the netting award, and in consequence the money was divided between two women, one of seventy, and the other of ninety-two, who were pronounced to be almost equal in skill.

There are many quaint traditions still retained in villages in relation to bees. One of these is the idea that it is right to inform the bees of the death of the bee-master, or any member of his family, and to fasten a strip of crêpe to each hive on such an occasion. Bees that are ignored on the occasion of a great joy or a great grief are said to take offence and to feel slighted, and at the earliest opportunity to forsake their masters. Old-fashioned bee-keepers invariably bear this in mind, attaching the little bit of crêpe directly after the death, to the hives, and then noticing, with a certain amount of glee, that from each hive in turn a few bees sail out to examine the crêpe with mild interest, and return to their hives, as the peasant would tell you— to inform all the rest.

There is no doubt that bees quickly get to know and to understand the character and the habits of their keepers, and I have watched a well-known bee-keeper in Sussex, pick out a handful of bees from a skep, and allow them to move about over his hands and arms, without the slightest fear of their stinging him, and he would put his ear to each hive in turn, and be able to tell by the sound whether anything was amiss, and would even, from the bench where he sat by the side of the skeps, tell me, from the colour of the bees' pollen bags, whereabouts they had been foraging.

This particular old bee-master invariably called his swarms by the old-fashioned sound of a frying-pan and a key, and many a controversy we had as to the reason for making this. Was it to set out the owner's claim ? Was it to prevent the sound of the queen's wings being heard ? Was it to warn other bee-keepers that a swarm was in progress ? Was it actually to attract the bees ? On one occasion, he had what he declared was one of the most fortunate things that could happen to any man, a swarm settling on his own neck and shoulders, and he declared that ever afterwards he was certain that prosperity would attend his efforts with his bees, because they had showed him such a marked sign of their attachment.

He was perfectly composed under what was, to me, as a boy, a rather startling ordeal, but he quickly detected the sound of the queen, picked her off, moved towards the skep, and when he had placed her, with some of the other bees, inside the skep the whole swarm gradually left him, and entered their new residence, and he was not stung.

He was just as punctilious about telling the bees of a wedding, and on the occasion of his granddaughter's wedding, brought her, after she had been married, to the bees, and announced the fact of her marriage to each hive in succession. He then fastened to each a tiny scrap of white ribbon, which the bride kissed before she handed it to him, and which, he declared, would have no advantage or information to the bees, unless she herself had marked it in this way.

I remember the anxiety of one of the bridesmaids that she should come and see the ceremony, and the old man's indignation that anybody should say a word to his bees about the marriage, or should hand the ribbon to him to attach to the hives, except the bride herself. On that occasion, he said, not even her husband was to be present, otherwise he was quite sure his bees would take offence, and on the following morning he would find these important members of his household had departed from him.

Kipling in *Puck of Pook's Hill* thus refers to this custom :

" Bees, bees ; Hark to your bees !
Hide from your neighbours as much as you please.
But all that has happened to us you must tell,
Or else we will give you no honey to sell."

Very interesting survivals in connection with village life are those which concern archery, and these are specially retained in Warwickshire. The village of Merriden in that county claims to be the very middle of all green England, and there the annual Wardmote of the Woodmen of Arden is kept up, in the fashion in which it has been held since 1785, except for two years during the war. The existence of the Woodmen of Arden belongs to a period very much more remote, however, than 1785. There have always been a group of these woodmen in existence, but it was not until the eighteenth century that they consolidated the rights and privileges belonging to various groups of wood-men into one society, and called it the Woodmen of Arden. The costume which the archers used to wear in the old days, green coats with gilt buttons and white trousers, was then adopted, and this uniform is still retained.

There is a competition every August, and a series of archery contests, the principal prize being a silver bugle horn, and the arrows are fired from long bows, about six feet in length, and of very much the same character as those that were used with such excellent effect at Agincourt and Crecy. A great portion of the yew from which the Agin-court and Crecy bows were made came from the yew forests in Surrey close to Merrow, now known as Fairyland. The yew-trees there are of very great antiquity, and some of them have even been stated, without, I am afraid, much authority, to go back to early British and Druidical times ; but it is quite certain that many of the bows used by the King's bowmen came from this district, because it is specifically referred to in the Exchequer records of the period as supplying the yew bows for the King's bowmen.

The winner of the bugle at the annual archery contest has to present a purse of shillings to the woman who had received his particular number in a draw which takes place earlier in the day, and this woman has the privilege of opening the ball at Woodman's Hall in the evening, with the winner of the bugle. The arrows which are used on this occasion are still marked in the manner which goes back to mediæval times, according to their weight in silver money, so that upon them would be stamped such figures as 4s. 6d. or 3s. 9d., which marks their weight in this ancient system.

The winner has his health proposed by the head marker, who wears a wonderful gold-banded top hat, green coat, white waistcoat and breeches, white stockings and low shoes, and he has to place a sovereign in a tumbler full of port, and then, drinking down till there is about a table-spoonful, has the duty of drawing the sovereign underneath his tongue. The present head marker has performed this ceremony for some thirty years, his ancestors for three or four generations were markers and makers of bows and arrows, and he is still in the same trade.

Another curious custom in connection with this society

is that toasts are proposed by the Warden, who at present is the Earl of Aylesford, and who has been a Woodman for fifty years, always beginning, " Mr. Adams and Brother Woodmen," although there is no Mr. Adams now present. The Vice-chairman of the society, when it was reconstituted in 1785, was a Mr. Adams, and if any of his descendants bearing his name becomes a Woodman, he is by right the Vice-chairman.

Archery has still been kept up in London, for the ancient society called the Finsbury Archers, and the Archers' Company of the Honourable Artillery Company, have never actually ceased to exist, and the latter still possesses a large silver shield, presented to them by Queen Catherine of Braganza, and many prize arrows of that period, and of an earlier one still ; but in 1781, the Royal Toxophilite Society came into existence, for the special purpose of bringing together those who were still interested in archery, and giving them a permanent home.

In 1832, a site was granted to this Society in Regent's Park, where the Archers' Hall was built, and until 1922 this important site remained in possession of the Society, and in the Archers' Hall were preserved the shield and arrows with numerous other mementoes connected with toxophilite contests, and many treasures that had been presented to the Society by different members. Lately, the Commissioners of Works required the ground for other purposes, and, after their very long tenure, the members of the Royal Toxophilite Society were driven out of their ancient premises, and accepted the hospitality of the Honourable Artillery Company, returning to land which had been, from almost time immemorial, used in connection with archery. To the premises which have been considerately lent to them by the Honourable Artillery Company, it is presumed they will presently remove their various treasures.

In Edinburgh the Company of Royal Archers still forms the most aristocratic of all regiments, and retaining their old green uniform and carrying their bows and arrows they claim the right of being the bodyguard to the Sovereign whenever he visits Holyrood. Admission to this favoured regiment is eagerly sought and a place in its ranks regarded as a position of great honour.

The name of Newington Butts, near London, reminds us that the land was once a vacant space set aside for the archery practice of the London train-bands.

Two strings to one's bow is a phrase that belongs to the days of archery. An archer would naturally have a spare string in his pouch, in case of accident, and the phrase has survived into modern use, although archery is no longer a form of warfare, and in fact even as an amusement or recreation is seldom alluded to at the present day save in the district mentioned, and in the Royal Toxophilite Society.

Lady Wolseley* has drawn attention to many survivals in the names of special days, which the peasantry still remember by their own old Catholic terms. " Collop Monday," for example, is the day preceding Shrove Tuesday, when pieces of meat called collops were salted, in pre-Reformation times, to hang till after Lent. Mothering Sunday, or Refreshment Sunday, is a day in the middle of Lent, when a certain amount of relaxation from the rigidity of Lenten habits was allowed, and when it was customary for visits to be paid to the mother of the family. These visits were accompanied by certain presents of cakes still known in some districts as Simnel cakes, a word derived from the name given to fine wheat flour.

Fig Sunday is an old name for Palm Sunday, and in commemoration of the story in the New Testament of the withering of the fig-tree, it has been the custom, from time immemorial, in some country districts to eat fig puddings on that day. By the way, caring " not a fig " for a person has nothing whatever to do with figs, but comes from an obsolete word in Italian patois, " fico," which implies a snap of the fingers. Plough Monday, the first Monday after Twelfth Day, is still the day for commencing ploughing in many districts. It is customary in some places on Twelfth Night to light twelve different bonfires, one very large one which commemorates the Christ, and one very small one, which commemorates Judas, and which it is the habit of the villagers, soon after it has been lighted, to stamp out, as a mark of their reprobation. The custom of rushing through the flames and escaping unscathed is probably of even more remote origin, and perhaps is a relic of Baal worship or Druidic custom.

* See her most interesting volume called *Countryman's Log-Book*.

Candlemas Day, when the lights are put on the altar, is still a festival carefully remembered in Scotland, although not so much known in England, but Candlemas term is a customary phrase in the north. Woolsack Day is another name for the feast of St. Blaise, and there are many persons who still invoke the assistance of St. Blaise in the case of throat difficulty, especially with regard to a bone having fastened itself in the throat, when St. Blaise is called upon to move it up or down. Blaise was the patron saint of the Woolcombers, and his initial is still marked on sacks of wool in some parts of the country.

The reference to the invocation of St. Blaise reminds me that, although invocations to the saints were regarded in the time of the Reformation as idolatrous and superstitious, and were done away with, especially in oaths, yet in one case, in the City of London, the invocation still continues, and the Master of the Merchant Taylors' Company, in taking his oath on St. John the Baptist's Day, still specifically invokes the assistance of that great Saint, in ancient and customary form, and the Masters of this great Company have so invoked the assistance of St. John the Baptist for many hundreds of years.

It has been pointed out, as an instance of the survival of names and customs, that some property in North Lincolnshire is known as the Hoodlands, and that tossing and various rough games take place at the village near by called Haxey, in commemoration of the fact that many hundreds of years ago a certain Lady Mowbray lost her hood in that piece of ground, and that the men of the village rescued it and brought it to her, when in gratitude she gave the land to the village, and her memory has been kept up ever since.

Some villages in England, I am told, still have an ecclesiastical official known as the " Cock-crower," whose duty it was, in the time of miracle plays, to cry the note of the cock, when the denial of St. Peter was commemorated, and although the symbolism has ceased, and the village mystery play has vanished, there are, I believe, two villages in Lincolnshire in which the cock-crower still exists. There was a Cock-crower at Court, down to the time of George II, and his habit was to sound the cry of this bird during Lent. George II did not understand the reason of the custom, and declared that the man's action was an insult to him, and it is said that this remark of the King caused the abolition of an old position, which had been in existence at Windsor for some hundreds of years.

Curious survivals remain in several of the almshouses of the country, in which the gowns worn by the bedesmen have to be of a particular colour, or are adorned with special ornaments, having reference to the founder. For example, in the Leycester Hospital at Warwick, the Brethren wear blue gowns with a silver badge, on which is the crest of the bear and the ragged staff, the armorial achievement of Robert Dudley, Earl of Leicester, who in 1571 converted the property of the dissolved guilds of the Holy Trinity, the Virgin and St. George the Martyr, into a hospital or asylum for twelve indigent men, and the representative of the founder, who now happens to be Lord De L'Isle and Dudley, still presents to the position of Master of this Hospital. Originally the Brethren had to be either tenants or retainers of the founder or of his heirs, or soldiers, especially wounded men, from certain Warwickshire and Gloucestershire parishes, and this latter clause proved, in these days that have followed the Great War, to be a very convenient one, enabling those who had to appoint the Brethren to make an easier choice.

In Guildford, in Surrey, bedesmen who reside at the Hospital of the Blessed Trinity, founded by George Abbot, Archbishop of Canterbury, a native of the town, wear blue gowns, adorned with silver mitres, as arranged by the founder, but at the time that Abbot lived, there was an important cloth industry existing in Guildford, and Guildford blue cloth was well known all over Europe. It was dark blue cloth of a fine quality that was especially in use amongst divines. A great deal of it was sent out to the Genevan clergy, and there is a specimen of it still to be seen in the museum at Zurich. Abbot assisted this manufactory, and one of his bequests was especially known as the Manufactory Loan. He ordered that the blue gowns to be worn by the bedesmen should always be made of " Guildford cloth." As, however, the manufacture has now entirely ceased, the only thing that the Governors can do is to procure cloth of something the same quality, and as near as possible the same colour as was the old Guildford cloth.

Some evidence of the existence of this manufactory still exists in the fact that the woad plant, *isatis tinctoria*, from which blue dye was extracted for the purpose, grows in the immediate neighbourhood of Guildford, in places where it was for a long time most carefully cultivated. It is a rare plant in England, but there are many places in the neighbourhood of that ancient town where it can still be found. The teazle, which was also used in connection with the cloth industry, also still grows in the neighbourhood, and a part of the river close to where the factory was situated, is spoken of in old days as " the fulling stream." Moreover, a piece of vacant land is still known as " Racks Close," from the large wooden racks which were originally put up in it, on which the cloth was hung out to dry.

It is interesting to notice that in the Leicester almshouses the badges worn by the Brethren are the identical ones that were worn by the first bedesmen who resided in the almshouses, and that the names of these original holders of the badges are still to be found engraved upon the badges, with the date 1571.

An old custom is still kept up in Scotland, where the first bird killed at an important shooting party is handed to the sportsman who was responsible for its death, that he might pluck a feather from it, and fasten it in his cap, and we still retain the phrase that such and such an honour or distinction is a feather in a person's cap, going back to the days of chivalry, when the knight received his helmet without any plumes, and won his plumes singly, as he won his spurs.

In early days in Hungary, it was a habit that no soldier should wear a feather but he who had killed a Turk, and the number of feathers in a Hungarian soldier's cap denoted the number of Turks he had killed. This custom was kept up till quite recent times in the Hungarian regiments, that only those who had fought against the Turks and had been successful, were allowed to have their standards crowned with feathers, and the same crowning belongs to one of the Austrian regiments, and to one that was raised in Poland, because both were successful, with John Sobieski, in driving the Turk away from Vienna.

On the anniversary of the raising of the siege of Vienna the plumes of feathers that commemorate the event are taken to the church of St. Stephen in that city, to be solemnly sprinkled with holy water.

Many curious country life customs yet remain in use in the county of Cheshire, and one of the most interesting is the practice of what is known as " sanding," which is carried on at Knutsford. No one can tell exactly the origin of this custom. It has been stated that the streets were always swept in front of the door of the bride's house, on the occasion of a wedding, and that some clever person once decorated his doorway with a sprinkling of clean sand of various colours, and that from that time till now, the habit has been adopted in Knutsford of sprinkling the doorways and streets with sand and dust which now takes the form of various devices.

It has been suggested by certain writers on Knutsford that this custom is one of considerable antiquity, and akin to the Egyptian one of placing a coffin in the middle of a banquet, to remind men of their mortality. Mr. Green, the historian of Knutsford, suggests that very possibly there was some early intention to teach that in the moments of the greatest joy we are but dust, and to dust shall our bodies return. Whatever may be its origin, it has existed in the little town of Knutsford for a very long time, and delightful devices are formed on the doorsteps of the houses, and even in the streets, with different coloured sand. The coloured sand is allowed to trickle through a funnel, so that inscriptions and emblems can be represented with it. On occasions of important festivity, the whole of the streets are decorated with white and brown sand, and the town affords an exceptionally pretty sight.

This is not, however, the oldest custom that is associated with Knutsford, because there is still the habit of people " going souling " as it is termed, on All Souls' Eve, when the girls wander round from house to house, singing a strange ballad, part of which runs " Soul, Soul, Soul, for a soul-cake pray you, good mistress, a soul-cake."

A certain kind of cake, rather resembling a bun, is still given away in certain houses in Cheshire on All Souls' Eve, and the practice of course goes back to early Catholic times, and is closely connected with the prayers and feasts which took place on the occasion of All Souls' Eve.

The same begging for "Soul-cakes" takes place in Chester on All Souls' Eve, and it is interesting to notice that the city retains one of the few remaining evidences of the existence of a miracle play, in the fact that playing at ball inside the Cathedral takes place once a year.

In Ledbury, on Palm Sunday, the churchwardens present to the clergyman and the congregation a small cake, which is known in the place as the "Sin-eating Cake," and which is declared to be evidence of a desire on the part of the people to cease from that moment from all enmities and to prepare for the Easter festival. In the same town, it used to be the custom when a corpse was brought out and laid on the bier, that a bowl made of maple wood was filled with beer and was drunk up by a person called the "Sin-eater," who, by this action, became a sort of scape-goat, and took upon himself the sins of the dead person, so as to free him from any excuse for walking about the place as a ghost after his decease. It is said that the habit is also known amongst the Tartars.

Another strange custom is still kept up in Cheshire, known as "lifting," and this is a very ancient habit. We are told that in 1290, Edward I paid a sum of money to the ladies of the bed-chamber and the maids of honour, for having at Easter taken their Sovereign Lord while he was in his bed, and complied with the usual practice of giving him a heaving or lifting, that is of raising him symbolically towards Heaven, emblematic of the rising of Our Lord, which took place at Easter time. Even now, this lifting habit is adopted on Easter Monday and on Tuesday, and those who are lifted present a gift to the members of their household who take part in the ceremony, and so keep up this curious old custom, which amongst the working classes of the district is always known as "heaving."

The festivals that were common in England in connection with May Day, and which are still kept up in so many places, have their origin in remote Roman times, for Virgil speaks of the Roman youths dancing and singing in honour of Flora in the Kalends of May.

Flora's festival, the Floralia, lasted for six days, from what we might call April 28 to May 3, and was characterised by excessive merriment.

"Jack-in-the-Green," which is carried about in certain

villages on May day, was, of course, a survival of the floral ceremonies, and there are a few villages where dancing round the maypole is still kept up.

In Minehead, on May day, the fishermen make a cardboard ship ten feet long, the sails trimmed with flags and ribbons. This is carried on a man's shoulders, and to the end of the ship is fastened a cow's tail. People who do not give largesse to the bearers of the ship are threatened with a beating with the cow's tail. The origin is said to date back to the beginning of the eighteenth century, when a ship was sunk off the coast and all hands lost, the only survivor being a cow.

At Saltash there is the survival of a heathen rite, intended to scare away demons from the houses. The children gather all the kettles, scuttles, tea-trays and pails, and drag them about in the evening, in and out of all the nooks and corners of the parish.

At Padstow, a hobby horse is dipped into the water, and with the water the spectators are sprinkled.

At Polperro, thorn blossoms and baskets are dipped in the water, and the persons who do not wear the white thorn blossoms receive an additional amount of the water sprinkled upon them.

There is a maypole in the village of Temple Sowerby in Westmoreland, and the Lord of the Manor has still the duty of providing a new one in the centre of the green, whenever the old one decays. There was a maypole in London, near to the spot now occupied by the church of St. Mary-le-Strand, and a part of an ancient one removed from there is said still to exist at Wanstead, having at one time been in the possession of Sir Isaac Newton and used in connection with the supports for his great telescope at Wanstead Park.

There are maypoles still standing in Wellow, Redmore, Hemwell, Welford, Donnington, and Preston Brockenhurst.

One of the most beautiful old customs that remains in England is in connection with what is known as " well-dressing " in the village of Tissington. On Holy Thursday, the five wells of the village, known as Holy Well, Coffin Well (from its shape), Hand's Well (from its owners centuries ago), the Town Well and the Yew Tree Well, are all decorated with much elaboration, flowers, berries, lichens and mosses being fixed to frames filled with layers of clay, so as to produce, in a kind of mosaic work, very intricate designs, and even pictures. After service in church, each well is visited in turn, and the Collects of the Day are said, appropriate psalms chanted, hymns sung, and a suitable Gospel read.

The origin of this interesting ceremony is declared to go back to the period of the Black Death (1348-49), when, out of a hundred and eight beneficed clergy in Derbyshire, seventy-seven died, and Tissington alone, of all the villages round about, escaped the ravages of the plague. The deliverance of the parishioners, Dr. Cox, the historian of Derbyshire, states, was ascribed to the special mercy of God, and the peculiar purity and abundance of the water supplying the village, and when the plague died out in 1350, on Ascension Day, the first festival was held, and it has been kept up ever since.

The Tissington water is certainly of peculiar purity, it comes from a very considerable depth, and is always of the same temperature, 47° Fahrenheit, both in winter and in summer.

In Lichfield there takes place, on September 8, the feast of the Nativity of the Blessed Virgin, an interesting ceremonial known as the " Sheriff's Ride." The Sheriff of the city perambulates the boundaries of " the city and county of Lichfield and the precincts thereof," accompanied by his officers, making temporary halts at various places which have always received this particular distinction. The perambulation is undertaken in virtue of a charter of Charles II, dated November 5, 1664, by which it is declared that the Bailiff and Brethren of Lichfield shall annually on the feast of St. James, July 25, elect any one of the citizens and inhabitants of the city (not being already one of the Brethren), to serve the office of the Sheriff of the city and county of Lichfield. If he refuses to serve, they have power, at their discretion, to fine him, to commit him to prison till the fine is paid, and to exclude him from all the privileges of the city, but if he serves, he is bound, under pain of " fine and amerciaments at the direction of that body," to perambulate the boundaries of the place, and this custom has been kept up since 1664, and is still observed with full accompanying ceremonial.

It is curious to remember that one of the most celebrated packs of fox-hounds in the country, that belonging to the Duke of Beaufort, was originally established for stag-hunting, and that its existence as a fox-hunting pack is a survival from an episode which took place in 1786. The then Duke of Beaufort had a most disappointing day's sport, and was leading his hounds back to their kennels, when the huntsman suggested that, for a change, they might be turned into a neighbouring covert. They searched one close at hand, quickly found a fox, and hunted him until the fall of night, with a satisfactory result. The Duke was so pleased with the run that he ceased to hunt the stag, and the Duke of Beaufort's hounds have been fox-hounds ever since.

There are several provincial survivals that may well be mentioned in this chapter. For example, since 1106 the burgesses of the town of Maldon have been exempted by charter from service on any jury outside the town and the borough. During last year, six were summoned to serve on the jury at Chelmsford Assizes, and the Mayor, Recorder and Town Clerk appeared before the Judge, produced the original charter and its confirmation made by George III in 1801, and in consequence the Maldon jurors were excused from attendance. It is stated that exactly the same privilege belongs to the inhabitants of Guildford, who cannot be summoned on the juries of any of the Assizes, even though they may be held in the town, and are never summoned to serve on juries outside the boundaries of their own borough.

A curious custom in Ludlow is that children suffering from whooping-cough are taken to the Castle, and if an echo is awakened by the child's voice, it is said that the cure will at once be effected.

In Leeds there is a street called Swinegate, the name having been derived from Sweyn, the father of King Canute, and it is said that from his time down to 1839 the inhabitants of Leeds were obliged to have their corn ground in the mills that were the property of the Crown. In 1839 the Corporation of Leeds paid over some thirteen thousand pounds to the then owner of the mills, in order to end the demand which had existed from Anglo-Saxon times.

In Lancaster the newly elected Mayor proceeds to the

Castle, and takes an oath before the Steward of the Duchy to conform faithfully to every ancient custom according to the best of his knowledge, and the Great Mace is lowered to the slope, as a token of acknowledgment to the power at one time held by the Dukes of Lancaster in the Castle.

In Winchester bull-baiting existed down to quite recent times, and in Hereford down to 1835. In Winchester the bull was baited before the Mayor's door, but later on at the bull ring, and the bull ring still remains in its place. It can also be seen both at Hereford and at Appleby.

In Canterbury the Mayor's wife has to be provided by the Mayor with a scarlet gown, and this habit has existed since 1556 ; if the gown is not provided, the Mayor is subject to a fine of ten pounds.

One of the most remarkable of old ceremonies takes place at Kirkby Ravensworth in Westmoreland, and was instituted in the time of Philip and Mary, when John Dakyn was the Rector. The method of selecting the Wardens of the important charity which Dakyn established in the village is very strange and differs from every other ceremony of the sort. The Vicar goes into the upper room of the almshouse, followed by six of his " gravest and honestest parishioners " nominated by himself and the churchwardens, and there he presides over the election of two out of the six. The six persons are each supplied with a piece of paper bearing their name. This is wrapped in a piece of brown paper, and handed to the village cobbler, who, with cobbler's wax kneads each packet into a warm ball of shiny wax. These balls are dropped into an earthenware pot which is full of water. One candidate stirs them briskly round, and puts the lid on the pot. The Vicar then removes the lid, takes out two of the balls, and puts them on the table, and as the water has made the wax brittle, it is easy to open the balls by a blow from the cobbler's hammer, and to reveal the names of the two persons who are to be Wardens of the Almshouses for the ensuing two years. These men then have to take a solemn oath for the performance of their duty, and they receive a fee of twenty shillings each, but that is only payable on the day that they cease to be wardens at the end of their two years of office. The four balls that are not broken up are considered to hold names which cannot be submitted again for four years, and the persons bearing these names are, according to this quaint deed of establishment, to be " expecting their election of chance with a contented mind, and without grumbling." The names of the unsuccessful persons are unknown, for the pot is shut up in the great muniment chest, with its three locks, locked with different keys, and the balls are only broken up immediately before the next election, when the names come to light. This curious system was established by Dakyn in 1556 ; it has to take place on the Feast of the Decollation of St. John Baptist, and it concerns the almshouses and the school which he established, " desiring now at last to pull in the reins of my youth, and to be conducted into the harbour of eternal rest."*

* I am indebted for the information concerning the Dakyn trustees to a local correspondence which appeared some time ago in the *Times*.

CHAPTER XIV

COMMERCE AND COSTUME

THERE are interesting survivals in connection with commercial life, coinage and banking. I referred in the preface to this volume to the use of the word guinea, and to its survival for reckoning professional fees although it is no longer in circulation as a coin.

There are two explanations of the origin of the coin. It is said that it was first coined in 1663, from gold imported from the Guinea coast by a company of merchants trading under a special charter granted by the Crown, and again its origin is dated three years later, when there was a great capture of Dutch sailing vessels, which contained bullion and gold dust from Guinea, and it is said that this was coined into gold pieces stamped with an elephant, called guineas to commemorate the capture. Certainly, some of the early guineas did bear a representaton of an elephant on one side.

It seems that pieces were issued for one guinea, five guineas, two guineas, and half a guinea. When first circulated, the guinea was only worth twenty shillings, but gradually the silver coinage deteriorated, and the guinea in 1694 was said to be worth thirty shillings. It fell to twenty-one shillings and sixpence in 1698, and to twenty-one shillings in 1717, retaining that value until it disappeared entirely from the coinage. The last guineas coined bear the date of 1813. Four years later the sovereign was coined, and the guinea was superseded, but it being worth a little more than the sovereign, it has been retained for professional fees, even though for over a hundred years there has been no coin to represent it.

Perhaps one of the most interesting guineas now in existence is to be seen in the Coin Room in the British Museum, and has a note attached to it, in the handwriting of Sir William Pulteney, to this effect :—

" This guinea I desire to be kept as an heirloom. It was won of Sir Robert Walpole in the House of Commons, he asserting the phrase in Horace to be ' nulli pallescere culpae ' whereas I laid a wager of a guinea that it was ' nulla pallescere culpâ.' He sent for the book, and being convinced that he had lost, gave me this guinea. I told him that I could take the money without any blush on my side, but believed it was the only money given in that House where the giver and receiver ought not equally to blush. This guinea, I hope, will prove to my posterity the use of knowing Latin, and encourage them in their learning."

The circumstances were that, in February, 1741, Sir Robert, who was accused of misdemeanour, made in his speech a long quotation from Horace to which Pulteney replied that the right honourable gentleman's language and Latin were equally inaccurate. Then ensued the bet, Walpole lost the day, tossed the guinea across the Clerk's table to Pulteney, who caught it, and held it up to the House, exclaiming, " It is the only money I have received from the Treasury for many years, and it shall be the last."

It will be remembered that Walpole himself said that he feared Pulteney's tongue more than any other man's sword.

The word " bank " we obtain from the Italian " banco," a table. The money-changers used to count out their money on such a table or bench, and when a man was unable to pay his way, and had got into disgrace, his bench, which was his counter, was broken up, and he was spoken of as " banco rotto," that is to say bankrupt. A great many of our modern transactions in banking date back to the days of the Medici family, who were the great financiers in Italy, and were the first to make a regular habit of advancing money upon pledges, hence it is that the three balls, which form the principal portion of their heraldic achievement, still hang over the door of the modern pawnbroker.

The memory of the fact that we derive so many of our banking ideas from Italy is perpetuated in the name of Lombard Street, denoting the district whence the early banking merchants came ; it is still more closely perpetuated in a strange characteristic of the Bank of England note.

The ordinary observer would almost certainly declare that the whole of the matter on the Bank of England five-pound note was printed in English, but he would be wrong, for the phrase concerning the Governor and Company of the Bank of England, contains "Cia," the abbreviation of "compagnia," instead of "company," the "ia" forming the evidence of its Italian origin.

The continued use of the letters "L.s.d." points back to the use of Latin words for what we now term the sovereign, the shilling and the penny, Libra, Solidus and Denarius.

The pass-books are so called because of the habit of the customers in the old days of banking of examining and passing, or *allowing* the account in which they were interested. At as late a period as 1715, this phrase appears at the end of many of the accounts in the oldest banking house in London, that kept by Messrs. Child & Co., "I allow, or pass, this account," The word itself has an Italian origin, and a similar word, *passare*, is now applied in Italy to current money.

The very odd use in a slang phrase of the word "tin" for money, reminds us of the existence of the valuable metal which England produced, the source of considerable wealth to the district in which it was found.

It has been suggested that there is a connection between the word "cash" and the name of the Tin Islands "Cassiterides," but it is generally believed that the word is derived from a Latin root, which implies to hold or contain, and that the word we now give to coin was originally applied to the box in which coin was kept, the cashier being more strictly the person who keeps the box for the money than he who actually holds the money. The words cask or case show the same origin; we also get casement and capsule and many other words from the same source. The French call a case a "casse."

Boodle, a slang phrase for money, is more strictly applied to money used for bribery or graft. The word boodle is a term of contempt.

Brass, another phrase, arises of course from the metal of which coins were composed (see St. Matt. x. 9). Spondulicks and oof I do not pretend to explain.

With regard to the origin of "spondulix," Mr. Brownson

has, however, suggested that the word was derived from the word " spondio " " I promise," which was always in use in the Roman market, and which emphasised the bargain. It is stated that the use of the word " spondio," in order to make a bargain quite certain, is still in practice in Italy.

Mr. J. Cohen has stated that in his opinion the expression " oof " was a corruption of the sentence " Auf dem Tisch," that is to say, " on the table," and he adds that the phrase is still in use in Germany in playing poker, where the bets are placed clearly before the players on the table. He says that the word should not be " oof " but " ooftisch."

Child's Bank retain one or two curious habits which are peculiar to that bank. For example, they still call their bank a shop, reminding those who enter it that the business commenced as that of a goldsmith, who, after a while, kept what are termed " running cashes," and took charge of the money for his customers, but who for a considerable time carried out the work of a goldsmith. Messrs. Child's books contain references to payment by customers for gold and silver cups, bowls and cisterns, and in many instances the ledgers give the actual designs for the cups. The back part of the banking house is still called the counting-house, this term also originating with the business of the goldsmith, but one of the most remarkable customs in connection with this bank is that all the clerks become partners in order of seniority, and this, Mr. Hilton Price— who wrote the history of *The Marygold at Temple Bar*— says originated in the apprentice to the goldsmith, having served his full articles, being taken into the firm in partnership with his master, and when banks discontinued having apprentices, that is to say, when they left off their goldsmiths' trade, the clerks who had risen from being juniors became head clerks, and eventually partners.

This custom has been steadily kept up since the seventeenth century, and continued down to 1924. Child's have also another strange old custom, by which three junior partners and two salaried partners take it in turns to sleep at the bank every night, so that it is never left, except in the evenings, without a partner being on the premises, in case he should at any moment be required. Amongst the pieces of silver which Child's Bank as goldsmiths delivered is a celebrated cistern, having a capacity of fifty-two gallons,

which was sold to the Earl of Rutland in 1682, and is still
in the possession of the present Duke. It is large enough
to hold three or four children, and the four children of the
present Duke, when he was Marquess of Granby, were
photographed sitting within it.*

It was Child's Bank that first introduced printed promis-
sory notes, really very similar to a modern cheque, and they
had the same representation of Temple Bar upon them that
appears on the cheques of the present day. It was an
undertaking on the part of Francis Child to pay a definite
sum, and it was practically like a bank note, and was
cancelled by tearing off part of the signature in exactly the
same way as the Bank of England at the present day cancels
its notes.

In that connection, it may be interesting to remember that
the Bank of England does not re-issue any of its own notes,
and a new note taken out on one side of the bank, if paid
into an account on the other side, has its career of circulation cut exceedingly short, because it goes out no more
and its number and history are at once recorded. These
records about every bank note are kept for a considerable
time, so that all the details concerning a bank note issued
by the Bank of England can be looked up at any time, and
a full history of its movements given so far as it bears upon
its own surface any proof of such movements. The actual
bank notes themselves are destroyed after a certain number
of years, but the story of all the bank notes, the life history,
it may be termed, is retained and is often most important
for reference.

For a long time Child's Bank was not in the habit of
allowing any interest for money on deposit, it is only comparatively recently that they have altered their custom in
that respect. It has been said that the ancestor of one of
the customers of the bank, only a hundred years ago, went
to various banks to consult them upon what terms they
would take his money. They were all anxious to accommo-
date him, and offered varying rates of interest, but the
reply he received at Child's was, " We shall be happy to

---

* It is to be feared that some of these old and interesting customs
may soon disappear, because owing to Lord Jersey's long minority,
the Bank has been swallowed up by Messrs Glyn & Co. and has to a
certain extent lost its original identity.

take care of your money for you, but we shall not give you
any interest at all upon it," and this reply seems so thoroughly to have pleased the customer, that he opened an
account forthwith, and his descendants still bank with
the old firm.

Child's and Hoare's are the only two banks now remaining
of the various banking houses mentioned in the London
Directory of 1677, still carrying on business under the
same name. There were at one time four of them, but
now Messrs. Martin, who traded in the seventeenth century
at the Grasshopper in Lombard Street, have become
absorbed with the Bank of Liverpool, and Stock's, who
were in business at the Black Horse in Lombard Street,
and whose successors were Messrs. Barnett and Hoare, have
lost all their identity in Lloyd's Bank.

Child's* and Hoare's still continue, the one at the Marygold, the other at the Leather Bottle, and of the two,
Child's is much the earlier. Sir Francis Child, whom
Pennant calls the father of the profession, is said to have
been the first goldsmith to lay aside the legitimate goldsmith's trade and become a banker.

Many of our words in connection with finance were more
or less derived from French and Italian sources. The
words " debt " and " debtor," " debenture," " credit "
and " creditor," which we get from the same root as we get
the words " creed " and " grant " ; " cash " ; " ledger,"
which simply means a book which is always lying open in
which to make an entry ; " diary " and " journal," which
have each the same meaning, are all words from foreign
sources. " Shilling " is a very odd word to apply to a coin ;
it really means the division of money into small parts,
coming from a word meaning " to divide," and is not actually
the name of a coin at all, but is a reference to money having
been made up in small form.

It must not be forgotten that the word " sterling " applied
to money, comes down to us from the Hanseatic League,
which had an important House in England. The Englishmen called its members the " Easterlings," because their
land lay " to the east of England," and hence the money
they paid was known as " Easterling money" and thence,
by an easy arrangement, the word became " sterling."

* In name certainly.

It was gold, very welcome in England in those days, and in return for gold the merchants were allowed important and highly valued trading privileges.

Professor Barnard* and Dr. David Smith† have both pointed out how the very work of counting or keeping accounts involves survivals from early days. The abacus, which is still used for children learning to count, and which nowadays consists of a series of strings or wires with balls upon them, is of remote antiquity, for as early as the twelfth century we are told that the Chinese had in use rods of sliding beads for the purpose of computing.

The phrase " abacus " itself goes back to the time when a board was used, covered with a thin coat of dust, whence the Semitic " abq," dust, gives us the origin of the name, and upon such a board, with a stylus, it was possible to write, and the figures could easily be erased. Our " blackboard " is a descendant of this type of abacus, which, amongst the Greeks and Romans, took the form of a wax tablet which could be written upon.

Horace speaks of the schoolboy with his bag and tablet, the tablet being probably covered with wax, and there are many references in classical authorities, such as those in Juvenal and Cæsar, to brass counters, in use for computing, and handled loosely or strung upon wires or rods. The common Roman name for these counters, Dr. Smith‡ says, was " calculi," the word being a diminutive of calx, a piece of limestone, the word from which we take our word " chalk." The " calculus " was therefore really a marble, and as these calculi were used in numerical work, we speak still of the " calculus," a branch of higher mathematics, and we use the word " calculate " for computing.

A boy in the sixteenth century who understood the use of the abacus, was said to know the lines, and the same sort of phrase still exists in modern school life. The counters were cast, it is pointed out, or thrown upon the computing board, and so, in mediæval times, they were spoken of as projectiles, from the Latin word meaning to throw ahead, and then, in translating from the French, we dropped the prefix, leaving only the word " jectile," which became

* See *The Casting Counter* and *The Counting Board.*
† See *Computing Jetons.*
‡ *Ibid.*

presently "jeton," with different variations, but we still speak of "casting up the account," going back to the days when the counter was actually thrown upon the computing board.

In the same way, we retain the use of the word "exchequer," because of the chequered board, or cloth in patterns of chequers, similar to that of a modern chessboard, upon which the computations were originally made. A jeweller makes use in his weights of the term "carat," which is derived from an Arabic word for a pod or a husk or seed, which had a certain definite weight, and became a unit of weight ; it is supposed to have been a part of the seed of the locust tree.

The word "cheque-book," one of the most familiar of commercial terms, comes to us in a curiously roundabout way. Skeat points out that the game of chess was one of considerable antiquity, and that from the Persian words used in this game we derive the expressions we use in the present day in connection with it. He traces it backward to a word meaning "to stop," and adds that the word "mate" used in connection with the game is the Persian word "dead," and the Persian expression "Shah mat," that is to say, "The King is dead," gives us our modern phrase, "The King is mate."

The squares of the game became known as "checkers," and we derive our phrase "Board of Exchequer" from similar checkers used in counting and reckoning, and our word "cheque," which Skeat declares is spelled in a pedantic fashion with the "q," from the word from the same origin, but it really implies an order for which we have a check or stop, that is to say, a counterfoil, by which, if necessary, we could stop its payment, so that, strictly speaking, the cheque is *not* the slip of paper which now passes by that name, but the counterfoil in the book, which is retained.

Other curious words used in connection with trades refer to the fact that they were at one time carried on in domestic life by women. We speak of a spinster as the person who spun for the household, but we are apt to forget that webster, saltster, brewster, even shepster (which is in use in parts of the country), all refer to branches of domestic industry regarded exclusively as women's work.

The phrase " a baker's dozen " takes us back to an old and constantly recurring difficulty as to short weight in bread, and the provision made specially in the City of London, that an extra piece of bread should be given in, in order that there might be no possibility of the weight being insufficient. In consequence, twelve with an extra piece were known as the baker's dozen, and at the present day we still speak of thirteen as a baker's dozen.

Why we double the final " er " in the word " fruiterer " is not clear, there is no particular reason for doing so, and the Scottish people, more correctly, say a fruiter. Other words in connection with trade, which have altered their meaning very much, are the names of three wines, claret, port and sherry. The word claret has nothing to do with the colour, although we do term a colour claret from the colour of the wine, but the word itself simply means clarified, *claretus*, and we retain that use when we speak of a clarified thing. Port is of course an abbreviation of the name of Oporto, from which district the wine came, and sherry an English transliteration of the Portuguese word Xeres, again the origin of the wine itself.

The double X which appears on barrels is probably the sign of the ten-shilling duty that was at one time demanded. In connection with another trade, we retain a name which takes us back to the days of tapestry : we still speak of a " paper-hanger." The original coverings for the wall of a room were known as the hangings, and were of tapestry or needlework. Presently, paper was introduced in lieu of these hangings, and as it was impossible, from the very nature of things, that it should be so put up, it was attached to the wall. We still, however, call the person who puts up the paper the paper-hanger, and the dealer in wall-paper declares that he deals in paper-hangings. It is said that the origin of the phrase " where one hangs out," applied by men to their apartments, goes back to the same origin.

There are but few of the signs formerly used over shops that remain in the present day ; the barber's pole with its brass basin is one which can however still be noticed, and reminds us of the days when barbers were surgeons, and blood-letting a part of their duty. It was on the pole that the patient put his hand when he stretched out his arm for the process of blood-letting, the basin, with its circular opening, fitting round the arm and receiving the blood, the strips of blue and white around the pole typifying the bandages placed round the arm after the operation was over.

With regard to another trade, that of the dealer in skins, we retain the old phrase "a fellmonger," taking us back to Anglo-Saxon and Danish words which imply a skin. The same suffix appears in connection with wood and with iron ; we speak of woodmongers, of ironmongers and of costermongers, that is to say, persons who traffic or deal in a variety of things, more or less connected with the trade which is typified by the prefix. The phrase "monger" really means a merchant who is dealing in a mixture of things, as we derive it from precisely the same root as we obtain the words "mingle" or "mix," "amongst" or "among," and even when speaking of an animal of mixed breed, we term it a "mongrel."

Perhaps I might add, in connection with commerce, how the old coaching terms are still in use on the railways, and how we speak of "driving" a train, and use the word "booking-office" as applied to the place where a man used to go to arrange for his seat in a coach, and have it duly entered in a book. He went to what is known as the coaching station, and we now book a seat in the train at the "booking-office," although in the present day the sale of the ticket is not entered into any book.

We still speak of the "way-bill," and term the official in charge the "guard," although now there is no need for him to be armed with a revolver, as was necessary in earlier times, to protect those who travelled by coach from highwaymen. Even now, the carriages connected with the train by which we travel are spoken of as "coaches."

We also speak of the "post" in the same way as we used to speak of a "post-chaise," and we refer now to the "post-office." It is simply *positus*, "placed," an official post is where a man is placed in his position, and to travel "post-haste" was to go where horses were held ready to expedite the journey. The "post-office" was just the building where the letters were placed, while to post accounts is to place the counters, which were used for computing, in correct and mathematical order.

The story of the survivals that exist in present day

costume is a very long and full one. It has been ably
treated by Mr. Skeat, and to his little book,* those who
want all the details of it are referred, but with every acknowledgment to what he has set down, it may be well in these
pages to mention a few of the interesting points.

The existence of the two buttons at the back of the
ordinary coat often cause enquiry, and the usual explanation is that these were the buttons which formerly supported
the belt from which hung the sword, but the more general
opinion, and one which Mr. Skeat sets forth with detail, is
that they are the buttons to which at one time coat tails
were looped back when found too long to be convenient, and
when, moreover, if used on horseback, it was desirable to
keep them out of the way.

The " V " shaped nick which we have on the lapel of the
coat also takes us back to the time when a collar was specially
needed for protection against bad weather, and the nick
was made so that it would easily turn up round the neck,
and it has been retained, even though now often cut by
the tailors in a way that would quite prevent its earlier
use being adopted.

Wigs are not worn nowadays, but if one regards the
levee dress of the present day, one finds a curious ornament
on the back of the collar of the coat, known as a " flash "
and composed of ribbon which really represents the tail
of the bag wig, as it lay upon the collar of the coat, and it
is still retained, although the wig itself has disappeared.
The shoes that are worn with the dress are known as pumps,
when in fact the word should be " pomps," because they
have to do with the pomp and circumstance which the
ceremonial of the dress involves.

The word frock, now used almost exclusively for a
woman's gown, really denotes the long robe as part of the
habit of the monk or the friar, and its original meaning
is retained in the term we still give to a person who is
deprived of his orders, and is said to be " unfrocked."
Moreover, we use the same word when we speak of a smock
frock, the old-fashioned dress of the agriculturist, and when
we designate the ceremonial coat known as the frock-coat,
but with these exceptions, the word has passed over to the
feminine sex, in the same way as many other words, originally

* *The Past at Our Doors*, W. W. Skeat (Macmillan, 1913).

applied to male costume, but now adopted as representing portions of women's dress.

In some parts of the South of England, the waistcoat, especially if it is made long, is still spoken of by labourers as a petticoat, or a half-coat ; the Cornish fishermen refer to a long kind of habit which they put over their clothing to protect it, as an oilskin petticoat ; but here again the word has now become a general term for use by women, and almost a symbol for womanhood.

In the use of materials from which we make our costumes, there are interesting survivals in the very names of the stuffs. Diaper reminds us of Ypres, where it was originally made ; cambric, for the same reason, of Cambrai ; muslin was first made in Mosul ; gauntlets made at Ghent ; the French word Gand giving the French name for the place and almost the actual word used for gloves ; calico we originally got from Calicut ; and in chintz we use an old Persian word, which simply means " spotty."

In blankets, oddly enough, we use the name of Thomas Blanket, who, in the fifteenth century, first made these very useful articles in Bristol. In linen we retain the old Latin word for flax, *linum*. In silk we take the word direct from the Chinese word " sei " in that language, and curiously enough, we get serge from exactly the same root, implying that that material, which is now wholly of wool, should be silken in its texture, and was originally made of silk. We still group up tapestries under the name of Arras, we speak of damask, which originally came from Damascus, and objects in metal are termed Dinanderie, because of the fine bronze craftsmanship which was originally carried out in Dinant.

Definite survivals of ancient costume exist in several directions, notably that worn by the boys of the Bluecoat School, which simply represents the ordinary boys' costume of Tudor times, and the similar, but less well-known costumes worn by the Red Maids at their schools at Bristol, the Blue Girls at their school in Chester, and the Castle Rising sisters in their delightful Jacobean habit, which they wear at the hospital founded by Lord Northampton in 1614.

The robes worn by the members of the various corporations are also survivals of far earlier ordinary domestic attire. A curious survival in Court costume came under my notice a short time ago, in the fact that the greyhound, one of the supporters of Henry VII, an heraldic emblem which he derived from his mother, Margaret Beaufort, still appears on the hilts of the swords worn by the Royal pages, though it seems to have disappeared from all other State apparel and from the Royal achievement.

The groom who goes out with a lady who is riding in the Park still wears the belt to which, if the lady had been riding pillion, she would have held tight in case of accident, and he wears it as a survival, although he rides separately from her and is simply there as an escort. The Bishop's apron is all that remains of the silk cassock which originally was the principal item in the Bishop's costume, and another curious survival is in the triple line of buttons that adorn the page's coat, where the two rows which curve down-wards towards the waist represent—Professor Skeat has pointed out—the buttons which were once worn for fastening back the lining of the front coat lapels, the two inner edges of the turned back coat being first hooked together, and then the hooks replaced by a central row of buttons, giving us the present three lines on the front of the coat.

The gift to the Prince Consort in 1846 of a machine-made watch-chain from Birmingham introduced the use of the word " albert," which we have retained ever since his time as the word which we use for a short watch-chain, extending across the front of the waistcoat, and which from that time superseded the longer gold chain which previously was in more general use. The mention of the page reminds us of the way in which certain men-servants are still known as footmen, although the days for their walking or running on foot to clear the way in front of a carriage have passed away for ever.

We call a particular shape of hat a " bowler " hat, simply because it was originally made by Thomas Bowler, the hatter, who lived in the Borough in Southwark.   This shape of hat was first introduced by William Coke, the nephew of Coke of Norfolk, and hence the hat is often styled a billycock hat.   He always said that he took the idea of it from the head-gear of a Greek statue ; there may have been some-thing in this, but it is certain that the first of that shape in England was made for him by the man whose name it still retains.

In connection with domestic habits, it is often forgotten that there is a distinct order or edict dealing with the shape of pocket handkerchiefs. It is dated June 2, 1785, and was issued by Louis XVI, at the request of Marie Antoinette. Up to her time, handkerchiefs had been of various shapes, dictated by individual fancy, oblong, round, triangular or square. The Queen thought it would be far more convenient if the square form only was used, and so the edict was made, and it decreed that " the length of handkerchiefs shall equal their width, throughout my entire kingdom." From that time, handkerchiefs have been square, and it seems that the edict issued in 1785 is likely to have an effect almost in perpetuity.

Madrid is one of the places where there are some interesting curious survivals. For example, at the changing of the guard in the Royal Palace, the ceremony takes place in exactly the same method as it has always done since it was instituted by Charles III, and the soldiers parade in full dress uniform, consisting of long blue trousers and tail coats, edged with silver, upon the upturned corners of which are the arms of Charles III embroidered in silver.

A similar survival of ancient custom takes place when the King and Queen of Spain drive to the race meetings at Aranjuez. They go with a postillion team drawn by six mules, and the postillions are in blue livery with black leggings, and a curious sort of bowler hat, slashed with gold, having its brims turned up at the side. They wear their mess jackets crossed with gold frogs, and this special livery has been in use for some hundreds of years.

CHAPTER XV

OUR CURIOUS WORDS, AND THE HABITS AND CUSTOMS OF OUR DOMESTIC LIFE

WE are curious people in England, with regard to our use of words, because we continue by force of habit and custom to use a word as it was first introduced, when long ago it has lost its original meaning, or when, as in some cases, it was originally misapplied, and is still so in its present use.

We speak of a country dance, we really mean a " contradance," those who dance opposite one another ; we talk about " briar pipes," as if the word had anything to do with a bush or a rose plant, whereas originally it belonged to the French word " bruyère." We speak of Indian ink and India paper, when the former came from China, and the latter had nothing whatever to do with India at any time.

We speak of rosewood, as though it had any connection with the plant on which the rose grows, and of cedar pencils, when cedar itself is not used in their manufacture. We call the entrails of a sheep " cat-gut," and usually speak of a particular kind of leather as " chamois " leather, when it never had anything to do with the animal that bears that name. We call cockroaches " blackbeetles," when they are not beetles, and are not black ; we speak of lobsters as fishes, when they are crustaceans ; there is, in fact, a well-known story of a writer on natural history, who spoke of a lobster as " a little red fish that runs sideways," a statement which Cuvier declared as being absolutely correct, save for three slight errors ; it was not a fish, it was not red, and it did not walk sideways.

We refer to Spanish fly, when we really mean a beetle ; we talk of French beans and French polish, which have no connection with France, and Kidderminster carpet and Brussels carpet, which never had anything to do with the

towns from which they are named. We use camel's-hair
brushes, which have nothing to do with the camel, and
galvanised iron which was never galvanised, and has no
connection whatever with the process. Our sealing-wax
contains no wax, and our plovers' eggs should be more
correctly termed those of the lapwing.

The silkworms our children keep are not worms but cater-
pillars, and if, when our children are ill, we give them sweet
spirits of nitre, it contains no nitre, while we have Chinese
drawings on rice paper which has nothing to do with rice,
but is made of pith. We eat marmalade which should be
composed of quinces (Portuguese " marmelo," a quince),
but it has no quince in it, and the Dutch clocks that hang
in our rooms are not Dutch at all, but German (Deutsch).
German measles is not a disease that belongs to the Germans,
or that has any particular connection with Germany ; its
rash resembles that of ordinary rubeola, and is a sort of
ficititous example of it. We also speak of German silver,
but when we talk of cousin-german, we use a word that is
allied to that of the word " germ," having to do with origin
and stock.

If we call a man a blackguard, we apply a term of oppro-
brium to him now, but we ought not to do that, because
it was simply the old term for the inferior servants of the
Crown, who in Tudor times were dressed in black. If we
put a person into our black books, we go back to much
the same period, because the original black books were
those that were compiled in Henry VIII's time, and contained an account of the misbehaviour that went on in
certain religious houses.

There is, perhaps, no word that we so completely misapply
as when we term a person " an idiot." As Dr. Brewer, to
whom we are indebted for many of these references, points
out, an idiot is simply an ordinary person, who is not employed in any public office. It is not that he is particularly
incompetent to do it, but he is just one who is neither a
priest nor an official, but an ordinary citizen, and from
that we have got an idea that this person was incompetent
to take such a position, and thence the word has gradually
assumed its present form, so that now it is applied to those
born lacking intelligence. In the present day some of us
are disposed to reverse this ancient use and give to the

persons *in* Public Offices, Treasury or Pensions, the term we now misapply.

There are few words that are more interesting in connection with their origin than those which we so frequently use, Lord and Lady, because they go back to the very beginning of domestic life. The Lord is simply the " loaf-ward," the guardian of the food, the band that keeps the house together, that is to say, the houseband or husband, and the protector of the food. The Lady is simply the " loaf-kneader," the maker of the loaf, the one who has to take upon herself the domestic duties that appertain to the household, exactly in the same way as the " spinster" is the person who undertakes other domestic duties in connection with the distaff.

There has been a long controversy over the origin of the phrase we use, " Hip, hip, hurrah ! " The " Hip, hip " has been said to be traceable back to the time of the Crusades, and to be an abbreviation of the cry when Jerusalem fell, " Hierosolyma est perdita," or " Hep," and the " Hurrah " is an old Jewish phrase, which we take almost direct from the Hebrew original. According to other authorities, it is derived from the cry to Thor for aid, which we get from our Danish ancestors, " Tur aie " or " Thur aie," but " hulla-baloo," the word we apply to the uproar that occurs when people are making these cries, has been traced back to an Irish phrase used for the crying out at funerals.

Mr. Charles Hofman informs me that shortly before the war there were anti-Jewish riots in Germany and Poland, and the statement was made : " Last week in the town of . . . certain evilly-disposed persons made an attempt to incite the mob against the Jews, by raising the cry of " Hep, hep ! "

" Hurrah " ought really to be pronounced differently ; it should be spelled " Huzzah," and in the Hebrew it is " Huzza " or " Hosannah," but Professor Skeat declared it had more to do with the Scandinavian phrase which meant to whirl or haste, from whence we get our word " hurry." The " biting " remark which is sometimes spoken of, Brewer says, comes from an ancient classical story. When Zeno the philosopher was ordered to be pounded to death in a mortar, and just before he died, he called to the tyrant to come near to him, to give him a great and important secret, and when he put his ear near to that of the dying man, Zeno bit it off, and so had his revenge at the last.

It may be worth while to refer to another phrase which is often used in conversation, and which is a direct quotation from the Bible, although the ordinary user does not remember that it is so. A person who does not desire to give away the source of his information, says that " a little bird told him " the story, and so quotes the words from Ecclesiastes x. 20, where it is said that " a bird of the air shall carry the voice, and that which hath wings shall tell the matter."

One of our words for a maidservant, when we term her an abigail, we obtain direct from Holy Writ, where Nabal's wife is named Abigail (1 Sam. xxv. 3), and it was she who described herself as a handmaiden to David, and by her skill and ability prevented David from repaying Nabal's provocation by the shedding of blood.

Another odd way we have in England is that of doubling the letters in some of our words. We should be much wiser if we wrote " wagon " and " fagot " and " bagage " and " lugage " and so retained the older forms of spelling. These and many other words are more accurately spelled in America, where they have retained the use of the old English words, and still spell them as they were originally. Their word " guess " is constantly found in Ben Jonson, and is part of the English phraseology of the day.

The intimate connection that existed between Scotland and France has left pleasant evidences in the Scottish tongue. There are many words used by Scottish people which would very likely be misunderstood by Englishmen, as they are derived directly from the French. An interesting little book was written in 1914 on this subject by Miss Isabel Sinclair, giving a vocabulary of words used by Scottish people having distinct connection with the French language. She gave chapter and verse for almost every word that she quoted, and her list was an extensive one. As the volume is out of print, and difficult to obtain, it may perhaps be permissible to quote a few of the words she mentions, in the order in which she gives them, and to mark against them the French word from which the Scottish one is derived.

A lawyer is, in Scottish term, an advocate, the word, of course, coming from " avocat."

A large dish, in which meat is served or carved, is called an " ashet," from the French " assiette."

A cupboard is an " aumrie," from " aumaire."

The word " avisement " is in occasional use in Scotland, coming from the French word of exactly the same spelling.

The official known as the " bailie," a municipal functionary or magistrate, gets his title from an adaptation of the French word " bailli."

The Scotsman sometimes uses the word " bien " in much the same way as the Frenchman uses exactly the same word.

For a washed out or dull blue, the Scotsman says " blae," and he speaks of " blaeberries " also, taking his word from " bleu."

A pale thing he characterises as " blankit " or " blunkit," from " blanc."

The Scotsman sometimes calls a mangle a " calender," and he speaks of " calendering works."

A diseased body was called " carmaladie," from " Cœur Malade."

In Scotland, to talk is to " crack," from " cracquer."

A neighbour is often called a " cummer," from " commere."

A riot has been called a " debosh," from " debauch."

Girls are spoken of as " demmysels," the explanation being easy.

The old Scotsman termed anything sweet, " douce."

Anything sad, he still speaks of as " doule," from the French term for mourning, " deuil."

Trouble in Scotland used to be styled " fasherie," from " facherie," and " canna be fashed " is still often heard.

The word " gawky " in constant use is derived from the French word " gauche."

A gooseberry* is termed a " groser," from " groseille."

Goldsmiths' work has been termed " orfarie," from " orfeverie."

Embroidery is sometimes spoken of as " passment," from " passement."

A cloak in old Scottish phrase was a " rokelay," from " roquelaure."

A watering-pot by Scott is termed a " rosser," a word derived from " arrosier."

A tray, termed a " servet," takes its name from the French word " serviette."

To " spairge " or to " spurge " is from " asperger."

" Watchful " used to be in Scotland " tentie," from " attendre," and a child holding a jug is still told to " tak' tent " of it, lest he break it.

" Vacance " is used in Scotland in exactly the same way as it is in France.

* Professor Reid suggests that the derivation of the word " groser " for gooseberry, allied to " groseille," may not be entirely accurate, as there are three forms of the word in use in Scotland—" groset," " groser " and " grosert "—and it is possible that they come from a Gaelic word, " grosaid."

An old friend adds :

" Cundie," a grating over a street drain, from " conduit."
" Canally," a mob, from " canaille," and
" Caussey," a paved road, from " chaussée."

Moreover, it is pointed out that there are many names of estates and houses in Scotland distinctly French, e.g. Montpelier, St. Germains, Picardie and Maison Dieu, and it is also stated that the plant *archangelica officinalis*, from which a certain liqueur and a candy are prepared, and which grows in the Pyrenees and in France, is extremely rare in the British Isles, but was introduced into Scotland in 1568 by Mary Queen of Scots, and still grows not only in the places where the Queen first planted it, but in other parts of Scotland, whence it has spread from its original home.

Gleaners in Cumberland still use the word " bever " for their eleven o'clock lunch, a corruption of the word " bouvoir," and early form of " boire," and going back to Norman-French times.

Sir A. Geikie reminded me years ago that the wild cherry, a little black fruit called in Scotland *geans*, takes its name from the word *guignes*, by which the French still speak of it.

A curious survival of Danish conquest remains in the existence of several Danish words in use in Yorkshire, especially in the Skipton Division. A man is spoken of as having " laaking fever," that is to say, he is lazy, the word coming from a Danish word which means to play about. A fight is spoken of as a " nevilling," from the Danish " neeve," for " fist," and " havver cakes " mean oatcakes, from the Danish " hafr," for oats.

Another curious notice appears in the windows of undertakers, especially in Yorkshire : " Pinking done here," and pinkers in Yorkshire are the persons who are called in to close the eyes of the dead persons. The name by which they are called is derived from an old Dutch word, " pinken," to half close, and scalloped borders (half circles) on linen are said to be pinked. Pinking is also a term used for cutting dress materials in half-circles or scallops, and " Pinking done here " is a sign that does not always refer to the dead, but often to the adorning of the living. A basin in Yorkshire, especially if it is a small-sized one, is often called a

" posnet," probably derived from the French word " poce-net," a small receptacle or basin.

In domestic life there are many habits that should be referred to, because of their origin. It may not perhaps have been noticed by everyone that when a servant announces formally that dinner or luncheon " is served," the statement is always made to the master, and never to the mistress of the house, although, after all, the latter has had more to do with the arrangements than has the husband, but the headship of the husband is always recognised in this phrase.

Some of us perhaps have not noticed the manner in which the hour of four is designated on our watches, that it is not by the usual Roman figure of IV, but by four strokes, a manner which was not adopted in Roman figuring, and does not occur on any other arrangement of figures that is known to me. This is said to have arisen in the time of Charles V, when the King complained that on his watch he confused the IV and the VI, and sent it back to the maker to have a change made, whereupon the courtiers decided to copy the King's example ; their watches were altered accordingly, and, ever since that time, this unusual method of marking the figure four has been used.*

We really do not, however, need any figures at all on our watches and our clocks, because we notice the time by the position of the hands, and not by the figures to which they point. When Lord Grimthorpe put up the big clock in Lincoln's Inn, he had each of the hours marked by a single stroke, but probably no one has ever noticed the omission of the hour numerals, because it is only necessary to glance up at the clock, and see the position in which the hands stand.

One of our unusual and vulgar phrases is " to walk your chalks," which goes back at least to 1620, when royal messengers coming into a small town and requiring accommodation for a large suite in attendance upon a royal personage, marked in chalk the houses they commandeered,

* The Dean of Christchurch reminds me of the fact that the four strokes signifying the figure 4 instead of IV, almost invariably occur in Vulgate MSS. from the fifth century downwards, and mentions that, in the Oxford edition of the Vulgate, the Press were careful to reproduce that method of enumeration in the capitula and dates.

and the persons in possession of those houses had to walk out, in order that the accommodation might be available as required.

We speak of " buckling to," and the phrase recalls to us the days of wearing armour. There are hardly any buckles in use in modern costumes at the present day, unless, perchance, they be the small ones used on the knee-breeches in Court costume, and those on waistcoats and trousers at the back, but when armour was worn, there were many of them, and all had to be fastened with great care and security before the wearer of the armour went into battle.

We say that a person takes " French leave," the allusion being to foreign soldiers, who had a habit of *looting* (a word derived from Hindi) whatever they desired, with or without permission, a habit that has been much adopted, unfortunately, by soldiery of various nations during the Great War, but the phrase has also been stated to have an origin far earlier, and to have been first applied to the men at Crecy and Agincourt as one of derision, because of the manner in which they ran away when exposed to the onslaught of the English bowmen.*

Judas is said to have had red hair, according to tradition, and hence came a rather widespread idea that red-haired people were dangerous and hot-tempered. Even now there is quite a general opinion that there is a tendency on the part of red-haired people to lose their temper more readily than do others.

Black has been a synonym for " bad " in many phrases of our language. We speak of " black-hearted," of " black envy," and when we use the word " blackmail " we refer to an Anglo-Saxon word for toll, and the word means a toll demanded by an evil person, so that in that case we do use a phrase which rightly expresses its meaning.

By the way, a vulgar phrase in which to die is spoken of as " to kick the bucket " has nothing to do with the ordinary bucket or pail, but comes either from a

* Professor Reid reminds me that there is in French a curious parallel phrase to the one used in English, " to take French leave." It is " S'esquiver à l'Anglaise." He also points out, as a curious fact, that the word " fun " was not used in England until nearly the end of the eighteenth century, and was regarded as a piece of Irish slang.

north-country word for a beam on which a carcass may be suspended, or else from a similar old English word used in another part of the country for a pulley, and so signifying the manner by which a carcass is drawn up into position.

We often retain in modern use old names for objects, as, for example, we call the balls used in bowling from the material of which they are made, " woŏds."

One of the curious words that we still use has come into special use lately, in connection with sales of rubbish, the word "rummage." It arose from two French words, " remuer " and " menage," and really refers to the complete clearance which is made on the occasion of moving. As late as 1787 it was spoken of as " remmuenage," and more than one writer of that period spoke of the bother and trouble that the remmuenage entailed. It has now come to be applied to the things that, in this particular clearance, have come to be regarded as of no special importance.

The ordinary names by which we speak of policemen, calling them " Bobbies " and " Peelers," reminds us of the reformation of the police force in 1829, under Sir Robert Peel, when he established a new body, known as the Metropolitan Police, and his Christian and surnames have been so perpetuated in these words.

One of our familiar phrases, " A Roland for an Oliver," we derive from an early romance of the period of Charlemagne. It is said that two of his Paladins (dwellers in his palace) had a contest, and decided to fight a duel, in order to settle a question that had been brought before the Emperor, which two knights were to settle on his behalf. The two combatants had been selected by their brother Paladins, and the visors of their helmets were kept down while they were fighting, so that neither knew who was his opponent. They fought for some prolonged period, and the contest waged was very severe, so much so that it is stated that one knight's sword was fixed in the other one's shield, and the sword of his opponent broken off at the handle. They then left their horses, and fought hand to hand, but eventually, tearing off one another's helmets discovered that each had been fighting with his dearest friend. Simultaneously, they yielded to one another, Roland to Oliver, the disagreement was at an end, and the saying took its origin from this curious romantic story.

A memory of the past is contained in the word cupboard. The original cupboards were shelves on which cups could be placed and exhibited. They were actual boards " made lyke stayres," as an old chronicle says, tier above tier, and quite an array of cups could be placed upon them. We still see very much the same in the Halls of the City Companies, where, behind the Master, are tiers of crimson-covered shelves, on which are arranged the pieces of the Company's plate, cups and their covers, dishes, salts and the like. From some such arrangement the word was transferred to its present use of a closed or protected place in which cups and other ornaments for the table are kept.

Our children talk of the story of Cinderella and the glass slipper, and in the tale the tiny slipper which fitted Cinderella is described as being of actual glass.

It was not so in the old French story from which ours is derived. It was " en vair," of fur, not " en verre," of glass, but the old mistranslation has survived, and it is almost sacrilege to dislodge it from the story now.

There is an attempt in the present day to try and alter the rule of the road in walking, and to compel people to walk on the left, instead of on the right. The original regulation goes back to the time when people carried swords, but it has to be varied at times, because a man, meeting a woman, should always walk on the outside of the pavement, theoretically the position of danger. This habit commenced in Norman-French times, the Normans having, it is said, introduced the practice in order that the woman should be protected by the wall and so avoid falling into the gutter. Gutters in old English times were really dangerous affairs, and down to the period of the early Georges there were in London gutters by the side of the paths which were more like ditches. It was feared that women might be pressed into these gutters, and such accidents did often occur, hence it was that the rule arose by which the woman was always given the wall, as the phrase runs.

It surely is unwise to attempt to alter old regulations, and still more to force a change so revolutionary upon the populace.

An interesting suggestion has quite recently been made by Dr. Saise in *The Times* relative to the words used by the mahout in India in directing his elephant. He finds that they are neither Hindustani, Arabic nor Persian, and he believes that they are relics of the language of those who first tamed the elephant, and have been handed down from generation to generation.

It will be noticed that there is an affinity in them to ancient Greek, and conceivably they may have had some connection with that tongue, and so date back to the time of Alexander the Great's expedition, or may belong to an even earlier language that has perished long ago.

The language is known amongst mahouts as Hathi Ki Bat, pronounced Hutti K'Baat. It was used by Syed Ali, the native mahout who was brought over to the Zoological Gardens in order to make Indarini, the big Indian elephant presented by the Maharajah of Cooch Behar, amenable to discipline.

Poker, the game that we play, is generally derived from two French words, " Pot et paire," a phrase used in connection with the game, but there is some diversity of opinion concerning its etymology.

One of the words we misuse is " asylum," which, strictly speaking, is not a place of confinement for lunatic people. It was a place for the protection of persons. The word comes from two Greek words which imply that you are not to pillage in that place, and criminals who were to be protected from attacks on the part of the public were to be assisted to a place that was called an asylum, a kind of sanctuary, which other people were forbidden to enter, and especially forbidden to attack and pillage.

A popular word in the streets is " cad," and this we take from a dead body, " cadaver." Originally, persons called cads were those living in a University but who were not members of that University. The graduates were divided into " men," and those who were not men, of the college, and thence grew up a habit of speaking of those who were not members as dead, and hence, by easy sequence, we came to the word " cad," which now has quite a different meaning.*

* Professor Reid suggests that " cad " might be a shortened form of the word " cadet," and that the word "caddie" used on the golf links is probably from the same source.

Amongst games, it is only quite recently that, near to my own house, I heard a boy, in throwing up his penny, make use, not of the customary phrase " Heads or tails," but of " York and Clark," an odd survival of an old scandal associating a former Duke of York with Mrs. Clark, and which was so much talked about that at one time the children in the streets adopted this method of describing the reverse and the obverse of the coin. I had no idea, until I heard this boy call it out, that the phrase still remained.

The Roman equivalent was " Heads or ships." The Roman " as " being thrown in the air descended either on the side that had the head of Janus Bifrons or that bearing the prow of the ship. Another method of expression, also having reference to the same Duke of York, is still occasion ally to be heard, " Duke or Darling," so indelible has been the mark left upon English life by that particular scandal.

The " Jew's harp " upon which the boy plays has nothing whatever to do with a Hebrew, the word is simply derived from the French " jou," a toy—and " gooseberry fool " has nothing whatever to do with a foolish person ; it is simply " foulé," mashed, the French phrase.

The schoolboy word to " pommell " somebody is not often recognised as having a distinct connection with the end of the sword, the boss on which the arms were placed in the case of a State sword, and called the pommell because of its resemblance to a small apple, from " pomum," an apple, so when it was desired to chastise a person, and it was not desirable to draw the sword upon him, he was often banged about the head with the pommell of the sword, in similar fashion to the manner in which schoolboys pommell one another with their fists.

We speak about our ears burning when people are talking about us, and here we have an exceedingly ancient tradition that is still accepted, for, as Brewer points out, Pliny in his History writes : " When our ears do glow and tingle, some do talk of us in our absence."

By the way, the word " talk " is one of the most extra-ordinary in the English language, because it is the only one that, so far as Dr. W. W. Skeat was aware, we derive directly from the Lithuanian tongue. He drew special attention to this remarkable survival. In Lithuanian " tulkas " was an interpreter, " tulkote " was to interpret, and there must have been some intercourse, says he, between the Scandinavians and Lithuanians by means of an interpreter, which brought that word into Scandinavian tongues, so that the word to interpret or explain is in Swedish "tolka," in Danish "tolké," in Icelandish "tulka," and hence our word "talken" originally, and now "talk." The word has nothing to do with the words "tale" or "tell," as many etymological books state, and to "talk" is, strictly speaking, to interpret or to explain, and a talker is an interpreter.

We have an odd proverb in England, by which we say we should first "catch our hare before we cook him," and we often attribute this statement to Hannah Glasse, who is said to have used it in her cookery book, first published in 1747.

No such phrase, however, appears in the volume. It has been suggested that the phrase should be "First scatch," but it is not so, though, were there a verb "to scatch," which seems highly doubtful, she might certainly have used it, for, in her preface, she apologises for not having "wrote in the high polite style," her intention being "to instruct the lower sort." What she did, however, say was not at all with reference to a hare, but when alluding to cooking a pig, she says, "When you have cleaned the pig, *scotch* him down to the bones "—using an old-world word which means to cut, score or gash.

It is declared that the wag Tom Hood was responsible for the original statement, that varied Mrs. Glasse's remark intentionally, "deliberately travestied it," as a recent writer has said, or it may be true that, in conversation, Mrs. Glasse may one day have said, "First scotch your hare before you cook him," but she certainly never made use of the expression in her *Art of Cookery made Plain and Easy.*

Children almost always break egg-shells at the breakfast table, in fact, my mother, than whom no one had less superstition, taught her children to break the egg-shells before we left the table, and never to leave a semi-perfect egg-shell on the table. Little as she knew it, the idea for this goes back to the old days of witchcraft. Witches could come in, it is said, to the table, and make use of an egg-shell that was at least half perfect, as a boat in which they might sail away, and the old superstition was that witches were always on the look-out for egg-shells to be used as vessels (aeroplanes ! !) in which they could fly away to another region.

We speak of smoking as conducive to peace and quiet, and it must not be forgotten that, amongst the Red Indians, the pipe has always had its distinct position when peace was to be made, and that quite recently, within the past year or two, this old use of the pipe was brought into prominent notice.

A formal reconciliation took place between the supreme chiefs of two groups of Indians, the Hurons and the Iroquois, who had been divided by a bitter feud for two hundred and seventy years, and who came together in the sight of some five thousand spectators, when a great council of Indians of Ontario met to draw the attention of the Government to a claim they still held to certain strips of land.

The two chiefs, accompanied by three representatives of the two respective nations, took their seats, and then the pipe of peace was produced, and the Iroquois, putting a match to the peace-pipe, handed it to the Huron, declaring " There is peace between our peoples." " There is peace," replied the Huron, who took the pipe and passed it on to one of his followers, who handed it back to the Iroquois. The two chiefs then solemnly buried their war hatchet, and, side by side, set out to hunt together.

Perhaps one of the most interesting domestic survivals exists in connection with Cornish clotted cream, because it is stated that the Cornishmen learned to make this cream from the Phœnicians, and it is only where the Phœnicians settled in Europe, that is to say, in Cornwall, Brittany and Devonshire, that this delicious clotted cream is to be obtained. Mr. Baring Gould says that the yellow saffron cakes that are given with afternoon tea in Cornwall are alluded to in papers relating to Phœnicia, and that the Phœnicians were acquainted with the use of saffron.

There is a curious tradition held by many gardeners in respect to parsley. It is said that, for some reason or other, it should never be transplanted, and also that it should be sown nine times before it will come up. The explanation given in Westmoreland is that the Devil is very fond of parsley seed, and takes all the nine sowings to himself, but the tenth he is powerless to remove. Another similar tradition states that if parsley is to be curly, it must never be sown on Good Friday.

Numerals in some of the Northern counties take rather curious forms, and the oldest are retained by the shepherds in counting their sheep. There are four different sets in existence in those two counties, resembling one another to a certain extent, but not identical; they run thus :—

KIRKBY STEPHEN DISTRICT.		BORROWDALE.
1.	Yaan	Yan
2.	Tyaan	Tyan
3.	Taedere	Tethera
4.	Maedere	Methera
5.	Mimp	Pimp
6.	Haites	Sethera
7.	Saites	Lethera
8.	Haoves	Hovera
9.	Daoves	Dovera
10.	Dik	Dick
11.	Yaandik	Yan-a-dick
12.	Tyanedik	Tyan-a-dick
13.	Taederedik	Tether-a-dick
14.	Maederedik	Mether-a-dick
15.	Boon buom buum	Bumfit
16.	Yaaneboon	Yan-a-bumfit
17.	Tyaaneboon	Tyan-a-bumfit
18.	Taedereboon	Tether-a-bumfit
19.	Maedereboon	Mether-a-bumfit
20.	Buomfit buumfit	Giggot

THE EPPING DISTRICT.		TEESDALE DISTRICT.
1.	In	Yan
2.	Tin	Tean
3.	Thera	Tether
4.	Fethera	Mether
5.	Fip	Pip
6.	Lethera	Sezar
7.	Methera	Azar
8.	Co	Catra
9.	Debera	Horna
10.	Dick	Dik
11.	Indick	Yan-a-dik
12.	Tin-dick	Tean-a-dik
13.	Tether-a-dick	Tether-a-dik
14.	Lether-a-dick	Mether-a-dik
15.	Bumfit	Bumfit
16.	In-a-bumfit	Yan-a-bum
17.	Tin-a-bumfit	Tean-a-bum
18.	Lether-a-bumfit	Tether-a-bum
19.	Mether-a-bumfit	Meth-a-bum
20.	Gigot	Jiggit

CHAPTER XVI

ON LAND AND WATER

IN a recent article Mr. Harold Spender* has pointed out how full the Universities are of interesting survivals. He refers to the life history of Oxford, and to the famous St. Giles's Fair, which has taken place every year, with hardly a break, for eight hundred years, and which goes back to a time before any University existed in the place, and alludes to the beginnings of the College life, and to the strange chances by which Oxford attracted the learning and teaching of the Middle Ages. The idea is set forth that very likely some wandering learned man may have begun the work of the University, by speaking amongst the tumult of the Fair, and by attracting the crowd into a tent, wherein he discoursed on strange things and carried on experiments which savoured of magic.

Whatever may have been the reason, in the early twelfth century students were flocking into Oxford in considerable numbers, and the University began to grow before the time of the Colleges, and so won its fame before any individual College corporation emerged. Then he speaks of the foundation of the early Colleges, Merton, University and Balliol in the thirteenth century, followed a hundred years later by the College which still is called " New," and yet has existed for five hundred years. There was a movement of rebellion passing over England, when people were beginning to fret against what they termed the sterility of the monastic ideal, and that, although many of these early Colleges were still half monasteries, and we have evidence of that in the present day in their cloisters, and in the continued use of many of their strange statutes; yet we see the beginnings of a struggle, to have a great effect later on.

There was the struggle with the town itself, in which the spirit of city life was beginning to rise, and Town and

* See his article on " Oxford after Many Days," *Fort. Review.*

Gown riots, which existed down to quite recent days, were
originally evidence of the conflict which was taking place
between the University and the town. One celebrated riot
took place in 1354, in which several students were killed and
others dangerously wounded, and it is mentioned that for
nearly another five hundred years, down to 1827, the custom
continued of the Corporation performing an act of penitence
at St. Mary's every year, to atone for that crime, while so
strong was the support given to the University by the State
and the Monarchy that, even to-day, the municipalities of
Oxford and Cambridge are more restricted in their rights
than are any other such municipalities in the country.

Then we have the evidence of the other struggle, between
the gradually rising Reformation spirit, and the stern
conservatism of the ancient faith, the Reformation breaking
in upon the world of Oxford, and dividing it into two
distinct parts. Startling evidence of this, it has been
pointed out, exists in the very stones of Tom Quadrangle at
Christchurch. On the right was the great banqueting hall
which Wolsey erected. Two sides of the quadrangle were
built by Wolsey, but on the left he had intended to build a
chapel, and the quadrangle was to be turned into a magnificent cloister. He fell before he could complete his scheme.
Henry VIII was then in rebellion against the Holy See.
The cloister never came into existence. The quadrangle
was left open to the light of day. The King took the Abbey
Church, and turned it into a cathedral and a chapel, and at
the same time destroyed the cathedral of Osney, so that
" the most orthodox College of Christchurch rests on the
muddy subsoil of a ruthless revolution."

Then with regard to survivals in words which still remain.
" Smalls," the phrase used for the preliminary examination
in Oxford, is based on a mistranslation of the Latin term
for the porch of a church or cloister, for it was " in parviso "
that the students were subjected to their first examination,
and there still exists a half built up room over the porch of
St. Mary's, where the examinations took place.

The " Moderators " were those who sat in judgment
over the debate, and, perhaps, moderated the language.
The " Collections," the phrase which now means a college
examination, then signified the occasions when the college
was collected at the end of the term, and when words of

praise or acts of punishment were decided upon. So strongly in Oxford does the tradition of early teaching linger, that even to-day the lecturer slows down his words to the pace of the average penman, keeping up the idea that the lectures are to be taken down in longhand, and the very possibility of printing is entirely ignored, while there follows the curious neglect on the part of Oxford students to take the trouble to read printed books, a habit of which one is reminded by the fact that no student in Oxford can take to his own rooms books from the Bodleian, although he can go there and read them. He is still encouraged to listen to lectures, to take notes of them, to talk about their subjects, and the *viva voce* examinations keep up the ancient tradition of disputation.

An important survival of the habit of consulting the books, when they were too important and too few to be taken to students' own rooms, remains in the various mediæval libraries in the Universities, where the books are still chained, the most striking examples being probably the one at Merton. The nucleus of Bodley's library commenced in one of the rooms in St. Mary's Church, for there were housed the original books given to the University by the great Duke Humphrey, and in the adjacent room, the first body called Congregation used to sit, and the mediæval students met there, in order to dispute.

The custom of disputation, which was so important in the mediæval universities, is still retained with much of its old vigour in some of the Continental universities, as for example at Bologna and at Padua, where there are still keen controversial disputes in which students have to take part before they are able to assume their degree.

Amongst the great schools, none is fuller of survivals than Westminster School, which was old when Winchester and Eton were founded, and Mr. McKenna, in a recent volume, has referred to the fact that Westminster School still uses a Latin Prayer-book, and has an annual Latin service in Westminster Abbey, and daily Latin prayers.

It is, by the way, a rather curious occasion for those who are interested in the pronunciation of Latin, as there are always two, and sometimes three different methods of pronunciation in use on the occasion of this annual service. The cry is still at the end of the afternoon school, " Instat

quinta," or on Thursday "Instat sesquiduodecima,"
although, nowadays, the hour is nearly one. The prayer
" Pro Fundatrice nostra Regina Elizabetha " is still said
before prayers at the school, the doors are still locked, and
a monitor put outside to guard against a possible raid of
the Volsci, known to the boys as " Scis."

There are also the singular privileges which still belong
to Westminster boys, that they may be present at State
functions and the opening of Parliament, and that they have
access to the gallery of the House of Commons, while their
presence at the Coronation and their cry of " Vivat Rex "
are intimate parts of that ancient ceremony, and they
are entitled to be confirmed in Henry VII's Chapel in the
Abbey, whenever there is occasion for such a ceremony
to take place.

In the Universities, the word " battles " is still retained
as a phrase applied to the food bills, derived from the
Scandinavian " batten," to feed, a word still in use when
we speak of " battening " upon anything. It should be
pointed out that the " buttery " and the " buttery bills "
have nothing whatever to do with butter, but are more
strictly concerned, not with what is eaten but with what is
drunk, the word coming from the same origin as that from
which we get the word " bottle," and whence we use the
word " butler," the bottler, the one who attends to the
bottles.

Again, the fees are still paid at the University, to the
Bursar, the man who holds what is now called the purse,
but which should more correctly be called the " burse,"
and which in French is still the Bourse, the place where
people meet for money transactions. The word itself
comes from the term for a hide or skin, from which the
original purses were made, and we have its original spelling
in the words " disburse " and " reimburse." A very similar
change of the " b " to the " p " occurs in the word " peat,"
which should really be " beat," the old English word
" beten " being to replenish a fire, and the word " beating "
was used for mending or making up a fire.

The Universities, in their meals, keep up with great attention the habit of seating the people above or below the salt,
and in many instances there are magnificent salt-cellars
of silver-work, which mark the position of the important

persons. It is curious that we still speak of the salt-cellar,
although it is a double phrase, because " saler " was simply
the receptacle for the salt, and it is an absurdity to speak
of a receptacle " for salt for salt." Persons of distinction
in the old days always sat above the salt, that is between it
and the head of the table, while the dependants and other
inferior guests sat below it. We now speak of a person
who is " worth his salt," that is that he has become entitled
to sit above the salt at the table.

It was, of course, from classical literature that we got
such phrases as " Fabian tactics " and " Parthian shots,"
and when we speak of persons getting their foot in, we are
reminded of the foot races that were so important a part of
the physical training of the students of the day.

Amongst the Colleges, Queen's has perhaps retained more
of its ancient customs than any other.

The President of Queen's reminds me of the fact that the
call for dinner in Hall has, in that college, always been
a horn, and that it is sounded in the back and front quadrangle five minutes before the meal. When the loving-cup
is carried round at Queen's, he adds, the ceremony has the
addition of the words " Poculum Caritatis " spoken before
drinking, and he also points out the exceedingly interesting
custom at Queen's of bringing in the boar's head on Christmas
Day with an ancient carol beginning :

> " Caput apri defero
> Redens laudes Domino."

It is carved before dinner, and pieces are eaten with a
special sauce. The lemon in the boar's mouth is handed
to the singer of the carol and the holly distributed to those
present. The custom is believed to date from the escape
of a scholar from a wild boar in the twelfth century, in the
woods surrounding Oxford. The President also alludes to
the quaint and characteristic May Day service, which takes
place at sunrise on the tower of Magdalen College.

The University presses and, in fact, most of the old
printing presses, still keep up the use of the word " chapel,"
which they apply to the group of printers who form a sort
of society or union in the printing office, taking us back to
the days when Caxton first of all set up his printing press
in a chapel in connection with Westminster Abbey. The
chairman of the little group is always called the " Father

of the Chapel," and another interesting phrase in use by printers is that of the " chase," which is the iron frame in which the type is held, derived from the French " chasse," a frame, a phrase which we still retain in " casement," but the " composing-stick," in which a compositor places the letters to be set up, is called a stick because the pieces of type are stuck into it.

The Theatre has one odd word in use which is clearly a survival. No one exactly knows, however, the meaning of the name, applied to one of the rooms at the theatre, of the " Green Room." Van den Hoff, in his *Leaves from an Actor's Notebook*, says that the term " green room " arose from the fact that the scene room was carpeted in green, probably in green baize, and that the covers of the seats or divans in it were of green stuff. George Augustus Sala had a theory that the green room got its name from the fact that in the old days of legitimate drama, the green baize cloth that was used for the performance of tragedy, was kept in a special room, which had this particular title, but other writers decline to accept Sala's theory, and say it is not a probable explanation. In the first Covent Garden theatre, there was a room called the green room, but it was a sort of drawing-room, and the decorations in it were not of a green colour. It was a room with large pier and mantel glasses, so that the actors and actresses could see that everything was satisfactory with regard to their costumes before they went on to the stage, and in this room they were supposed to wait and talk to one another, until summoned to take their positions.

In Drury Lane Theatre, it is said that there were two green rooms, a first and a second, the first being devoted to the important actors or actresses, the second to what were termed the " little people " of the theatre, excluding the two principal dancers, who had the privilege of using the first green room.

In the theatre erected at Covent Garden in 1809, there were three green rooms, but neither of them was decorated in green. It has been said that the Prince Regent was fond of smoking green cigars in the withdrawing room of the theatre, and that he called the room the green room, but this seems a theory as little likely to be correct as was the one adopted by Sala. It is, in consequence, decided

that either there must have been some scene room or withdrawing room in the seventeenth century that was decorated
in green, which gave the name to the room, or else, as has
been suggested by a later writer, that it is a variation of the
word " scene-room," and that gradually the word became
" green-room " instead of " scene-room."

It seems impossible to arrive at a decision in a more
satisfactory fashion than this.

There are many curious survivals in the Army. I am
not sufficiently acquainted with military usages to be able
to give many of them, but I know that the Cameronians
still sit at the royal toast. No regiment could be more loyal,
but out of old attachment to the Stuarts, they have preserved this strange tradition. They also still use the
claymore.

I am indebted to Sir Robert Baden-Powell for information
concerning a curious survival that exists in connection with
the 13th Hussars. He tells me that a hymn-tune is always
played by the band every evening, and that the origin of
this custom goes back to the days of the Peninsular War,
when it is stated that the regiment, contrary to orders,
attacked a convent, and did some damage to the building,
and injured some of the persons who were dwelling within
it. The Duke of Wellington ordered that a hymn-tune
should be played every evening by the band as a sort of
penance, and in recognition of the fact that it had disobeyed
its instructions, and this has been kept up ever since.

I am also told that so intimate is the connection between
the regiment of the Guards and the Sovereign, that it is not
regarded as necessary that the Sovereign's health should
be toasted except on very formal occasions.

A certain official of the Yeomen of the Guard is still
known as the " Exon," a phrase which does not hold in
any other regiment. It simply implies that the man
has a certain delegated authority, is *exempt* from certain
special duty, and the exon, I believe, sleeps at the palace,
and is in charge when his superior officer is absent.

About the name of the " Beefeater " there has been a
good deal of controversy. The usual explanation is that
the word is derived from the Norman-French " Buffetiers,"
and that they were waiters at the sideboard, but it is really
not so. They were originally ordered to be big, stout men,

and one regulation in the papers by which they were founded, refers to them as being big men, who were " good eaters." The words " loaf-eater " and " wine-bibber " are still used, and the " beef-eater " was a common phrase applied to the man who was strong and whose strength had been nurtured by a considerable consumption of beef.

The Broad Arrow, with which Government articles are marked, goes back to the later part of the seventeenth century. It was the " pheon " which formed part of the armorial bearings of the Earl of Romney, in those days Master-general of the Ordnance, and the things he had marked with his badge were regarded as belonging to the Government Ordnance, and hence the derivation of the broad arrow mark which appears on all Government property at the present day.

The Welch Fusiliers proudly bear, as part of their uniform, the strange ornament that has been referred to in another part of this book, that which is known as the " flash," a bunch of black ribbons fastened together in the form of a rosette attached to the back of the coat at the centre of the collar. This is all that is left of the black silk tie and the bag wig that the officers formerly wore, and this regiment is the only one that retains its use.

There is a curious tradition, I am so informed, in connection with the sea, by which a rowing boat takes precedence of a sailing ship, and the latter again of one that is driven by steam, the rowing boat being the earlier method of progression on the water, and I believe that, if three vessels come near to one another, at the entrance to a port, both the sailing ship and the steamship have to give way to a boat that is being rowed.

The " Blue Peter " which the ship hoists, takes its name from the French " partir," to go ; it has nothing to do with the Apostle whose name it bears. " Davy Jones's locker " reminds us of the old Bible story of Jonah, the word " Jones " being a corruption of the name of the prophet who was sent to prophesy to Nineveh. The phrase, so Brewer points out, really means that the person has gone to a place of safe keeping where the ghost or " duffy " of Jonah was sent to, the " locker," of course, being the sailor's customary phrase for the place where he keeps his own little treasures.

One of the curious customs still kept up in connection with

the water, is the race that takes place on the Thames during August between London Bridge and Chelsea for what is known as the Doggett coat and badge. This race has been going on for over two hundred years. Thomas Doggett was a comedian, who lived in the reign of George I, and died in 1721. On August 1, 1716, being the day " of His Majesty's happy accession to the Throne," he gave an orange-coloured livery with a badge representing Liberty, to be rowed for by six watermen " that are out of their time within the past year," and he established an endowment, by which this livery and badge was to be competed for annually, on the same day, for ever, and the men were always to row from London Bridge to Chelsea. Funds to provide it were left in the hands of the Worshipful Company of Fishmongers, and they still hold the money and arrange for its bestowal. The coat is now a red one, and has upon it a large metal badge bearing the white horse of Hanover. The race has been immortalised by Charles Dibdin in his operetta, " The Waterman," when the hero, Tom Tugg, " the jolly young waterman," sings of how he won the trophy. Of the men who competed for it in 1922, two came from Greenwich, and the others from Erith, Richmond, Bermondsey and Putney.

The winner in 1922 was a Putney man, T. J. Phelps, and it is of interest to notice that he was the son of Charles Phelps who carried off the prize in 1884, the brother of Harry Phelps, the winner in 1919, and the nephew of another member of the same family who won it in 1875.

A curious tradition with regard to the water is that fishermen and sailors raise every possible difficulty when asked to take a clergyman on board one of their boats, saying that he invariably brings them bad luck. It is possible that the origin of the superstition goes back to the time of Jonah, for it will be remembered that the crew would have been lost, if Jonah had not been cast into the sea, and it was only then that the waves ceased from raging. It has also been said that the devil will visit any ship to get a parson.

Other fishermen have an objection to anything that is white, and endeavour to throw out from their ballast stones that are pure white. They also do not like to have stones that have holes in them, having a theory that the fish would slip through the net, if any of the ballast stones were perforated. For some strange reason or other, perhaps going back to early Mosaic days, they have a strong antipathy to the hare, and if a hare runs across the path of a fisherman when he is on his way to his boat, he will turn homeward, and refuse to sail. To carry a dead hare on the boat would be considered to be quite enough to spoil the chance of a catch, and to have a live hare on board would mean a much more serious catastrophe, probably the wrecking of the boat and the loss of the lives of all on board. Even a hare's foot, tossed on board by a rival fisherman when a boat was setting out for sea, has been known to cause great consternation.

There was, until quite recently, a Company in the City, known as the Watermen and Lightermen, but it was never actually included in the list of the Livery Companies. Its Hall still exists, and there are persons who still belong to the Company, while it is in possession of some almshouses at Sydenham and some cottage homes at Ditchling. In other respects, the Company is in a state of suspended animation.

It originally controlled the traffic on the Thames of watermen, wherrymen and bargemen, and it settled the fares they were to ask. It yet has to do with the licensing of the watermen and lightermen, and the tariff of their fares has not been altered since an Act of Parliament was passed in 1729. Previous to that, the tariff had been fixed in 1559.

There are still certain rights of drifting which belong to the free watermen, and are regarded as a great nuisance to persons who are yachting on the Thames, to whom these drifting boats are very often both a terror and a danger, but the watermen claim to retain the privilege of free use of the Thames, and it seems to be probable that, under the original charter, which goes back to 1372, and which has never been abrogated, the right does still exist. The charter was granted to the Lightermen, the Watermen themselves not having had possession of a separate charter. The Watermen's Company will always be proud of the fact that John Taylor, the water poet, was a member of it.

The City of London has always had certain rights and privileges over the Thames. At one time it actually ruled over the whole of the river from its mouth, and over the Medway also, and in 1605 a charter of King James admitted that the City for time out of mind had exercised the conservation of the Thames. This privilege has now been merged in the Port of London Authority, constituted by the Port of London Act in 1908, and this did away with the special power of the Thames Conservancy that had succeeded the City, but the City still retains the right of nominating a representative on the Port of London Authority.

A curious privilege which still belongs to the Crown is that of claiming any whale or sturgeon captured on the coast of the United Kingdom, and brought to land. The sturgeon is a royal fish, and both of these perquisites date back to the days of the Norman Conquest and are still in force.

A curious survival of days that are past remains in the very road in which I have the pleasure of writing these words. Its name of Well Walk, and the adjacent street called Flask Walk, remind me of the days when the chalybeate well of Hampstead was regarded as one of great importance, and invalids were often sent to reside in the village of Hampstead, in order that they might drink its waters. The spring still remains, and the well gives its name to various adjacent properties and to an important charity known as the " Wells Charity."

It was in order to drink these waters that Mrs. Johnson was brought by Dr. Johnson up to Hampstead to reside in a little cottage close to where the well now is. There were many such springs round about London, and some actually close up to the City. Holywell Street, recently destroyed, reminded us of one, and there is still a Holywell Lane in Shoreditch, while Sadler's Wells, Spa Road and Spring Gardens all refer to the existence of medicinal springs, very popular in their day, but now only remembered by the names they have given to adjacent streets.

There are certain noblemen who are still known as " Admirals of the Coast," and who, by reason of the possession of estates bordering on the sea-coast, had duties given to them to overlook the defences of their particular districts. Upon them was laid the burden of seeing that the guard of the coasts was properly maintained and supervised, and they were, in Tudor times, frequently called upon to supply ships and men for the protection of the country.

The office was hereditary in the families who possessed the land, and although in some cases the possessions on the sea-board have actually passed away from the estates, yet the privileges still continue in the hands of the owner of the remainder of the property, as though he yet held a sea-board estate. For example, Lord Hothfield is Hereditary Admiral for the coasts of Westmorland, and has the right in consequence to fly an Admiral's flag, and Lord Lonsdale holds a similar position over Cumberland. The latter does actually still retain lands bordering on the sea-coast, but the Clifford lands that were sea-board have some time ago passed away from the possession of Lord Hothfield. The hereditary privilege has, however, still remained.

A very interesting survival of the use of the crucifix still exists on the man-of-war. Everyone who goes on to the quarterdeck brings his hand to the salute as he does so. The idea in the mind of many persons is that this is to salute the flag, the ensign that flies over the taffrail, but it is not so. In Catholic days there was always a crucifix, or else images of Christ and the Blessed Virgin, on the mizen-mast of every ship, and the men saluted or crossed themselves as they passed it. Nowadays there is not even a mizen-mast, but the habit of saluting is kept up.

Another interesting and very similar survival consists in the fact that the lightermen of the Thames, when passing Lambeth Palace, invariably still remove their caps. The origin of this custom was the mark of respect to the niche which at one time contained a representation of St. Thomas of Canterbury, but which is now empty.

CHAPTER XVII

NORMAN-FRENCH SURVIVALS

I HAVE already referred, in the chapter on the House of Peers, to the manner in which the Royal Assent is still given to Acts of Parliament in Norman-French, instead of English, but if we desire to understand more fully concerning the survival of this ancient tongue in current life, we must visit the Channel Islands, and study the customs that the Islanders have still retained. We still mark the divergence between English habits and those introduced by the Normans, when we refer to the two different methods of weight that we have in use in England, avoirdupois and troy, the avoirdupois being the old French word for the weight of goods in general, and the troy weight meaning, as Brewer points out, simply London weight.

There have been some philologists who have insisted that the origin of this weight came from Troyes, that it was in use in the great fair that took place in that town, and came into England by way of the Crusades, the Crusaders finding it in use in Egypt, brought thence by traders from Troyes. It was pointed out long ago, however, that this was an untenable idea, because the word troy applied to a weight (and also, curiously enough, to a measure) was found in England in Anglo-Saxon times. London used to be called New Troy, or Troy Novant, having no connection whatever with any refugees from Troy, who at one time were said to have founded the town, but being simply an old English word, meaning the inhabitants of the New Town. Thus, of these different schemes for weight, we have on the one hand the old English habit, and on the other the new one introduced at the Norman Conquest.

In virtue of the fact that the Channel Islands were ruled over by the Duke of Normandy, they retain an ancient custom known as the " Clameur de Haro." The cry of " Haro ! " is understood to take its derivation from " Ha Rollo," referring to the first Duke. To Rollo Normandy was ceded by Charles the Simple in 912. Franco, the Archbishop of Rouen, was sent to him with overtures. " Will you, mighty giant," he said, " go on to make war with the Franks so long as you live ? What will become of you if death surprises you ? Do you think you are a god ? Are you not a mortal man ? Remember what you are and will be, and by Whom you will one day be judged." Rollo, impressed by this address, became, it is stated, a Christian, and a champion of justice, and hence, tradition says, he is appealed to in cases of encroachment or invasion of privilege. If a prompt remedy is required, the aggrieved party calls upon the name of the Duke, falling on his knees and crying out, " Haro ! Haro ! À l'aide, mon Prince, on me fait tort ! " The appeal dare not be disregarded. All workmen employed have to cease their work until the matter has been settled by the Royal Court. But if the great name of Rollo has been invoked unlawfully, the party so doing is subject to a fine, losing his case, and paying costs.

In 1923 an inhabitant of La Motte, St. Heliers, owing to a dispute which had arisen regarding a right of way, uttered this Norman formula in the presence of his opponent, Mr. Luxon, and immediately all further argument as to the disputed right of entrance to a flat, which was the point at issue, had to be dropped, because the cry for justice must be respected, and the trespass or tort, has to cease until the matter is thrashed out and decided in the Courts.

There are curious survivals in these islands with respect to the coinage and weights and measures. Many rents are still expressed in what is known as " monnaie Tournois," and the coinage of Tours (at one time the capital of French Touraine, when the province of Tours was united by Henry II with England) has always been, and is at present, the legal standard of coinage in the Island States. The Tournois pound was set in 1709 as equivalent to a fourteenth of an English pound sterling. There are many payments, however, of rent that are not made in money. For instance, a Guernsey paper of 1887 refers to the sub-tenant of the holder of a fief in Guernsey who owes annually to his landlord one donkey and one cake made from a bushel of wheat. In a somewhat similar case, either the fief or the tenancy had become subdivided, and a suit had to be brought for the proportional share of the rent, which amounted to one fowl, one half and one sixteenth of a fowl, one fortieth and one four hundred and eightieth part of a fowl, twenty-eight eggs and three-fourths, and one eighth of an egg. The action, ridiculous as it may sound, was declared as necessary in order that proper title should be maintained.

In a work recently issued on the Channel Islands it is stated that one person paid as rent to another a cartload of ashes or its money equivalent, and in another case eighteen eels, or the equivalent in money, while a firm could be called upon to provide, when required, the rope for the bell of the parish church, and the rent demanded by the owner of another property from his tenant was a chicken, the tail of which must be at least one inch long. Property, it is stated, changes hands very little in the Islands, and one manor, that of St. Ouen, is said to have been in the possession of the Carterets, who still occupy it, for more than nine hundred years.

Other curious survivals are in names of measures; for instance, a pint of milk is called four noggins, an acre of ground spoken of as two and one-fourth vergees, and for the bushel the word cabot is used—this is a measure of varying capacity, because a cabot of wheat is equal to ten pots, but a cabot of potatoes is equal to thirteen pots plus a pint and a half.

It is always interesting, in talking to a native of the Channel Islands, to find how clearly he understands that his part of the world is all that remains under the British Crown of the original Dukedom of Normandy, and that he and his people were never conquered by the English, but they were the conquerors! The Channel Islanders have always been devoted adherents of the Crown, and proud of their British citizenship; yet, at the same time, they are equally proud of their Norman descent, and in spite of the constant warfare between them and France, they take a keen sentimental interest in the welfare of the country that lies nearest their shores.

I believe that while their official language is modern French, and the use of English is optional, their own dialect is a genuine survival of the Norman-French language. It has variations and differences according to the island in

which it is spoken, and it has always been stated that the
Norman-French spoken on Sark is the purest of all, and is
most closely akin to the speech of the invaders who came
over with William the Conqueror.

The Islanders have retained many Norman-French
institutions, and specially so with regard to their system
of land tenure, which has hardly altered since the time of
the Conquest, while they retain also many of their ancient
feudal tenures and feudal ceremonies of which they are
exceedingly proud, and which were gladly rendered to the
King and Queen when, after a period of nearly a thousand
years, the monarchs reigning over England paid a *state*
visit to the Islands.

It is strange to recall that, although they have been
attached to the Crown for such a long time, there has been
but one formal visit of the Sovereign to their shores, within
an exceptionally long period, and that was the one occasion
when Queen Victoria visited both Guernsey and Jersey in
1846.   Previous to that time they had been visited by
Henry III, who landed in Jersey in 1230, by Henry VII
when Duke of Richmond, and by Charles II twice—in 1646
when only sixteen and Prince of Wales, and again three
years afterwards.   To find an earlier visit, one had to
go right back to King John, who is said to have once landed.
The King is still regarded as Duke of Normandy in the
islands, the cry is " Vive Le Roi, notre Duc," and the
addresses that are presented to the Sovereign refer to him
as " Le Roi, notre Duc."

In solemn fashion, the seigneurs of Jersey paid homage
to the King, a homage which is only due when the Sovereign
actually visits the island.   The leading seigneur, who
represents St. Ouen, knelt before the King with his clasped
hands in front of him, which were grasped by the King,
and, surrounded by the other twelve seigneurs, they all
together recited, " Je suis votre homme lége, à vous porter
foi et hommage contre tous."   Then the Seigneur of Trinity,
according to ancient custom, advanced to perform his
Crown Serjeantry, by presenting a silver dish, on which
were two mallards in their plumage, with their beaks gilded,
and the birds and the dish were handed over to the Receiver-
General, who bore them away in triumph.

I have already alluded to this curious word mallard.

The homage in Guernsey was not quite the same as that in Jersey. There were four holders of Guernsey fiefs who came up in succession to the King, representing the fiefs of Sausmarez, Bruneaux St. Martin's, Henri de Vaugrat and Cannely and Fantosne. Then they were followed by the Seigneur of Sark, who did homage for his fief. They each made three deep bows, and knelt at the King's feet, holding their hands closed, palm to palm, in front of his face. The King enclosed the fief-holder's hands with his own, and the kneeling man declared thus, " Sire, je demeure votre homme, à vous porter foi et hommage contre tous," and the King replied to this statement, also in Norman-French, " Nous vous acceptons, advouants tous vos légitimes droits et possessions relevants de cette teneure de nous sauf pareille-ment à tous nos droits de régalité."

All these fief-holders were introduced by the person who in Guernsey is called the Greffier, and then a lady, who represents an important fief, in ancient form presented to the King, on a red velvet cushion, a pair of gilt spurs, left with her ancestors by Charles II, to be kept for the King's use whenever he visited the Island. The King touched them, and returned them to their owner.

The ancient costume is kept up more tenaciously in Guernsey than in Jersey. The persons who are termed the Jury justicers have purple gowns with grey silk facings, and they wear the old flat caps, the shape of which has been in use in Guernsey for many hundreds of years.

The Islands still retain their own local administrations, and very proud they are of it. The local Parliament has its own halberdiers, who carry halberts that were in use in the time of Sir Walter Raleigh when he was Governor. Their head official is still termed His Majesty's Viscount, the Mace-bearer and Banner-bearer are called Denunciators, from a privilege they originally possessed, and they carry a mace given to the island by Charles II, and the flag of Normandy, with its three lions in white and scarlet. That flag had not ever been used since the time of George III, until it was flung out before the King on his recent visit.

Another curious point is, that in the Jersey courts the Bailiff (to show the superiority of the civil head of the island, a claim which has always been made with definite emphasis, and is similar to that claim made by the House of Commons in England) is placed some six inches higher than the military governor, to signify that the people are rulers in the House, and that the military power, which is under the control of the Sovereign, is held to be strictly subordinate to the rights of the Norman people.

It would be impossible to refer to all the curious survivals that still exist in these islands. They constitute a little museum of ancient habits, and almost all their customs date back in origin to very early days. For example, in the island of Sark there were originally but forty colonists, and they had held the island since Queen Elizabeth made it into a fief in 1565 and gave it to one of the Carterets with his heirs and assigns. Representatives of these forty men still exist in Sark, and hold their land by a totally different tenure from any that prevails in the other islands.

Again, the question of sanctuary has always been an important one in the Channel Islands. At one time, all the churches were sanctuaries, as well as the road, by which they were approached, and it is only in comparatively recent times that these sanctuary roads have been done away with.

The constitution of the courts is also unusual, and differs in the different islands, while the Islands also afford evidence of the tenacity with which small nations hold to their original tongue, a tenacity which has another proof in the continued existence of the Eisteddfod in Wales, which is regarded as of the greatest value for keeping up the attachment of the Welsh for their native tongue. It is, by the way, a curious thing that one can go into the crypt at Canterbury Cathedral and hear a service going on in French, still conducted by the descendants of those Huguenots who, on fleeing to England, were permitted to hold their services in that part of the great Cathedral, and who, ever since the days of the Edict of Nantes, retained that privilege, and still retain it.

Another evidence of attachment to language exists in the fact that in Berlin there is still a colony which represents the descendants of some French Huguenot refugees who settled there two hundred and fifty years ago, and who, although distinctly German in their habits and ways, and possessed of great attachment to the Prussian laws and regulations, insist upon using the French language, and have done so ever since they came to Berlin. They teach it to their children, they speak it in their own households, they use French books, they even use the French language on their tombstones, and there were many monuments inscribed, during the time of the Franco-Prussian War, to the effect that the persons who were commemorated died " Pour le Roi et pour la Patrie," although " Le Roi " and " La Patrie " referred to the Kaiser and the German Empire. The little colony has always kept very much to itself, it is a colony of well-to-do people, and a very generous one, and many churches and hospitals and schools have been supported by these descendants of the French Huguenots, who, in the midst of their German associations, have retained their attachment to the country from whence they came.

The King and Queen were attended, on the occasion of their visit to the Channel Islands, by those known as the Hallibardiers, whose duty it is to form a guard of honour for the Governor, the Bailiff, and the members of the Royal Court. They were originally the freehold tenants of the Crown fiefs in the parishes of St. Martin, St. Saviour and Grouville, and they had the duty of escorting prisoners from the prison to the Court and back, because, at the original Court of Heritage, there were called to the King's Peace any fugitive criminals, and if they did not come, they were regarded as prisoners, and handed over to the custody of the Hallibardiers.

In the old days, all the Hallibardiers were entitled to partake of a dinner when they came to the Court of Heritage, at the expense of the Governor, but presently he found it more economical to do this work of escorting prisoners through the soldiers of the garrison. The guard of honour therefore degenerated down to a sergeant and twelve privates, instead of the large number of persons who were the Crown tenants. The original Hallibardiers were, however, called together on the occasion of this visit, but the actual guard round the Governor consisted of soldiers, although they were styled by the same name as that which the tenants themselves originally held.

The land for which the spurs are presented in Guernsey is still called " Les Eperons." According to the ancient law, there should be two pairs of spurs one of gilt and one

white, probably of silver. In connection with the visit
of the King to the Vinerie, Sir Havilland de Sausmarez
performed the duty of handing the cups of tea for the use
of the King and Queen. The original tenure of course never
dreamed of such a drink as tea—it was something far stronger
that was partaken of in those days—but the custom of providing cups for the use of the King goes back to 1299, when,
at the assizes that were held in St. Peter Port, Mathieu de
Sausmarez acknowledged that he held his fief from the
Crown, as his ancestors had done from time immemorial,
by the service of being a cup-bearer to the King.

The Seigneurs who did homage at the Court of Heritage
were those who represented the following fiefs: St. Ouen,
Rozel, Trinity, St. Germain, St. Jean la Hogue Boete,
Augres, Hague, St. Brelade, Poingdestres and St. Heliers,
two out of the number being called franc fiefs. The tenures
of two of these fiefs were not paid in customary fashion.
The original arrangements were that the Seigneurs of Rozel
and Augres should both wade into the sea on horseback,
up to the girths of their saddles, to meet the King when
he lands in the island, and should similarly accompany
him on his departure. The Seigneur of Rozel has the
additional duty of acting as the King's butler for as long
as the King remains on the Island.

These incidents of feudal tenure are clearly set out in the
documents preserved in Jersey, dating from 1331 and
onwards, and the first duty—that of wading into the water
on horseback—was actually performed by the Seigneur of
Rozel when Charles II arrived in Jersey on September 17,
1649, when Sir Philip de Carteret, who then held the fief,
went to meet the King in the sea, as the King was about to
land from his pinnace at Elizabeth Castle.

THE END

NOTE.—I am greatly indebted to Miss Gertrude Metivier, and to
the works of Mr. Osborne, for information contained in the preceding
chapter.

INDEX

THE YEOMAN OF THE GUARD CARRYING THE SILVER DISH WITH THE
PURSES CONTAINING THE MAUNDY MONEY. THE THONGS FROM THE
PURSES HANG DOWN IN A FRINGE.

London News Agency. Photo.

The City Solicitor chopping the Faggots in the presence of The King's Remembrancer and other High Officials. The Horseshoes are on the Table.

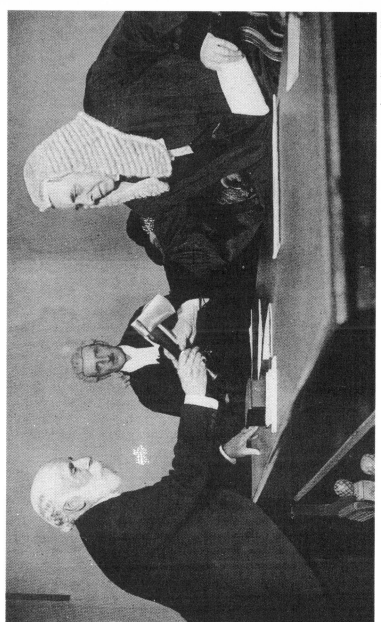

London News Agency, Photo

THE CITY SOLICITOR HANDING THE HATCHET AND BILL HOOK TO THE KING'S REMEMBRANCER.

The Lord Mayor (Sir William Treloar) with the Mace, the City Sword Bearer and various High Officials.

The Ceremony of The Keys in The Tower. The Keeper of the Keys at the Door.

THE MASTER AND WARDENS OF THE WORSHIPFUL COMPANY OF GIRDLERS WEARING THEIR HISTORIC CROWNS.

Interior of the House of Lords, showing the Throne and the Woolsack.

Stone, Photo.

THE YEOMEN OF THE GUARD SETTING OUT TO INSPECT THE VAULTS AT THE HOUSES OF PARLIAMENT PRIOR TO THE MEETING OF PARLIAMENT. THEY ARE CARRYING THEIR LIGHTED LANTERNS WITH THEM.

THE CHAIRS SET READY FOR THE GOVERNOR AND THE BISHOP ON THE TOP OF THE TYNWALD HILL, ISLE OF MAN, IN PREPARATION FOR THE CEREMONY OF PROMULGATING THE LAWS IN THE OPEN AIR.

The Dole at the Hospital of St. Cross, Winchester.

THE TOWN CRIER OF HUNGERFORD BLOWING THE HORN AND
USHERING IN THE HOCKTIDE FESTIVITIES.

The Closed Entrance to Corby Fair. All comers have to pay in accordance with the terms of the Elizabethan Charter.

Stone, Photo.

Dancing the Furry Dance in the Streets of Helston.

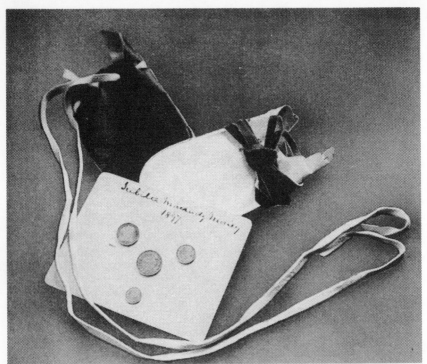

THE MAUNDY MONEY AND THE RED AND WHITE LEATHERN PURSES
IN WHICH IT IS PRESENTED.

TWO OF THE BIDDENDEN CAKES.
(The Postage Stamps are put in order to show the size of the cakes.)

Stone, Photo.

THE ALMSWOMEN AT CASTLE ACRE IN THEIR INTERESTING COSTUME.

THE FEALTY-CEREMONIES OF THE SEIGNEURS IN GUERNSEY ON THE OCCASION OF THE VISIT OF
THE DUKE OF NORMANDY TO THE CHANNEL ISLANDS.